Edward Rogers

Reminiscences of military service in the Forty-third regiment

Massachusetts infantry during the great Civil war 1862-63

Edward Rogers

Reminiscences of military service in the Forty-third regiment
Massachusetts infantry during the great Civil war 1862-63

ISBN/EAN: 9783337223427

Printed in Europe, USA, Canada, Australia, Japan

Cover: Foto ©ninafisch / pixelio.de

More available books at **www.hansebooks.com**

REMINISCENCES OF MILITARY SERVICE

IN

THE FORTY-THIRD REGIMENT.

Massachusetts Infantry,

DURING THE GREAT CIVIL WAR, 1862-63.

By EDWARD H. ROGERS,

COMPANY H, CHELSEA, MASS.

BOSTON:
FRANKLIN PRESS: RAND, AVERY, & CO.
1883.

F
8349
.469

Rogers, Edward Henry, 1824–
　Reminiscences of military service in the Forty-third regiment, Massachusetts infantry, during the great Civil war, 1862–63. By Edward H. Rogers, Company H, Chelsea, Mass. Boston, Franklin press, Rand, Avery, & co., 1883.
　　210 p.　front., illus., plates.　23½ᶜᵐ.
　　Title vignette.
　　Appendix: A. Historical portion of the address of Hon. R. C. Winthrop on the presentation of the colors of the Forty-third. B. Roster of the companies composing the Forty-third regiment, M. V. M.

Dawes
F
8349
.469

　　1. Massachusetts infantry. 43d regt., 1862–1863. 2. U. S.—Hist.—Civil war—Regimental histories—Mass. Inf.—43d. I. Title.

2—1885

—— —— another copy.
Library of Congress　　E513.5.43d

[4¹f¹]

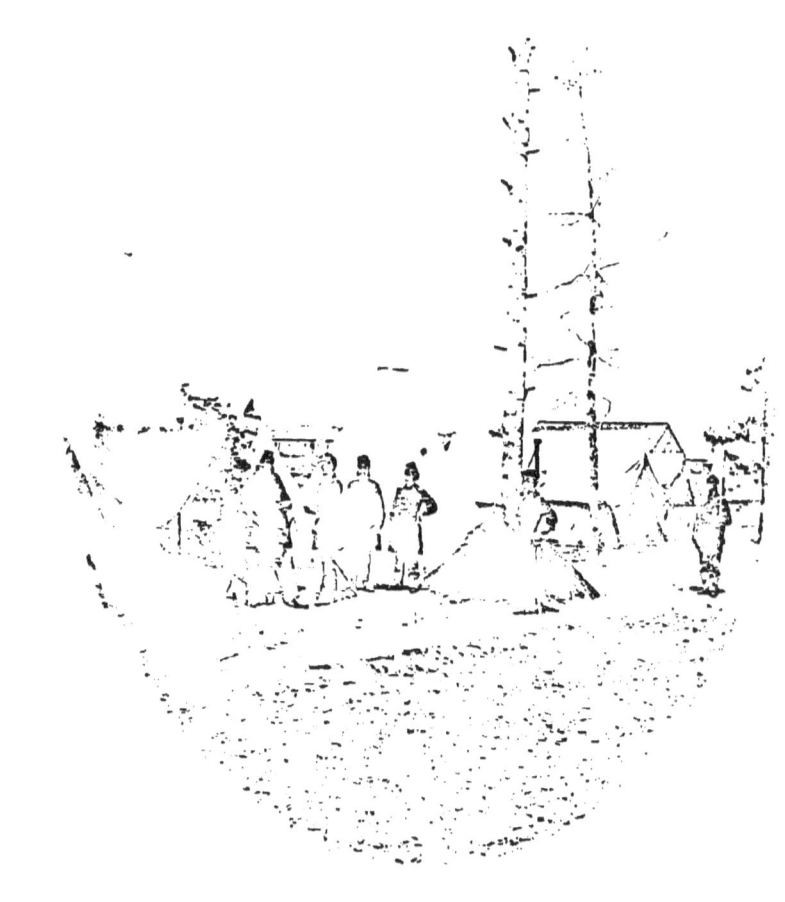

PREFACE.

THE veterans of Chelsea who served in the First, the Thirty-fifth, and the Fortieth Regiments, have a right to ask why this book precedes the record of their own memorable deeds. In answer, it may be said that its separate issue was not decided upon until after a persistent effort had been made to unite with others in the compilation of a complete military history of our city during the war. This was found to be, at present, impracticable. The effort, however, has resulted in the preparation by the various interested parties of a large part of the material for such a history. It is still confidently hoped, that, before many years elapse, our community will be favored with its publication.

There are, however, sufficient reasons why this history of the Forty-third should be given to the public without the abridgment to which it must have been subjected if bound with others. The regiment was a fairly representative organization of the "nine-months men" of Massachusetts. Very little has been written concerning this levy of troops. Our fields of action in North Carolina and Louisiana were distant, and slightly known; and our operations seemed insignificant in comparison with the marches and battles of Virginia and the Central States.

I have shown that we were really an outpost of the great army which threatened Richmond. Not a movement could take place in Virginia without affecting us; and the fact foreshadowed the grand

combinations which took place around Goldsborough at the close of the war.

The loss of the coast of North Carolina was a great disaster to the Confederacy. It is reckoned that it cost us a hundred millions of dollars to capture and defend it. But it proved to be worth that sum. Its secure possession by the Union forces throughout the war, in spite of several determined efforts to recapture it, enabled Gen. Sherman to shape his northward course without opposition, except in the open field. Not even a single fort hindered him, as at Savannah, from effecting a union at Goldsborough with our troops from Newbern, who left an open passage to the sea behind them. United with the forces of Gen. Schofield from Wilmington, the great army carried despair into the hearts of the rebels. With Grant victorious, and Sherman close at hand, resistance was hopeless.

All this would have been changed for the worse, if Burnside's fleet had waited until the spring of 1865. It is with some degree of satisfaction, then, that I look back to the eight months of the darkest period of the war, during which the security of this vital point depended very largely upon the militia of Massachusetts.

My thanks are specially due to Col. Whiton, Major Lane, and Lieut. Turner, our quartermaster, for counsel and assistance. Nor can I omit, in this connection, our recently deceased comrade, Chaplain Manning, whose interest was very marked. It will be seen that I have quoted freely from his letters to "The Boston Journal," over the signature of "Old South," of which church he was the pastor. The same acknowledgments should be made to Capt. Hanover and Orderly Edmunds, with other comrades of the company.

Henry Mason, Esq., editor of "The Pioneer," has placed our community under obligations for the generous manner in which his paper has been put at my disposal, not only for the first printing of this work, but also for much fuller reference to its files than appears here. I have thought it best not to change the familiar forms of expression which were used in the original publication.

I had prepared most of the material which is quoted, with a view to placing it in the hands of some one of sufficient leisure, and more competent than myself. That it does not still lie in waiting for such a person is because diligent search has failed to discover any one who has the two requisites.

Nearly twenty years have passed since the war closed. Several attempts at a permanent record of the deeds of the soldiers and sailors of Chelsea have proved abortive. Under these circumstances, I ask a friendly judgment for my own imperfect efforts, and also for those who may follow me.

Reluctant, for various reasons, to assume responsibility in so important a matter, my reserve has been overcome, first by the encouragement, and then by the approval, of our highest local authority in literary matters, that of Judge Chamberlain. The action of Theodore Winthrop Post 35, G. A. R., in placing this, and even more honorable duties of the same kind, under my control, has also cheered me with the appreciative support of my associates in arms.

To the group of public-spirited citizens of Chelsea who met the first request for funds with such liberality as to insure success, I return my grateful thanks.

E. H. R.

CHELSEA, MASS., Dec. 25, 1882.

CONTENTS.

CHAPTER I.
THE ENLISTMENT, AND THE CAMP AT READVILLE.

The Chelsea Rifle Corps. — Cessation of Recruiting. — National Disasters. — The Sabbath Enlistment. — General Statement of the Services of the Company and Regiment. — War Speeches in the Square. — Note from Capt. Hanover. — War Circular. — Patriotic Ballad, "Six Hundred Thousand more." — Choice of Officers. — First Letter from Camp. — Details of Life in Camp. — Sworn into the Service of the United States. — Roster of the Company. — Necrology. — March to Chelsea, and Reception at City Hall. — Visit and Speech from Hon. Frank B. Fay. — Incidents, Tragic and Comic. — Orders to the Scene of War. — Presentation of Colors on Boston Common by Hon. Robert C. Winthrop 11

CHAPTER II.
THE VOYAGE.

The Storm in Boston Harbor. — Colliding with the Buoy on Monomoy Point. — Sea Letter. — Nauseous Condensed Water. — Accident to the Quartermaster, Lieut. Henry A. Turner. — Arrival at Morehead City. — Railroad Ride to Newbern. — Description of Scenery in Vicinity of Camp Rogers. — Letter from Chaplain Manning. — The Regiment. — Roster of Field-Officers. — Details of Companies during Term of Service. — Desertions. — Formation of the Brigade. — The Camp. — Marching Orders 29

CHAPTER III.
THE GREAT MARCH. — KINSTON.

The March on Goldsborough. — Scenes in Newbern. — The Veterans. — First Day's March. — Cooking, Sleeping. — The Road blocked by Trees. — Crossing the Streams. — Home of a "Poor White." — Engagement at South-west Creek. — Battle of Kinston. — Musical Bullets. — Rebel Battery. — The Charge. — Chaplain Manning's Letter. — The Flag of Truce. — The Witty Colored Girl. — The Twenty third and Forty-fifth Massachusetts Regiments. — Firing on Kinston. — Loyal Verses. — Troops advance on Kinston *en echelon.* — Foster's

8   CONTENTS.
                                                                    PAGE.
Despatch. — Ravages of War. — Weight of the Soldier's Load. —
Plundering. — Countermarching over the Battle-Ground. — Dead
Heroes. — Experience in First Fight. — Description of Plantation. —
Sad Scenes in the Ambulances. — Letter of Chaplain Manning . . 39

CHAPTER IV.
WHITEHALL AND GOLDSBOROUGH.

The Battle of Whitehall. — First Gun. — Go down into the Valley. — Procession of the Wounded. — Under Fire. — Ordered back. — Sheltered in the Forest. — Advance again. — Heavy Artillery-Fire. — On Hands and Knees. — Back again to the Cover. — Death of Private Smith. — Rally again. — Placed in Front of Battery. — Sleeping under Fire. — Narrow Escapes. — Chaplain Manning's Letter. — Situation of the Twenty-third Massachusetts. — Placed in Charge of Baggage-Train. — Under Sharpshooters' Fire. — Interview with Comrade of the Ninth New-Jersey. — Experience with Baggage-Train. — Regiment ordered to Spring-Bank Bridge. — Devotional Exercises. — Recall of Sentries at Midnight. — Capt. Hanover and Orderly Edmunds lost. — The Forest-Fire. — Mirage. — Description of the Rebel Charge on our Artillery. — Witherby. — Services of the Seventeenth Regiment and Barney Mann in burning the Bridge at Goldsborough 63

CHAPTER V.
REVIEW OF THE GOLDSBOROUGH MARCH.

Killed, Wounded, and Missing. — Gen. Foster. — Able Strategy. — His Wife. — Our Guide. — Whitehall a Naval Station. — Capture of Plymouth. — No Pomp, but some Impressive Sights. — The Sound Fleet. — The Blockade. — Singing. — "Stonewall Jackson's Way." — The "Battle-Hymn of the Republic." — Sacrificial Exposures of Officers. — Colored Camp-Followers. — Recruiting in North Carolina for Colored Regiments. — The Freedmen 90

CHAPTER VI.
THE TRENTON MARCH.

Rest. — Christmas Rejoicings. — Letter of Chaplain Manning. — The Chapel Tent; Religious and Masonic Meetings. — Personal Eccentricities in Morals. — Visits of Mr. Bond, Charlie Farnum, and Capt. Dale. — Letters. — The Great Expedition to Charleston. — March to Trenton. — The Swamp. — The Child. — The Chapel. — The Rock Ledge in the Road. — The Mill-Dam. — The Skeleton File-Closer. — Young's Cross-Roads. — First Picket. — Under Water. — The March back 103

CHAPTER VII.
THE CAMP AT NEWBERN.

All quiet on the Trent. — Full Description of Camp Rogers. — Letters. — Our Cook, Mr. William B. Bryant. — Our Sutler, Mr. James Q. Gilmore. — Gambling. — Drinking. — Drill. — Grand Review. — Artillery-Practice. — Avocations. — Visit to Newbern 119

CONTENTS. 9

CHAPTER VIII.
ATTACK ON NEWBERN.
PAGE.

Notice to March. — Artillery Duel on the Road to Kinston. — Firing on Fort Totten. — On the March. — See Longstreet's Camp-Fires. — Meet the Twenty-fifth Massachusetts and the Forty-sixth. — Follow the Enemy to Deep Gully. — The Quaker Cannon. — Scripture Welcome. — Visit of Major Rogers of Boston. — Colors on the Steeple in Newbern. — Reviewed by Gen. Palmer. — Siege of Little Washington. — Letters. — Affair at Blount's Creek. — Full Account. — Gen. Spinola . 130

CHAPTER IX.
PAMLICO SOUND.

On Board a Transport Schooner. — Gen. Foster runs the Blockade. — "The Escort" comes alongside. — Companies H, C, and D left on Board the Schooners. — In Camp at Hill's Point. — Meet C, D, and I of the Forty-fourth. — Short Rations. — Company E runs the Blockade in Schooners. — The Rebel Artillery. — Appearance of "The Escort." — The Siege raised. — Reconnoissance in Force. — The Rebel Grave. — Blowing up the Earthwork. — The Alarm on Picket. — Return to Camp Rogers. — Another Advance on Kinston 147

CHAPTER X.
NEWBERN.

Letters. — Guard Duty at Newbern. — Swiss Settlers. — Moral Deterioration. — Colored Carpenter. — The Newbern Palm. — The Newbern Battlefield. — Burnside's Strategy. — The Resurrection. — Gun-Shot Accidents. — Thunder-storms. — Mosquitoes. — Vermin . . . 161

CHAPTER XI.
THE RETURN HOME.

Exchange of Arms with the Seventeenth. — Letter from York River. — Letter from Chesapeake Bay. — Our Voyage on "The Vidette." — Copper Poison. — Hampton Roads. — Company G, Fortieth. — Passage to Baltimore. — Drunken Delirium. — Camp Bradford. — Wounded Officers. — Volunteers go to the Front. — Part of the Regiment returns. — Repulse the Last Enemy. — Report of the Comrades from the Front. — Invalids from Newbern by Sea. — Reception. — Bounties of Nine-Months Men. — Chelsea Rifle Corps. — Boston Light Infantry (Tigers). — Causes of the War. — Prevention of War. — Celebration of Peace at City Hall, Chelsea. — Te Deum Laudamus 171

APPENDIX A. — Historical Portion of the Address of Hon. Robert C. Winthrop, on the Presentation of the Colors 195

APPENDIX B. — Roster of the Companies composing the Forty-third Regiment, M.V.M. 199

ILLUSTRATIONS.

[The two camp scenes are from photographs taken by Lieut. NICKERSON of Company E. The battles were sketched by Private MERRILL G. WHEELOCK of Company F, Forty-fourth Regiment. They were painted in oil for Col. LEE, and photographed. The heliotypes in this volume are reduced from the photographs.]

PAGE.

HEADQUARTERS OF THE FORTY-THIRD REGIMENT, M.V.M.,
WITH THE FIELD AND STAFF . . . . . *Frontispiece.*

    Col. HOLBROOK is seated on the left. Quartermaster TURNER is at his side. Lieut.-Col. WHITON stands in front of the colonel. Chaplain MANNING and Surgeon WEBBER are next. Adjutant WHITNEY reclines at the foot of the flagstaff; and Major LANE is last.

CAMP ROGERS 35

    Encampment of the Forty-third Regiment, M.V.M., Newbern, N.C., March 12, 1863.

CAPTURE OF KINSTON 51

    This scene is located after the battle. Morrison's Battery is firing on the town: the troops are passing over the bridge, and forming their lines on the meadow. The "earthwork" is seen in the foreground, with soldiers engaged in filling their canteens from the river.

BATTLE OF GOLDSBOROUGH. . . . .

    The "covered bridge" is located on the right of the picture. It is nearly concealed by trees. The Wilmington and Weldon Railroad, along which the Seventeenth passed, can be traced from the bridge, across the battle-ground, to the left-hand side. The forest from which the Confederates emerged is visible on the left side, beyond the railroad; and their assault upon our artillery was upon the knoll represented in the foreground.

HISTORY

OF THE

FORTY-THIRD REGIMENT, M.V.M.

CHAPTER I.

THE ENLISTMENT, AND THE CAMP AT READVILLE.

THE "Chelsea Pioneer" of March 22, 1862, contained the following item: —

"CHELSEA RIFLE CORPS. — This company is now filling up its members fast, and, as soon as weather will permit, intend to turn out for street drill. As they own their arms and equipments, we would recommend any of our young Chelsea men who intend to join in this healthful and useful exercise to make early application, *so as to be among the number who will* (D.V.) *shortly do escort duty to our Chelsea Volunteers* (Company H, First Regiment) *on their return home from the field of victory.*"

Extraordinary as the lines which I have italicized appear, they undoubtedly represented the state of the public mind of the North at the time they were written. The Western armies were making rapid progress. Burnside had achieved brilliant victories in North Carolina; and McClellan was moving down the Potomac with a mighty host, which, it was confidently believed, would soon capture the rebel stronghold, Richmond, and put an end at once to the Rebellion.

These hopeful events had deceived the authorities at Washington; so that during the spring, recruiting for the

army was stopped, as it was deemed certain that we had a sufficient force in the field to effectively crush all opposition to the national forces. Before three months were gone, events had transpired which changed the whole aspect of affairs, deferring for three long and sorrowful years the hopes of the loyal people of the North. In one of those years of gloom and disaster the following experiences were cast, and they are now offered to the public as an humble portion of the nation's record of patriotic effort.

Early in the afternoon of the sabbath, Aug. 31, 1862, the writer enrolled himself as a member of a military company afterward known as Company H, Forty-third (Tiger) Regiment, Massachusetts Volunteer Militia, for nine months, unless sooner discharged, and was present with the company and regiment, with a brief exception, until its arrival home.

The most noteworthy events of our term of service were connected with what took the name of "The Great March" from Newbern to Goldsborough, N.C., in which we formed part of a column of from twelve thousand to fifteen thousand men under Major-Gen. John G. Foster. During this march, which occupied eleven days of the month of December, 1862, we were under fire three times, either as a regiment or company, — at Kinston, Whitehall, and Goldsborough. When Newbern was attacked by Gen. Longstreet's troops, in March, 1863, we were sent to the outer posts on the road to Kinston, several miles from town, and while there were in the immediate presence of a large rebel column. Later on, while the same forces were besieging Little Washington, N.C., the regiment was under arms for several weeks in active operations, and on one occasion, at Blount's Creek, was subjected to a vigorous shelling. On the passage of Gen. Lee into Pennsylvania in 1863, we were ordered north, in company with several other nine-months regiments, and formed for a few days a part of the troops, supposed to be about eighteen or twenty thousand men, which were gathered at White-House Landing, on the Pamunkey River, under the command of Gen. Dix. From here we went back to Fortress Monroe, going into camp at Hampton, and remaining until July 2,

when we took the steam transport "Kennebec" for Baltimore, reaching there on the afternoon of July 3. We remained for several days at this place, after marching through the city on the morning of the 4th, and camping in elegant private grounds in sight of the Washington Monument and a large fountain. From this place, the colors of the regiment were carried, by two hundred and three officers and men who volunteered for that service, to Sandy Hook, near Harper's Ferry, Md. The remainder of the regiment and company availed themselves of the expiration of our term of service to return home, which we reached on July 10. A portion of our company had preceded us, being sent as invalids direct from Newbern to Boston by sea. Ten days afterwards, the comrades who went to the front in Maryland rejoined us in Chelsea, and on the 30th of July the company came together for the last time at our old camp at Readville, and were mustered out.

The materials for composing this history consist mainly of a series of letters written to my own immediate friends, though other sources of information are at hand, and will be freely drawn upon. The interest of much of what I wish to write will be limited to surviving comrades and their families, or to the friends of those who are deceased. The honorable record of the city of Chelsea in its dealings with its soldiers will be evident, and is of sufficient local importance to be impressed upon our community. But, above all these considerations, there will still remain enough of incidental allusion to the great contest in which we were engaged to fix the attention, and command the respect, of the general reader. If the record of our comparatively brief service and slight exposures contributes in any degree to set in its true light the sacrifices of the veterans of the three-years term, I shall feel that a desirable object has been gained.

Returning to my opening paragraph. On the sabbath in question, public worship in the churches had been interrupted early in the morning service by the terrible news from Washington, that the disasters of the Peninsula were being repeated on the banks of the Rappahannock, and that the

forces of Gen. Pope had been hurled back in a second Bull Run defeat upon Arlington Heights, our own Company H, First Regiment, being disastrously involved in the repulse. We scattered to our homes for the preparation of hospital stores, and Chelsea for several hours afforded an unusual change from its ordinary sabbath stillness.

I had for some time been quietly but earnestly considering the duty of enlisting as a matter of religious as well as patriotic obligation, for I had no other reasons. In order to insure a calm conclusion, I had avoided the stimulating war meetings which were being held, and at the moment of decision, after circling Winnisimmet Square anxiously for an hour, I was so far from enthusiasm, that it was only by a supreme effort of moral power that I forced myself into the recruiting-tent, which was located near the centre of the old square, and signed my name to the enlistment-roll. There were but three or four present: of these I can only recall the name of the one whom I shall have occasion hereafter to introduce as our respected orderly. Much to my surprise, they instantly, as was the custom, rose to their feet, joined hands, and gave three lusty cheers. I confess I felt like any thing but cheering; but still, this first earnest of the friendly relationships of the soldier's life, which endured throughout the rough experiences of a year's campaigning, and which is still in existence, was very encouraging to me.

During the early hours of the evening of the same day, the square was thronged by our citizens, of both sexes, who were addressed by several public speakers, the Rev. Dr. Copp being one of them, and some of the members of our company; and on that sabbath, or the next one, the evening meeting at Walnut-street Methodist-Episcopal Church was largely devoted to recruiting-speeches from Capt. J. E. Round, a preacher of the New-England Conference, and Lieut. John W. Fletcher, afterwards mayor of Chelsea. Both of these officers were connected with Company K of the Forty-third. Lieut. Fletcher left us soon after we reached Newbern, and joined the expedition to Charleston, S.C., as an officer of the Signal Corps.

THE ENLISTMENT, AND THE CAMP AT READVILLE.

As nearly as I can remember, there were over eighty names upon the list before my own; and the patriotic motives of the signers were demonstrated by the fact that *most of them had volunteered before any bounty was offered;* then fifty dollars was promised, then a hundred dollars. After we were in camp, an additional hundred dollars was given, in the benefits of which we all participated. This last action was taken by the city government without pressure from us. The quota of Chelsea was not filled, the draft was impending. and citizens who were of military age were urgent in their entreaties for relief. There was also a sincere conviction that the families of the enlisted citizens could not be supported on the scanty pay of the government, — thirteen dollars per month, — without a liberal local supplement. The following note from Capt. Hanover shows the spirit with which the company was organized: —

BOSTON, Nov. 8, 1882.

Mr. E. H. ROGERS.

Dear Sir, — . . . I would like to make a suggestion or two in order to strengthen what I deem a fit and proper thing to say of our Company H, and its really patriotic impulses at the beginning. I have thought that some allusion should be made to the circumstances of its origin.

A few members of the Rifle Corps sent in to the city government (at their Saturday evening session, Aug. 16) a petition for permission to raise men for the nine-months service. We waited anxiously in the armory in the Square, until after midnight, when a note from Mayor Fay was received, granting the prayer of the petitioners. We immediately obtained an express-wagon, and went to Boston, procuring a new Sibley tent. Returning, we broke ground in the Square, — so hard that crowbars had to be employed to make holes for guy-pins. On sabbath morning we displayed the *first tent* pitched in Chelsea for war purposes, showing to city government and citizens that we meant business.

GEO. B. HANOVER.

Perhaps there is no way in which I can more vividly recall the influences and scenes of those times than by reprinting a local flier which was distributed throughout the city some

time during the month of August, 1862. It was the first of several which I have (the last dated 1864), forming very conspicuous guides to the development of the war-spirit among us.

WAR COUNCIL.

This (Thursday) Evening, at 7 o'clock.

RALLY FOR YOUR COUNTRY!

And show that you are in earnest in bringing this unholy Rebellion to a close by immediately re-enforcing the Army of the Potomac.

Remember! if the city has to resort to draft, that no Bounty or State Aid will be paid!

RALLY ONE AND ALL!

☞ Let the Chelsea boys in the Army of the Potomac know that you are ready to sustain them at any cost!

I should also have associated with the above the circulation and singing of spirited ballads, one of which I will send down to posterity. The "six hundred thousand more" refers to the levy of the three hundred thousand three-years men of 1862 and our own contingent of the same number of nine-months men, which followed immediately.

SIX HUNDRED THOUSAND MORE.

We are coming, Father Abraham, six hundred thousand more, —
From Mississippi's winding stream, and from New England's shore;
We leave our ploughs and workshops, our wives and children dear,
With hearts too full for utterance, with but a silent tear;
We dare not look behind us, but steadfastly before:
We are coming, Father Abraham, — six hundred thousand more.

If you look across the hilltops that meet the northern sky,
Long moving lines of rising dust your vision may descry;
And now the wind an instant tears the cloudy veil aside,
And floats aloft our spangled flag in glory and in pride ;
And bayonets in the sunlight gleam, and bands brave music pour :
We are coming, Father Abraham, — six hundred thousand more.

If you look all up our valleys, where the glowing harvests shine,
You may see our sturdy farmer-boys fast falling into line;
And children from their mother's knees are pulling at the weeds,
And learning how to reap and sow against their country's needs ;
And a farewell group stands weeping at every cottage-door :
We are coming, Father Abraham, — six hundred thousand more.

You have called us, and we're coming by Richmond's bloody tide,
To lay us down for freedom's sake our brothers' bones beside,
Or from foul treason's savage grasp to wrench the murderous blade,
And in the face of foreign foes its fragments to parade.
Five hundred thousand loyal men and true have gone before :
We are coming, Father Abraham, — six hundred thousand more.

Some time during the first week in September, the company met for the choice of officers, resulting in the election of Messrs. George B. Hanover as captain, and William Bradbury and D. C. Colesworthy, jun., as first and second lieutenants. Mr. John Edmunds, jun., was appointed first sergeant, or orderly, with four other sergeants and eight corporals. On Tuesday the 9th, we met at the armory of the Chelsea Light Infantry, in Gerrish's Building, and made our first march over the ferry and across the city, past the State House, to the Providence Depot, taking the cars for Camp Meigs at Readville, about nine miles from Boston.

As we passed over Beacon Hill, the body of Col. Fletcher Webster of the Massachusetts Twelfth, who had been recently slain at the head of his regiment, was being borne to its last resting-place at Marshfield, within our hearing; and the mournful notes of the "Dead March" which fell upon our ears were not calculated to elevate our spirits. But the day was pleasant; we were hopeful as well as patriotic; our situation had the charm of novelty: so gloomy thoughts were soon dissipated, and we arrived at camp, where we found matters as introduced in the following note: —

IN CAMP, READVILLE, MASS.,
Sept. 10, 1862, 38th Birthday.

——— ———, I am glad that I am able to write my first note to you in such good spirits and such favorable circumstances. We reached our camp about one o'clock; and after feeling the first restraint of the soldier's life, in being kept in line half an hour before our dinner was ready — on account of the tendency to straggle — we had the liberty of the camp, or rather one of them (for there are five distinct ones), the others being occupied by the Forty-second, the Forty-fourth, and the Forty-fifth Infantry Regiments, with the Eleventh Battery. During the afternoon our rubber and woollen blankets were delivered to us, and at nine P.M. we were mustered in line, and the roll was called. At half-past nine the lights in the tents were ordered out, and we retired. There was plenty of straw; but I am obliged to say that we all had rather an uncomfortable night: the reason lay partly in our inexperience, and partly in a very piercing valley mist, which soaked our tents, — they were old and thin, — and reduced the temperature. We feel more hopeful for to-night.

As to eating — some of our meals are very good; but coffee and tea are poor. I am to-day put in uniform. . . . There were about sixty-three of our company came out; but they are coming and going all the time, averaging about twenty-five present. This is written in the centre of my tent, which will accommodate about twenty men. I am surrounded by a group of talkative young fellows. It is late, and I must bid you good-night.

The camp to which we had come was first occupied by the Boston companies, on the 27th of August, and it was already known as that of the Forty-third Regiment, which was being recruited on the Boston Light Infantry — Second Battalion — as a base. This was an old organization long known under the appellation of "Tigers:" which term the new regiment appropriated. Several companies were on the grounds, which presented a scene of activity new to most of us. Our own company had been filled nearly to its maximum, and on Sept. 20 we were inspected and sworn in by Capt. N. B. McLaughlin of the regular army, afterwards in command of our friends of Company H, First Regiment. I noticed that all the recruits of advanced years appeared to

THE ENLISTMENT, AND THE CAMP AT READVILLE. 19

have stopped in their growth at the age of forty-five: the reason was obvious. One man admitted that he was older, and was immediately rejected. When the officer came to any one who was evidently older, but who would not admit it, he cross-questioned him sharply. If the age was persisted in, and the man appeared reasonably vigorous, he was passed.

I quote here the full roster of the company, from the report of the adjutant-general of the State, appending, also, a memorial of the dead. Ninety-three are given as residing in Chelsea, but this is an error. The word "quota" should be used instead of "residence." A very large majority, however, were citizens of Chelsea.

The company was homogeneous and harmonious. We were all of American birth and parentage, with the exception of six, who were English or Scotch, with one French Canadian, — all of them acceptable as comrades.

ROSTER OF COMPANY H, FORTY-THIRD REGIMENT.

Names.	Rank.	Age.	Residence.
George B. Hanover	Captain	42	Chelsea.
William Bradbury	First Lieutenant	38	"
D. C. Colesworthy, jun.	Second Lieutenant	27	"
John Edmunds, jun.	First Sergeant	23	"
Charles G. Butts	Sergeant	33	"
John H. Perry	"	28	"
Horace P. Eldridge	"	26	"
Daniel P. Ilsley	"	23	"
Charles T. Adams	Corporal	20	"
Thomas King, jun.	"	33	"
Southworth Bryant	"	28	"
Charles M. Coburn	"	19	"
John T. Pitman	"	26	"
Franklin O. Barnes	"	21	"
Alfred M. S. Butler	"	21	"
George E. Colesworthy	"	18	"
Charles L. Humphrey	Musician	18	"
Norman Wilson	"	18	"
Samuel P. Wilkinson	Wagoner	24	"
Charles R. Fisher	Armorer	38	"
Adams, Sylvester R.	Private	24	"
Adams, Jonathan S.	"	44	"
Bryant, William D.	"	44	"
Baxter, Gilbert	"	22	"
Blanchard, Edwin B.	"	18	"
Beatly, Charles S.	"	23	"

ROSTER OF COMPANY H. — Continued.

Names.	Rank.	Age.	Residence.
Bassett, Charles Z.	Private	19	Chelsea.
Burtt, Joseph A.	"	21	Andover.
Butts, Edwin H.	"	18	Chelsea.
Balledon, George	"	35	"
Banner, Edwin	"	22	"
Bettis, Jonas A.	"	45	"
Carruth, Isaac S.	"	22	Andover.
Colesworthy, Charles J.	"	22	Chelsea.
Cao, William	"	21	"
Dade, David B.	"	32	"
Emerson, George H.	"	18	"
Evans, Thomas H.	"	33	"
Evans, Frank S.	"	19	"
Folsom, William J.	"	18	"
Farley, James A.	"	23	Boston.
Fracker, John W.	"	21	Chelsea.
Forrest, Henry	"	30	"
Gooding, George	"	42	"
Goodwin, Clement F.	"	33	—
Gilling, William F.	"	30	Chelsea.
Geary, George W.	"	27	"
Giraghty, John F.	"	20	"
Hayden, John	"	19	"
Harlow, Dexter	"	45	"
Hopkins, John P.	"	22	Malden.
Hall, Charles W.	"	18	Winthrop.
Harrison, John L.	"	18	Chelsea.
Hemmenway, George S. H.	"	20	"
Haney, Thomas	"	23	"
Hoyt, Charles H.	"	—	"
Judkins, Hiram	"	27	"
Jones, John T.	"	21	"
Johnson, Samuel W.	"	24	Weston.
Kimball, James H.	"	18	Chelsea.
Knowles, Henry F.	"	18	"
Lombard, George E.	"	18	"
Le Blanc, Remi	"	26	"
Lovejoy, Joseph T.	"	22	Andover.
Loach, James W.	"	22	Chelsea.
Lord, George F.	"	18	"
McIntyre, James	"	24	"
McKenzie, William	"	26	"
Maynard, Cornelius D.	"	42	"
Morrill, George E.	"	18	"
Mason, Walter	"	18	"
Mears, George	"	27	"
Merritt, Martin	"	21	"
Patrick, Albert E.	"	21	"
Perry, Almon	"	33	"
Pierce, George F.	"	19	Malden.
Parker, Merritt	"	18	Boston.
Perkins, Charles W.	"	30	Chelsea.
Pratt, George W.	"	19	"
Pickford, Henry	"	31	"

THE ENLISTMENT, AND THE CAMP AT READVILLE. 21

ROSTER OF COMPANY H. — *Concluded.*

Names.	Rank.	Age.	Residence.
Richardson, Zanoni A.	Private	18	Winchester.
Racklif, Benjamin	"	40	Chelsea.
Rogers, Edward H.	"	38	"
Stanwood, William E.	"	40	"
Spaulding, William A.	"	21	Malden.
Sinclair, John G.	"	21	Chelsea.
Spooner, John F.	"	18	"
Swords, Edward K.	"	25	"
Swett, Cyrus E.	"	18	"
Scott, Frank J.	"	19	"
Thompson, Henry F.	"	24	"
Twombly, Charles W.	"	19	"
Tilden, Colman, jun.	"	22	"
Tufts, John	"	34	"
Teel, Abner G.	"	26	Weston.
Whittemore, Thomas, jun.	"	24	Chelsea.
Whitford, Reuben	"	29	"
Whiting, Edward	"	44	"
Warren, Theodore B.	"	19	"
Watson, John A.	"	19	"
Wilson, Henry	"	44	"
Wylie, Isaac	"	39	"
White, William R.	"	42	"
Wood, Joseph A.	"	26	"
Waters, John	"	28	"
Young, George W.	"	39	"

NOTE.—Cao, Forrest, and Waters deserted at Readville; Judkins and Swett were discharged for disability in March, 1863.

NECROLOGY OF THE COMPANY.

	Died.		Died.
Lieut. William Bradbury	1874	John Hayden	1867
Lieut. D. C. Colesworthy, jun.	1867	Hiram Judkins	1868
Corporal Charles T. Adams	—	James H. Kimball	—
Musician Chas. L. Humphrey	—	George F. Lombard	1872
Musician Norman Wilson	1864	James W. Loach	—
William B. Bryant	1866	William E. Stanwood	1893
Jonas A. Bettis	1878	John F. Spooner	1867
Isaac S. Carruth	1882	Edward K. Swords	1877
David B. Dade	—	Abner G. Teel	—
Thomas H. Evans	1881	William R. White	—
James A. Farley	1880	Joseph A. Wood	1866

The above includes only the names of those who are known to have passed away. The date, in some cases, is conjectural.

Here, then, amid the beautiful scenery of the southern suburbs of Boston, at the base of the Blue Hills, was to be our home for nearly two months. The three-years regiments

immediately preceding us had been hurried to the front without the instruction necessary to enable them to manœuvre under fire, and it was understood that Gov. Andrew was unwilling that we should leave the State until we were thoroughly drilled. To this end the movements of the squad, company, and battalion, with the daily dress-parade and guard-mounting, were pursued with diligence. The perfection of our movements, however, was much impeded by the fact that our arms (Springfield rifles) were not furnished to us until the eve of our departure. We made several marches into the country, and on one or two occasions the regiment visited the city: during one of them we were provided with a bountiful collation on Beacon-street Mall at the expense of the city of Boston. A short time before our departure, the Chelsea members of the company, which comprised a large part of our number, came home in a body, being met at the Providence Depot by the Chelsea Rifles, and escorted to the Square by the way of the ferry: here we were dismissed to our homes. During the evening we again assembled under the following circumstances:—

MILITARY OVATION.

"A pleasant re-union of friends, a mingling of partially dissevered households, took place at the City Hall on Wednesday evening. Capt. Hanover and his company (Fourth Company Chelsea Volunteers) — H, Forty-Third Regiment, attached to Col. Holbrook's 'Tigers,' and encamped at Readville — visited the city of their homes on invitation of the Chelsea Rifle Corps, citizens and friends co-operating to make the reception worthy of the occasion.

"The company arrived at Providence Depot in Boston at five o'clock, where they were received by the Rifles. Capt. Hilbourn, fifty guns, with the Chelsea Band. Under this escort the Tigers reached Chelsea by the ferry, the band playing 'Sweet Home' with the quick movements of a march as they passed through our streets to the armory, where they were dismissed till eight o'clock, at which hour they marched to the City Hall under the same escort. The hall was flanked with richly spread and brilliantly decorated tables, and made attractive with kindling eyes. . . . Capt. Hil-

bourn delivered a reception-speech to his guests, which was responded to by Capt. Hanover with ardent brevity. The Tigers then filed round the tables, and commenced to fill with rations of palatable viands not common to soldiers' haversacks. Meanwhile the band discoursed melodious strains.

"After the repast, W. R. Pearmain, Esq., in behalf of the ladies, presented Capt. Hanover with a magnificent bouquet, and to the other officers and non-commissioned officers similar floral favors. These bouquets, for the most part, were very choice, and were supplied for the occasion by Mrs. Isaac Stebbins and other ladies.

"After a period of social conversational intercourse, the music indulged in livelier and more impulsive measures, terminating in the dance. . . . Next day, at two o'clock P.M., they re-assembled at the armory, and returned to Camp Meigs, highly delighted with their visit." — PIONEER, Oct. 18, 1862.

Among the incidents of our stay at Readville, one, in which Lieut. Bradbury was the principal actor, deserves recording. One of the younger members of the company was somewhat free with his tongue while on duty, and the lieutenant was aggravated by it to such an extent as to cause him to lose command of his temper. Catching the offender by the coat-collar, he sat him down quite suddenly in a mud-puddle. The incident caused some feeling among the men, and also in Chelsea. The lieutenant, learning of it, took the first opportunity to make a handsome public apology to the whole company; and justice to his memory calls upon me to say that his conduct throughout the whole term of service amply vindicated his sincerity.

Having said this, I will add that all our officers were "gentlemen." Just how much is comprised in this term no one can tell until he has been under the strict control necessary in military affairs. I am justified in saying that there was not an angry altercation or word between any of us and our officers, commissioned or non-commissioned, during the whole time of service; nor was there any harsh or severe treatment experienced by us at their hands.

A short time before our final departure, the Hon. Frank B. Fay made us a visit, and addressed the company assembled

in line in our street. I recall enough of his speech to know that it was characteristic of the man, — both sensible and practical. We listened with profound attention to the advice which he, by his familiar intercourse with the army, was so well qualified to give to us. He complimented our appearance, and expressed his confidence in our ability to establish a good record; he urged us to take good care of our health, not to drink too much coffee, never to sleep on the bare ground if it could possibly be avoided, — to get a fence-rail, or a barrel-stave, or a bunch of weeds under our back-bones to protect us from moisture, — to be sure to mark our names on our knapsacks, clothes, etc. In concluding, he warned us to expect to be treated unjustly.

Some time during the autumn the regiment had quite a sensation, coming in the shape of what appeared to be an accident to a member of the Abington company. He was engaged in splitting wood, during which he cut off one of his great toes, exciting much sympathy, until, on looking at his boot, it was found to be chalked at the spot where the axe had passed through it, thus proving that the mutilation was intentional. From all that could be learned, homesickness, instead of cowardice, seemed to be the impelling motive of the deed.

Our stay at Readville was enlivened by the daily presence of a Boston band, hired by the regiment, and also by the frequent visits of our families and friends. We had our full share of the exuberance of spirits natural to men released from the dull and engrossing routine of daily labor, and many were the pranks that were played. As I recall them, I wonder that we had not broken some of our necks. On one occasion I saw a sutler's building, that must have been at least fifteen feet by twenty-five, taken off its foundation by as many men as could get under it, and moved several hundred feet, to a more appropriate location than its original one, with the most side-splitting scenes of laughter. After it was set upon its new base, it was broken open, and the contents of pastry, etc., were tumultuously scrambled for, and eaten. Rather rough on the owner, the reader will

think. In some respects it was; in others, not. It would have cost him something in money to have moved the building himself, so that his cakes were not an entire loss to him; then the transaction was an open one, done in the broad light of mid-day; it was impromptu, and without malice, and it passed off without any further notice.

At another time, as I was standing in our company's street early one evening, I noticed one of the tallest and liveliest of our men, whom I shall speak of as "the deacon," coming quietly along past me, having with him six or eight of the fun-lovers of our number. I saw by their manner that something was up, and kept my eyes upon them. They passed up to the head of the street, and stopped opposite the sergeant's quarters,—a low A tent large enough for four men. It was closed; but it was apparent shortly afterwards, that our orderly was in it, engaged in writing, and one or two of his associates were also with him. Absolute stillness prevailed. As quick as the tent was reached, and without any talk or even signs, the "deacon" laid himself down flat upon his face, on the ground; his comrades in mischief ranged themselves on either side, and placed their hands under his body, raising him about eighteen inches; they then swayed him to and fro, still preserving perfect quiet, until, at a final word of command, he was hurled head first into the tent, and, as the flap was not fastened, he disappeared completely from our sight. The effect was very observable. The group of astonished sergeants put in an appearance on the street as soon as they could pick themselves up, and get out of the fallen tent. It was soon apparent to them that the world had not come to an end, after which an explanation was in order: this was made in such circumstances of uproarious merriment from all concerned, as to render anger out of the question. "John" thought that it was rather "steep," hoped, in his courteous manner, that they "wouldn't do so again," and the incident passed off without serious consequences, either physical or moral.

There was often a strange blending of the grave and the comic in connection with our countersigns: these were

usually taken from the scene of war, — Antietam, etc.; and on one occasion a German recruit, who had hardly acquired the ordinary use of our language, challenged the grand rounds "to advance the 'South Mountain,' and give the countersign."

A pleasant memory of Readville recurs in chronicling the fact that the neighboring residents on several occasions made us the honored sharers of their crops of fruit, bringing them into camp by loads, and emptying them upon the ground in our streets.

Finally, during the last of October, various floating rumors as to our departure and destination took definite form in an order, dated Oct. 24, to our colonel, to go on board of the steamer "Merrimac," at Boston, and on arrival at Newbern, N.C., to report to Gen. John G. Foster, commanding the Eighteenth Army Corps.

The preparations necessary for our departure delayed us until Wednesday, Nov. 5, when we took the cars for Boston. Several regiments besides our own were in motion on that day, destined for North Carolina and Louisiana; so that our progress was slow, and we did not reach the parade-ground on the Common until late in the afternoon. We here received our colors from the hands of the Hon. Robert C. Winthrop, accompanied by a lengthy and interesting historical address, the closing words of which I give, as follows, with Col. Holbrook's reply: —

"Sir, I may detain you no longer. These historical reminiscences and allusions, which I should hardly have been pardoned for omitting on such an occasion, have left me no time for dwelling on the circumstances under which you have been called forth, or of the cause in which you are engaged. But the banner at my side will more than supply all such deficiencies. Indeed, however precious and however sacred may be the freedom of opinion and of discussion to the citizen at home, to the soldier in the field, the order of his commander and the flag of his country are the only and all-sufficient chart and compass of his duty. I will make no vain effort to give a new glory, or even a new gloss, to that flag. All that could be done to invest it with the charms of elo-

THE ENLISTMENT, AND THE CAMP AT READVILLE. 27

quence and poetry has already and long ago been done. The genius of our land has inwoven itself upon every tint and thread and fibre of its hallowed texture. Yet its own majestic presence is more eloquent and more inspiring than all that ever has been or can be said of it. It is the flag of our fathers, the flag of Washington, the flag of the Union. It is the symbol of no party less comprehensive than the whole people, of no policy less broad and general than the whole constitution, of no region or territory or district or section less extensive and wide-spread than our whole country. The stars are all there, shining out from its field of blue and red, like the glory of those who first unfurled it from the fields of their wounds and blood — the stars are all there: we count them wistfully day by day, and hail each one of them still and always as the cherished emblem of a sister-state. And most fervently do we hope and pray, that, by the blessing of God, the day may again soon return when each one of them may again be hailed as the emblem of a loving and loyal sister, when a spirit of reconciliation may have been poured out effectually over all those alienated hearts, and when the blessed radiance of our whole glorious constellation may once more illuminate the pathway of constitutional liberty for all the nations of the earth.

"It only remains for me, sir, to present to you, as I now do, the standard which has been prepared for you. In the name of the Boston Light Infantry Association and of the friends of your regiment who are gathered around me, I commit it to the sacred guardianship of the regiment under your command. And may the blessing of God attend you whenever and wherever you may be called on to display it or defend it; and not upon you only, but upon all your gallant compeers who have been your associates in yonder camp, and who go forth with you this day to a common field of duty and of danger. God bless and prosper and protect them all!"

This eloquent address was listened to with earnest attention, and was frequently applauded.

Col. Holbrook, in behalf of the regiment, responded as follows: —

"MR. WINTHROP, AND GENTLEMEN OF THE BOSTON LIGHT INFANTRY ASSOCIATION, — The fatigues of the camp this morning have completely unfitted me for making any remarks, and beside

your own. I feel that there is nothing for me to say further than that, without making any promises or pledges of what we shall accomplish, we shall endeavor to do our duty to the best of our ability. And, sir, from the knowledge I have of the officers and men under my command, I have no hesitation in saying that whatever I call upon them to do, and whatever dangers they may be called on to brave, they will nobly sustain their part with honor to themselves and members of the Boston Light Infantry Association.

"I thank you, sir, and through you the members of the Boston Light Infantry, for this beautiful flag. It will not only serve to remind us of the present moment and of friends at home; but it will ever remind us of the motto of our noble corps: 'Death, or an honorable life.'"

It was nearly dark before we were allowed to take leave of our friends. They had been patiently waiting, for long wearisome hours, for the final parting, upon the dear, familiar grounds where most of us had been accustomed from our boyhood to scenes of patriotic rejoicing and festivity upon our national anniversary. It was so late, that but a few moments could be allowed us for this purpose, after which we formed column.

> "With hearts too full for utterance,
> But with a silent tear,
> We dared not look behind us,
> But steadfastly before,
> For farewell groups stood weeping"

as we moved past the State House, down School, Washington, State, and Commercial Streets, to Battery Wharf at the North End. Here occurred one of those tedious delays which formed so marked a feature of military life, and it was late in the evening before we were fairly on board, and moving down the harbor.

CHAPTER II.

THE VOYAGE.

WE awoke on the following morning, and, to our surprise, we found ourselves lying at anchor under shelter of Deer Island. It was understood that we were to wait until the gunboat "Huron" could be prepared at the Navy Yard to act as a convoy. The Confederate cruiser "Alabama" had been capturing shipping off the coast, and it was deemed unsafe to trust unarmed steamers, like our own, at sea.

Meanwhile a severe and long-continued easterly storm, a gale indeed, with rain and snow, set in. The large size and corresponding draught of our ships had compelled us to anchor at some distance from the island. The storm occasioned a heavy swell to heave in from Broad Sound; and the action of the tide caused the vessels to lie, much of the time, in the trough of the sea, or sideways to the waves: they rolled considerably, and this made the situation quite uncomfortable to us all, and specially so to those, of whom there were many, who were inclined to seasickness.

I should have stated previously that the Forty-fifth Regiment from Readville was under the same orders as ourselves, with the exception that they were on board "The Mississippi," a sister-ship of "The Merrimac;" and the Forty-sixth, a nine-months regiment from the western part of the State, was also with us, half being on board "The Merrimac," and half on board "The Mississippi." This made nearly fifteen hundred men on board each ship, which would have tasked their capacity to the utmost, even in pleasant weather. The ships were well ventilated, and fitted for troops; but the number on board was too large. And the privations and ex-

posures were sufficiently marked to cause much fault-finding and some suffering.

The national authorities at Boston sent down another steamer, "The Saxon," as soon as our condition became known. Part of the men of the Forty-sixth were removed from each ship to her, and peace and comfort prevailed among us. The storm abated on Sunday, our preparations were completed; and on Monday afternoon, Nov. 10, we saw the gunboat coming down the harbor. All three of the transports immediately weighed their anchors, and proceeded to sea, accompanied by our friends in harbor-tugs, who finally bid us good-by as they went over the side while we were passing Boston Light at sunset.

I remained upon deck long enough to enjoy the sight of the four ships steaming rapidly to sea, one after the other, the regulation-colored lights at each bow, and a light at every masthead. Going down to my place on the after-orlop, I slept quietly until about three o'clock in the morning, when I was startled by a slight collision, with a peculiar noise. For the moment I was mystified. The ship's propeller stopped at once, and it seemed a long time before the sound, which was a rasping friction of something with the ship's side her whole length, ceased. But she finally ran clear of it, and we soon learned, what I had suspected after my first bewilderment was over. Our ship was built of iron, and we had struck the iron-can buoy located at Monomoy Point, the extreme south-eastern extremity of Cape Cod. The sound was as unearthly as the bray of the mules with which we afterwards became so familiar in North Carolina. The men were, for the most part, cool; but there were tendencies to a rush to the gangway-ladders, which might have been disastrous to some of us. This was happily averted, however, by the loud and clear voice of Capt. Hanover, who had leaped upon deck at the first alarm, and, after learning its cause, came to the hatch, and calmed our apprehensions with an explanation. It was fortunate for us that we had been relieved of some of the men of the Forty-sixth. We were so fearfully crowded while they were with us, that we should

have struggled desperately, if a panic had happened, to get on deck.

At daylight we were passing Edgartown, and, on clearing Vineyard Sound, directed our course to the south-west, which soon brought us to the open ocean; and by ten o'clock A.M. we had sunk Block Island (the last land in sight) so low, that it only showed as a speck upon the horizon. We were at sea. The last local association had been sundered, and we became conscious that henceforth our country demanded all our time and strength in her service.

Of the voyage, as of the camp, I have but one letter, which I will copy, and afterwards supply its omissions.

STEAMER "MERRIMAC," OFF BEAUFORT, N.C.,
Friday, A.M., Nov. 14, 1862.

—— —— I am on deck this morning, under a summer sky soft and balmy, with showers falling in the horizon, as with us in August, endeavoring, as best I may amid the constant interruptions incident to such a crowd, to pencil a few lines. We are supposed to be close in to Beaufort, as we passed Hatteras Light last evening, though the shore is so low that it is invisible. With the exception of three or four passing vessels and our own squadron, we have seen nothing but sea and sky since Tuesday morning. Our passage has been very pleasant, and, with the exception of one day, very smooth. There has been, however, some seasickness on board. The length of our voyage has been owing to the dull sailing of our convoy, "The Huron;" there being a constant necessity of slacking speed, of stopping, and even of going back and circling around her, in order to keep within the shelter of her powerful armament.

SATURDAY, A.M., Nov. 15.

Last night "The Mississippi" ran away, and this morning "The Saxon" and ourselves are following suit, driving ahead with the full force of our engines. We expect to be in Beaufort before night.

Our officers have been very kind and considerate, and we are favored with the presence of one lady, the colonel's wife, who stands to us as an earnest of what a thousand other wives would do, did circumstances permit. You can't think how grateful we are to the kind friends in Chelsea, who at the last moment sent our

company five barrels of apples. They are so admirable, both for the palate and above all for health, that we have been the envy of the regiment. I believe that Mr. Butts was conspicuous in this kind deed: if so, I could wish to extend to him our hearty thanks. I have fared well during the voyage, having my haversack so well filled by loving hands on the Common. We have had two meals a day, which has been enough. As we are so crowded, there is no room for drill, and we have but little to do. What privation there has been has been mainly due to the fact that we are entirely dependent upon condensed water, as all the fresh water that we have has to be given to the officers' horses, who will not drink a drop of the condensed water: this is limited in quantity, and it tastes so strongly of oil as to be nauseous. Many can taste it even in tea and coffee. (Interrupted by arrival.)

The only incident of general interest which happened during our voyage was an accident of a serious nature to our quartermaster, Lieut. Henry A. Turner. He, with quite a number of other officers, was on the quarter-deck, at the extreme after-end of the ship, on the most windy day of our voyage. The ship was very uneasy, making it difficult for landsmen to preserve their balance. The officers had gathered a quantity of joiner's chips, pieces of board, and the like, and one by one they were throwing them overboard, and then firing at them with revolvers, as long as they remained within easy range. It was quite exciting sport, as the water showed where the balls struck: and encomium or ridicule rapidly followed upon each shot, according to its success or failure. All at once, we of the ranks, who were debarred from the official precincts above us, noticed a sudden cessation of the firing, the laughter, and talk, and it quickly appeared that the services of our surgeon were required. It proved that Lieut. Turner, while waiting for his chance to fire, had prematurely discharged his weapon while holding it downwards; and the ball had gone through the centre of his foot.

I will finish the record of the voyage by using a portion of the first letter home from Newbern.

IN CAMP, NEAR NEWBERN, Nov. 16, 1862.

—— —— I wrote to you on board ship, sealing my letter on discovering land, and leaving it on board for transit home. We were unfortunate enough to ground on a bar shortly after entering

the harbor, giving the other regiment the start of us in respect to railroad facilities; so that we did not get clear of the ship until Saturday noon, nine days after coming on board. What should we have thought if we could have known this when we embarked!

From the same letter I quote as follows:—

"We had a pleasant and interesting railroad ride to Newbern, through rough forest scenery. We passed over the battle-field which resulted in the capture of the town six months before, without being aware of its proximity, and stopped on the south bank of the Trent River. From here we marched north-westerly, along the course of the Trent, about two miles from Newbern, and halted very nearly upon the spot, at nightfall, where our regiment was to be located. 'Camp Rogers' was the name afterwards given to it, in honor of Major C. O. Rogers of 'The Boston Journal,' a patron of the regiment."

THE CAMP.

For a day or two our situation was one of uncertainty and discomfort while waiting for our material and stores from "The Merrimac;" but gradually order came out of disorder, as we adjusted ourselves to our new circumstances. My first impressions of the place are recorded as follows:—

"Our camp is very pleasantly situated on an elevated rolling plain, more extensive than Readville, about two miles and a half long, and a mile wide, having been a plantation. The soil is a porous, sandy loam very much resembling the Cape, but more arable. It is thinly clothed with grass, and contrasts strangely with the luxuriance of the meadows and water-courses. If you can bring into your mind all that you have read of the verdure of Brazil, and suppose it by some incomprehensible process wedded to the barren sterility of our sandy Cape, you will have some idea of what I am seeing here in respect to natural scenery."

I afterward ascertained that there were large beds of delicate tropical shells, barely hidden beneath the surface, within a few hundred feet of our camp; thus proving that the low part of North Carolina is of very recent origin.

In the location of the camp the north-western corner was

bounded by the Trent for a hundred feet or thereabouts.
At this point there was a beach of hard soil. The river was
perfectly fresh, there being no regular tide, though the
volume of water varied considerably. This beach was a great
convenience to us. The whole regiment resorted to it in the
morning to wash or bathe; and parties were present at all
hours of leisure engaged in washing clothes.

Just below the camp, a few hundred feet, there was a
bridge, which connected with what was called the Trent
Road, leading toward Kinston. This bridge, I should judge,
was about four hundred feet long. About a quarter of a
mile nearer Newbern, the navy was represented by a New-
York canal-boat, which was doing duty as a floating battery.
She had a rifled pivot-gun on her deck, and was a fixture,
although afloat all the time of our stay. During the stillness of the night we could hear her bell striking the time in
nautical style. This was a great convenience in regulating
our watches, and the associations were also pleasant to those
of us who were accustomed to the sea.

The Chaplain writes concerning the camp as follows:—

TIGER REGIMENT (CAMP ROGERS), Dec. 8, 1862.

Our camp is on the right bank of the River Trent, a broad and
tortuous stream which creeps northward to the Neuse with a flow
so sluggish as to be hardly perceptible; while on its left bank, and
between the two rivers, is the city of Newbern. We are two miles
from town by direct course and the railroad-bridge; some four or
five miles, if we choose a pleasanter route through woods, crossing
the Trent by an old bridge near the barracks of the Forty-fifth
Massachusetts Regiment. Our regimental line extends north and
south, the left toward Newbern, the right resting on the river,
which at this point wears gently inward upon us. The rising sun
looks into the tent-doors of the field and line officers, and up the
company streets.

At dress-parade, when the day is withdrawing through the west,
amid its setting splendors we fancy ourselves at Readville again.
True, the glories of Blue Mountain are not in front of our line of
battle; but just over the extreme right, between our hospital and
chapel tents, and beyond the river and the far-stretching marsh, we

CAMP ROGERS.

ENCAMPMENT OF THE FORTY-THIRD REGIMENT, M. V. M. NEWBERN, N. C., MARCH 12TH, 1863.

see the sun go down precisely as at our first encampment in old Massachusetts. There are the same officers in the same relative positions, the same commands in the same ringing tones, the same glistening bayonets, polished musket-barrels, shoulder-scales, and various housings, burnished by the same peaceful radiance; and the surface of the Trent, no longer dark and sullen, but beaming with the brightness of the descending sun, whose benignant smile has overlaid it, seems no other than that of the little lake which spread so sweetly between us and the Forty-fourth hardly more than a month ago.

THE REGIMENT.

There was no time previous to our arrival in North Carolina which could be devoted to a description of our regiment, for changes were taking place from day to day, which now measurably ceased, and the battalion took permanent form. The history of the company involves, to a large extent, that of the regiment, and especially so in our case, as we were the color-company, and on that account were the less liable to be detached: in fact we were only separated for a week or two during the whole time of service.

The field-officers were as follows: —

CHARLES S. HOLBROOK, *Colonel;* JOHN C. WHITON, *Lieutenant-Colonel* (afterwards Colonel of the Massachusetts Fifty-eighth); EVERETT LANE, *Major;* A. CARTER WEBBER, *Surgeon;* AUGUSTUS MASON, *Assistant Surgeon;* JAMES M. WHITNEY, *Adjutant;* HENRY A. TURNER, *Quartermaster;* JACOB M. MANNING, *Chaplain;* J. E. GILMAN, *Sergeant-Major;* W. W. TUTTLE, *Quartermaster-Sergeant;* A. C. JORDAN, *Commissary Sergeant;* W. H. MANSFIELD, *Hospital Steward.*

The details of companies for special duty apart from the regiment during our term of service were as follows: —

Nov. 30, Company C, Capt. William B. Fowle, jun., was ordered to Beaufort, N.C., where it remained until the 4th of March, 1863, when it reported back to the regiment. On Dec. 31, 1862, Companies A, D, and E, were ordered on picket-duty at Bachellor's Creek, about ten miles from camp, where they remained till Jan. 11, 1863. They were under

the command of Capt. T. G. Whytal of Company D. Jan. 11. Company I, Capt. George O. Tyler, was ordered on picket-duty at Evan's Mills, about seven miles from camp, where it remained till March 2, 1863. On the 15th of April, Companies C, D, and H, as further stated, were detailed for special duty in Pamlico Sound, under Major Lane, from which we were relieved on the 24th inst.

The report of the adjutant-general gives seventy-one desertions from two of the Boston companies, A and B, while only twenty-four are reported against the rest of the regiment, of which nine are set against the other Boston Company, C, three only being credited to our company. The reason for this is to be found in the fact that Boston was slow in offering bounties, and the country companies profited by her delay. In justice to the whole regiment it should be said that there was not, so far as I know, a single genuine case of desertion after we left the State. The whole battalion was patriotic and loyal, without ostentation or vanity.

We were united with the Twenty-third, the Seventeenth, the Forty-fifth, and the Fifty-first, all Massachusetts regiments, and formed the First Brigade, and first division of the Eighteenth Army Corps. Col. Thomas J. C. Amory of the Seventeenth was acting brigadier.

Of our camp, which I have previously located, I should say here, that, although it proved to be in some senses a permanent one, yet this fact could not be assumed beforehand. Every thing in the soldier's life is, and must be in the nature of the case, uncertain. We might at any moment have been driven out or captured by the Confederates, or, without notice, have been ordered up into Virginia, or sent to the Southern coast with the great expedition which was fitted out in our department during the winter. In fact, the regiment was often absent (at one time as long as two weeks, during the movements around Little Washington); but we always finally returned to the first camp, so that we came eventually to regard it as our home, and cheerfully devoted time and labor to its grading, improvement, and ornamentation. Of the details of this work and of our life in camp, I

will write more in future. We had been a month in North Carolina when events matured as indicated in the following letter: —

CAMP ROGERS, NEWBERN, Dec. 9, 1862.

—— ——, I despatched a letter to you this morning, and, shortly after sending it, our orderly came to my tent, and told me that I was one of the three who had drawn the privilege of a day's liberty to visit Newbern. So, after cleaning my gun from yesterday's firing, off I started for the Fifth Regiment, by way of Newbern, which I found a place hardly worthy of a second visit, looking as though nothing had been done to it for thirty years. I had, however, a very pleasant call on Chaplain Snow of the Fifth, and also on my Navy-Yard acquaintances in the Charlestown City Guard.

But the item that prompts this note to you is the fact that we have received re-enforcements to-day (how many I cannot tell, but I suppose not a very large number); and to-night, on dress-parade, orders were read for us to be ready to march within thirty-six hours, with three days' cooked rations, two blankets, one extra pair of socks, without knapsacks, and, as is understood, without breaking up the camp, and with seven days' rations in bulk. It is probable that it is an expedition similar to the Tarboro march; but of this we cannot tell, as we cannot even guess our destination. I do not know what reports may reach you, so, little as it is, I thought best to send you all I knew, as it is not likely that I shall have a chance for some time of writing again. . . .

Our cooks were busy all night preparing our extra rations, and in various ways our time during the next day was fully taken up. Such articles of clothing and bedding as were not wanted, together with other personal articles, were either packed in our knapsacks or strapped to them, and were carried to a transport schooner, "The Skirmisher," which was brought up to the upper bridge across the Trent. This led us to think that we were not to return to Newbern, as we reasoned that the schooner was to follow the column with our equipments; but it appeared afterward that it was only for their safe keeping. The tents were allowed to remain standing, and were unmolested during our absence.

Some of the young men of the regiment were wild with delight at the certainty of an engagement; but to most of

us the thought of the untried scenes which were before us, possibly of wounds, imprisonment, and death, was not specially exhilarating. There was no depression, however, and no indication of irresolution; nor was there in either of the engagements which ensued.

Early on the morning of Thursday, Dec. 11, we were in line on the parade-ground, prepared, as ordered, for the march. Our colonel made a brief speech, enjoining us to obey orders, to keep in our places, and assured us that he did not want us to go anywhere that he did not lead. We gave three cheers, started in the direction of Newbern; and "The Great March" was begun.

CHAPTER III.

THE GREAT MARCH.—KINSTON.

THE morning was foggy. Our movement was made in connection with Burnside's attack on Lee, at Fredericksburg, Va., and, at the moment we started, the pickets of both armies were firing across the Rappahannock, through the mist, at the flashes of their rifles, without seeing each other. I will say here, that most of our marches in North Carolina were made, more or less, in connection with the course of events in Virginia. The great railroads were in operation within the rebel lines; and troops were moved with such facility upon them that we could have been driven out of Newbern at any moment. And we should have been, undoubtedly, were it not that the gunboats would instantly have recaptured the place.

We entered Newbern by the railroad-bridge, and found its streets thronged with troops of every arm, all under similar orders with ourselves. The town had been abandoned by its inhabitants; but their places had been filled by fleeing slaves from the interior. There was also a considerable number of officers' wives, and some families of civilians connected in various ways with the public service. The morning was warm, the windows were open, and the faces of our fair countrywomen told but too plainly of the severity of the strain which the terrible experiences of war imposed upon them. All shades of sorrowful expression, accompanied in some cases with deathly pallor, were to be seen; and I noticed one instance of a lady, presumptively the wife of a general officer, who was pacing to and fro in her parlor, wringing her hands, with every indication of poignant suffering. On the following sabbath we were passing through the

streets of Kinston, and the few women who remained in their homes received us in much the same manner. Whoever, hereafter, succeeds in bringing the true causes of the war to light will find the richest veins of basic truth lying just below the refined feminine sensibilities of the cultivated women of the South. Their action in throwing their almost omnipotent influence on the side of armed resistance to law was a crime against the gentle nature of the sex.

The moving columns, slowly and with frequent delay, converged upon the road to Kinston; the fog vanished; and by nine o'clock we were fairly on our march. Two-thirds of the column was composed of us raw recruits, nine-months men from Massachusetts: most of the rest were the remnants of Burnside's original army, with which, six months before, he had captured the seaports of the State; the recent re-enforcements being mainly regiments whose depleted ranks told an impressive story of the exposures of the Peninsular campaign. Gen. Foster was an artillery officer, a veteran of the Mexican war, one of the gallant band who had been shut up in Sumter. He favored his own arm in fighting, and to this, I apprehend, was due the fact, that, though our little army only numbered at the most fifteen thousand men, we had sixty pieces of artillery. His policy seemed to be to get his guns within easy musket-range of the enemy, to pack his infantry as closely around them as possible, lying on our faces, and then to blaze away.

One of these batteries, Morison's of New York, was composed of brass guns called Napoleons. They were of very large size and bore for field artillery, firing a six-inch round shell. Their appearance was imposing; but the reverberation from their brazen throats was terrific. One of the most impressive sights that we witnessed was when they were planted on the river-bank at Kinston, and opened their fire upon the town.

We untried soldiers gazed with something of awe upon the faces of the veterans of Roanoke Island and the fight at Newbern. We heard them say to each other with easy *nonchalance*, "Something up now, sure!" "You bet your life on

that!" "This means business," etc. The Erie Canal of New York, and the mines of Pennsylvania, had sent their quotas of sturdy men. Massachusetts, Rhode Island, and Connecticut were well represented among the veterans. New Jersey was there in the gallant Ninth, and, by our association with these brave men, we returned to Newbern with sufficient experience and reputation to be intrusted with the defence of the coast, while most of the veterans were withdrawn to other departments.

Our march the first day was to a plantation on the Newbern side of what afterwards became known to us as Deep Gully. We were not opposed, and rested quietly during the night. Much to the surprise of us new-comers, no tents were furnished. We had supposed that flies, at least, would be provided; but they were not, and it was a puzzle to us to know what we should do in case of rain or snow. We learned however, before our return, that rubber blankets can be so utilized, even in the open air, as to answer nearly, if not quite, as well as the thin, small, inconvenient sheets of cotton-cloth, two of which united constitute a fly-tent. In cold weather, soldiers are obliged, when on the march, to sleep as close to each other as is possible for the sake of the warmth. This liberates at least half of the blankets, as they are not needed underneath the body: in such cases, the half thus liberated are placed on top of the sleeping ranks, protecting the soldier and his woollen blanket. These last, it should be further stated, are duplicated by the same process; so that each man has at least one thickness of rubber, and two or three of woollen, both underneath and over him. I have repeatedly seen men sleep quietly, while covered in this manner, during a drenching thunder-shower. As the warm season approached, flies were given to us; but they were not acceptable, and, if circumstances allowed it, we hutted ourselves in preference to using them.

As the regiments and batteries reached the plantation, they were ranged in line, and released from duty, with the exception of a detail for guard, and the pioneers. The first matter to be attended to was the gathering of fence-rails for

our fires, to be kept up during the night. These were usually close at hand, and of excellent material, as the plantations of this portion of the State are fenced, in zigzag style, with hard-pine split rails without posts. Our fires kindled, we cooked our coffee in our tin dippers, with as much jarring, jostling, and wrangling with each other, as if we had been English sparrows, instead of friendly and social comrades. "There, you've upset my dipper! 'Twas just ready to boil. I thought you would. Confound you, you clumsy lout! why couldn't you be a little more careful?" Sometimes it would seem as though two of the best fellows in the company had sworn mutual and deadly enmity to each other for the rest of the term of service. But somehow or other, though nearly all of us fell from grace more or less in respect to these exposures, the circumstances were so trying, that we forgave each other immediately.

This done, we devoted ourselves to levelling the hills which remained from the last crop of corn or cotton, spread our blankets in the manner I have described, and composed ourselves for the night.

With the first gray light of the morning we were up, and engaged in cooking our breakfasts, in which I should include the roasting, in the accumulated ashes of the night, of what sweet potatoes we had been able to lay our hands on. The lack of utensils prevented us from cooking any meat or poultry, with the exception of one night during which we were encamped in the streets of Kinston, when we made a free use of the pots and kettles found in the houses.

When our regiment was near the head of the column, we moved early: if we had no intimation of this, we prepared ourselves fully for a sudden start, and rested upon our blankets after they were rolled up, ready to be slung over one shoulder, which was the way we carried them. During the night we heard the axes of our pioneers employed in removing the first obstruction we had met. The Confederates had got sufficient notice of our coming to block the road for some distance by the felling of large trees. It requires but one cut to level a tree; but, as it lies across the highway, it

takes ordinarily two cuts to remove it: at any rate this
was the case in this instance. Our men had had a hard
night's work; but they had accomplished it, so that we were
not delayed an instant. This was a foretaste of one class of
the obstacles which were met by the column. Bridges were
burned, or sawed in such a manner as to require propping.
Mill-dams were sluiced, so as to deluge us with water; and,
in various ways incidental to the possession of the enforced
labor of the slaves and the irregular action of guerillas, we
were harassed and delayed to give time for the collection of
the trained forces of the army to resist us.

One incident of our march must not be omitted. The
small streams and creeks of North Carolina run through gullies, or low places, which they have worn for themselves in
the course of ages, and we found them quite swollen with
water. They recur at frequent intervals, and were, in some
cases, well up to our thighs. They were corduroyed; that is,
the lowest and muddiest parts had been covered with logs or
thick plank. Our artillery in passing through would crush
these in their centres so as to raise their ends sufficiently
high to trip us, yet not high enough to show above the
water. The consequence was, that all of us were wet up to
our bodies; and quite often some luckless fellow would get
a plunge into the muddy stream, not very favorable to his
health or comfort, or the preservation of his ammunition.

Many of these low places had a line of trees, which had
been felled, and placed end to end with each other on the side
of the road, and elevated sufficiently above it on crotched
sticks to make a rude bridge, which we passed in single file.
This, however, was usually more or less out of order and
unreliable. Being round sticks, we jostled each other as we
crowded upon them; so that after we were once wet, many
of us preferred to take our chances in the road rather than
run the risk of being thrown off from the bridge.

Early in the forenoon of the second day, we came to the
primitive dwelling of one of the "poor whites." Its owner
and his family were out in front of it. Their appearance,
in connection with their local surroundings, was unthrifty

and illiterate in the extreme. They seemed in dread of personal violence; but they appeared to have been unmolested. In deprecating our anger, they had extemporized the national colors out of white cloth with stripes stitched on it. By a ludicrous blunder which illustrated their ignorance, the "colors" were set "union *down;*" so that what was evidently intended to conciliate us was really, in its outward form, an insult. The trepidation, however, of the family was too evident to allow us to take offence at the mistake. A lieutenant of our regiment contemptuously tore the rag down, and we left them to their ignorance and poverty.

As we passed on in our march, we came, at frequent intervals, to the ruins of what had been large plantation-houses; the chimneys now, for the most part, being all that was left. These were the sad memorials of the fierce contests with rebel pickets and guerilla parties, which had raged during the previous summer. To the great credit of a worthy citizen of Massachusetts, of the Masonic order, who had visited the State as a peacemaker previous to our arrival, these bloody and useless contests had ceased by mutual consent.

Towards the afternoon of the second day we began to have evidence that we were in an enemy's country by seeing occasionally a dead body by the roadside, slain by our cavalry, and also prisoners. On Saturday there was continuous though not rapid firing of artillery on our right, in the direction of the River Neuse, as we approached Kinston: this proved to be an engagement at South-west Creek.

This stream crossed our march at right angles. At the point where we were expected by the rebels, they had prepared formidable intrenchments; but Gen. Foster avoided these by crossing the creek farther to the west. The firing which we heard was from our cavalry, which was provided with light howitzer cannon, with which they engaged the attention of the enemy, while the Ninth New Jersey and Twenty-third Massachusetts forded the stream above and below a bridge, and captured their guns.

We were halted for an hour while this transpired, and while the bridge, which the enemy burned, was replaced.

We lay in line of battle, but were not further engaged. At this time we saw at a distance a sight which reminded me vividly of the experience of our English ancestors here in New England. Some guerillas, closely pressed by our cavalry, took refuge in a large plantation-house, and defended themselves from their foes, with their muskets, from the chamber-windows. We saw the guns pointing downwards, and the light clouds of smoke which followed the report. The sight brought forcibly before my mind the time when our forefathers were subjected to similar exposures, in the early history of our country, in resisting the French and Indians.

On Sunday forenoon, about ten o'clock, rapid artillery-firing commenced at the head of our column, which at the moment was about a mile in advance of our regiment. The infantry was immediately halted, and opened to the right and left of the narrow road; while cavalry and artillery went to the front at headlong speed. The artillery-firing continued, increasing in volume without being very rapid. One after another, the infantry regiments went into position as they came up, and opened their fire; the first volley being well defined and massive, as when an ocean-wave falls heavily upon a beach, and then being followed by the confused uproar of firing at will. Our eyes, however, aided us but little in observing these occurrences, as the action took place in the forest, there being barely openings enough to handle the troops. While we were watching and listening with all our faculties, expecting every moment orders to go in ourselves, I observed that shells were exploding in the tops of the trees, which were about a hundred feet high. I supposed that our gunboats had succeeded in passing the obstructions in the river, and were attacking the enemy, as I did not think that our field-batteries could throw a shell so high in the air at so short a range. But I soon noticed that the missiles were smaller than the fleet would be likely to use, and I was mystified. When we reached the guns, a short time after, I found that their trails were buried deep in the ground, so that the cannon pointed up into the air.

While these matters were transpiring, we remained a half hour or more in the road. We were then taken into a field, or open place on the right, to support a battery. We were formed in line of battle, and enjoined by our officers to keep our places, and fire coolly and low. After a while we were marched out into the road, and toward the front. We soon met the wounded and dead being brought out on stretchers and ambulances, and immediately found ourselves on the scene of action. We could see nothing, however, but the forest, with narrow openings; but our ears gave us abundant evidence of a hotly contested battle within the leafy coverts before us. As we continued to advance, we became conscious that a shower of bullets was whistling in the air at some distance over our heads, and we received orders to lie down. While here, I was conscious of a singular and unexpected experience. The rebel arms must have been mostly smooth-bores. There was none of the whizzing, screeching sound so characteristic of rifle-balls; but in its stead the noise of the leaden storm which was upon us was a soft and impressive sighing, like that of zephyrs in a forest of pines,— somewhat louder, it is true, but in a high degree soothing and pleasant. I thought of the story of Washington, wherein he is asserted to have said, when he was young, that musket-balls made the sweetest of music to him.

In a few moments we were again ordered forward. Proceeding some five hundred feet, we filed sharply to the right, marching between two lines of battle, composed of New-York and Pennsylvania troops,— so near them on either side that we could speak with each other. Their officers stood with drawn swords, composed and soldierly; but the bearing of the men was different. Almost without exception, they were pale: most of them were excited. Some cheered us: others greeted us with slang. Many seemed ready to drop to the ground with fatigue and anxiety: some, indeed, had lain down in sheer exhaustion. Passing them, we came out of the forest into a large open space at the extreme right of our line, five hundred feet wide or more and a quarter of a mile long. Here we also found the battery with their trails

buried in the ground: they had ceased firing. At the extremity of this field, as it appeared to us, an enemy's earthwork was visible; whether occupied or not, we could not tell. Our hearts flew quick for a few moments at this discovery. We had just noticed, as above stated, that the troops we had passed were in a peculiar condition of excitement, and we understood afterwards that they expected that the rebels would open fire on us the moment we emerged from the forest. We ascertained at the close of the action that the Neuse rolled between us and the fort; but, if the enemy had been in condition to prolong the fight on the other bank, we should have been no better off on account of the river, for the fort was evidently built to sweep the plain upon which we had entered.

We were now at the very tiptoe of expectation. For more than an hour we had been in a suspense that weighed heavily upon us. Every face showed sharply cut lines. The officers had dismounted, and it seemed to us that we were to plunge at once into the thickets in our front: they seemed as solid as a stone wall. We knew that we could advance but a short distance in that direction without receiving a volley. The men began to throw away their blankets, but were instantly checked by the colonel. One of the boys of our company replied, in respectful expostulation, "Colonel, there is no fun in fighting with our blankets on." The colonel replied with gravity, "Fighting is not fun anyway."

We did not, however, enter the swamp, but moved slowly, in line of battle, diagonally along the field, our right flank being somewhat in advance, occasionally halting, using great caution, and keeping our hands, as it were, on the triggers of our guns, as we were likely at any moment to receive the enemy's fire, and would undoubtedly have done so were it not that they were hotly pressed by our regiments in their front and right. By this time it was long past noon. The heavy volleys in the woods ceased, and the cheers that followed told us that our men were successfully charging. We could dimly see through the undergrowth long lines of men centring upon the rebel position, and could note the few

desultory shots that were fired, the despairing efforts of the brave men who for nearly three hours had resisted our attack.

What a colossal war! Ten thousand men had grappled each other by the throat, and fought for hours with desperate energy; and yet, in comparison with the gigantic contests of Virginia and the West, this and other engagements of North Carolina are hardly thought worthy of a few lines in the records of the Rebellion.

CHAPLAIN MANNING'S LETTER TO "THE BOSTON JOURNAL."

DEC. 23, 1862.

The battle of Kinston, which began near noon, was over between three and four P.M. Then it was that ghastly and horrible sights met the eye on all sides. The buildings taken as hospitals were soon crowded with the wounded and dying. Friends and foes mingled together, and receiving the same prompt attention from our busy surgeons. It seemed strange that no rebel surgeon had staid to care for his comrades. But in our kindness we forgot that they were foes, and gave them all the heed which our duty to the loyal would admit. The Tenth Connecticut and the Hundred and Third Pennsylvania had been the chief sufferers. The Forty-fifth Massachusetts, also, lost several men. . . . In answer to the inquiries of friends as to the behavior of Massachusetts soldiers during the battle, I can say freely that they showed no signs of flinching, but only eagerness to be foremost in the fight. To lie still under fire, hearing the tremendous discharges of artillery, and sharp volleys and irregular rattle of musketry in the woods, tried their courage not a little. . . .

Shortly after we came upon the open field, a rebel soldier was seen in the road which ran along the river-bank, waving a white flag: this, as we afterwards understood it, was a ruse to gain time for the retreat of his associates. He was not molested, however, because he was so far from us that we could not tell at once, with certainty, whether he was a friend or foe. Meanwhile a company of cavalry, and section of artillery, which had been moving down the field upon our right flank as slowly as ourselves, went rapidly forward to

the river-bank as the foe retreated. The cavalry were armed
with repeating-rifles. They formed line in our sight, and fired
upon the fleeing army, as they crossed the bridge, till their
pieces were empty, and then reloaded and fired again with
great rapidity. The artillery did not reach the river-bank in
season to fire. We could not see the enemy; but, when we
crossed the bridge shortly after, it gave good evidence of the
accuracy of the aim of the cavalry. The rebels made desperate efforts to burn it, without success. One of our colonels
lost his life at this point. And the brave fellow who was
intrusted with the application of the torch fell lifeless into
the flames, and his body was shockingly burned before the
fire was extinguished. Very much to our vexation, we could
not see the struggle at this point, as the forest still intervened. The Massachusetts Seventeenth, with which regiment Col. Fellows and his son of Chelsea were honorably
connected, had been closely following the artillery and horsemen, moving by the flank down the field upon our right.
At this point the action may be said to have ceased, though
there was an afterpiece. Our regiment stacked arms near
the road, which we had reached; and the men, by the permission of the colonel scattered for foraging, being allowed
to take any thing upon which we could lay our hands without the use of fire-arms. Before we had all dispersed, however,
a somewhat ludicrous incident happened, quite appropriate
to the occasion in some respects, but in others so singularly
contrasted with the scenes through which we had just passed,
as to forcibly remind us that it is but a step from the sublime
to the ridiculous. On and around the battle-field were a
number of the humble houses of the "poor whites" of the
South. Suddenly, and much to our surprise, an aged couple
of this class appeared before us, and passed slowly along the
regimental line. They were followed at a respectful distance
by a smart colored girl, quite attractive in her bearing and
appearance. I must say that the man and his wife were
about as forlorn-looking old crones as ever I laid eyes on.
In dress and manner their appearance was abject and humili-
ating to the last degree. If the Gibeonites were half as

effective in their counterfeit woe as these poor people were
in their real one. I do not wonder that the heart of the great
captain, Joshua, melted at their sight. By themselves alone
they would only have been looked upon with pity by the
most thoughtless of our number. But the best part of the
story remains to be told. The "gal" was bright enough to
take in the comic side of the situation, and make the most
of it. She was all gayety and fun. Not a word did she say;
but by facial expression, attitude, and gesture, she read, in
her irresistibly sarcastic manner, an indictment of the whole
South, about as follows: "Aren't they a set of fools? Here
they have gone and stirred up all this row on our account,
and now we are being liberated, and they are losing, not only
us, but all their movables." Oddly enough, the squealing
of swine and the distressed cackling of poultry was being
heard all around at the same moment, proving that the appeal for protection that the poor old people were making was
altogether too late. As I have intimated, the effect upon
our risibles was irresistible. The whole regiment was convulsed with laughter at the superb by-play of the wench, and
its contrast with the woebegone aspect of her former owners.
They were so engrossed in their sorrow, that they did not
notice that she was making game of them. If they happened to look back an instant, she was apparently as demure
and downcast as a nun. Evidently they did not have the
least idea of what was going on behind them. I have no
doubt but that in their hearts they roundly cursed us as a
set of cruel wretches.

I have spoken of the after-scene. We had stacked arms,
and most of the men were gone to the field of action through
curiosity, or to the farms for food. I had found a few
moments to step into the lines of the Forty-fifth, which had
lost heavily, — fifteen killed and forty-three wounded. They
were looking very grave. I also passed into the ranks of the
Twenty-third, finding this gallant regiment in a high state of
mental exaltation on account of their satisfaction at whipping
the South-Carolina Twenty-third, with which regiment they
had been fighting, taking sixty-three prisoners, with small

CAPTURE OF KINSTON.

loss on their own part. On returning to my own company I got back just in time to receive the order to "fall in" for an advance. The line-officers were shouting vehemently, and all was excitement and confusion. Those of us who were present obeyed the order, leaving the guns of our comrades lying on the ground, as we unstacked them in a manner not laid down in the manual.

The whole brigade was marched across the bridge to Kinston. Simultaneously with this order, two of the brass Napoleons on the river-bank close to us opened on Kinston. firing over the town, which lay plainly in sight about a half-mile off across a meadow. Our comrades who had scattered heard the noise, and followed us as fast as posssible; so that, by the time we reached the town, our ranks were full.

The occasion of our sudden and unexpected call was as follows: it appears to have been the intention of Gen. Foster that we should remain over night where we were; but the rebels made as though the fight would be prolonged on the northern outskirts of Kinston: hence the artillery-fire, and our own change of camp.

Months afterwards I came across a rude lyric, deeply tinged with the wail of humanity, with which I will close the account of this, our first engagement. As originally printed, some repetitions give room for suspicion that the brave fellow who wrote it enlisted and went to the front in such a hurry, that he left his book of "synonymes" at home. I have endeavored to act a comrade's part in making a few omissions and corrections.

THE BATTLE OF KINSTON.

WRITTEN BY J. L. AULT, COMPANY C, HUNDRED AND FIRST REGIMENT, PENNSYLVANIA VOLUNTEERS.

Oh, listen! while I tell you, boys,
  Of Kinston's bloody fight, —
The deafening peals, the cannon's noise:
  Perhaps you saw that sight.

The morn had dawned, — the sabbath day
  That God has made and blest
For all his people on their way
  To the land of heavenly rest.

But a sullen foe before us waits;
  A furious storm is near;
And each one thinks of coming fate
  Approaching very clear.

What's this that's coming down the lane,
  Making such a rattle?
'Tis our guns: you see the iron train
  Rushing into battle.

"Bang, bang!" the mighty cannons roar
  In awful thunder dread;
And through the trees our missiles tore
  The branches o'er their heads.

We met them in a swampy mire,
  Where they were all concealed,
To rise, and pour a deadly fire,
  And drive us from the field.

Oh, fearful is the uproar now
  Of arms on every side;
While blood is gushing from the brow,
  And wounds are opened wide.

"Charge on, brave boys!" our colonels shout,
  "We'll surely make them yield;"
And pressing on they drove them out,
  And won the battle-field.

Quick, quick! the bridge they're passing o'er;
  They are making for the town;
They're trying to reach the other shore
  Before the bridge burns down.

The fire's put out — we flanked them there;
  But some have crossed the stream:
The deafening shouts that rend the air
  Give grandeur to the scene.

My first look across the Neuse, when I came up to the river, which at this point was a rapid stream three hundred feet at least in width, was for the retreating enemy, and then for our own army. The first were not visible. I understand that they took to the woods on the northern bank of

the river as soon as they had crossed. Our own troops made a more imposing display than I saw at any other time. They had deployed, and were crossing the meadow toward the town in three or more lines of battle, marching *en echelon*, as it is termed,—a French military phrase frequently used in drilling by brigade. In advancing in this manner, the several lines of battle lap past each other; so that, if the front line should lose heavily, the one next in the rear can fill the vacancies by moving to the front, or, if the nature of the ground and the points to be assaulted require it, the width of the front of the column can be extended or reduced, something as a brass slide is pulled out of a carpenter's measuring-rule.

The Forty-third marched by the flank, in ranks of four, across the meadow, and through Kinston, over to the northern side of the town, observing as we went the effect of one of our shells which had exploded in the attic-chamber of a cottage, shattering the gable-end of the house. We noticed no other damage of that kind to the place. By this time the afternoon was far advanced, and, finding that the rebels had retreated, we returned to the centre of the town, and prepared to pass the night in the streets and back-yards.

During that night Gen. Foster sent the following despatch to Washington:—

HEADQUARTERS DEPARTMENT OF NORTH CAROLINA,
KINSTON, N.C., Dec. 14, 1862.

To MAJOR-GEN. HALLECK, *General in Chief.*

I have the honor to inform you that I left Newbern for this place on the 11th inst.; but owing to bad roads and the consequent delay to my trains, etc., I did not reach the South-west Creek, five miles from this town, until the afternoon of the 13th inst. The enemy were posted there; but, by a heavy artillery-fire in front and a vigorous infantry-attack on either flank, I succeeded in forcing a passage, and without much loss.

This morning I advanced on the town, and found the enemy, strongly posted at a defile through a marsh, fording a creek. The position was so well chosen, that but little of the artillery could be brought in play.

54   HISTORY OF THE FORTY-THIRD REGIMENT, M.V.M.

The main attack, therefore, was made by the infantry, assisted by a few guns pushed forward in the roads. After a five-hours' hard fight, we succeeded in driving the enemy from their position. We followed them rapidly to the river. The bridge over the Neuse at this point was prepared for firing, and was fired in six places; but we were so close behind them, that we saved the bridge. The enemy retreated precipitately by the Goldsborough and Pikeville roads. Their force was about six thousand men, with twenty pieces of artillery.

The result is, we have taken Kinston, captured eleven pieces of artillery, and taken from four hundred to five hundred prisoners, and found a large amount of quartermaster and commissary stores. Our loss will not probably exceed two hundred killed and wounded. I am with great respect,

     Your obedient servant,
    JOHN G. FOSTER, *Major-General commanding.*

It seems to me, that, in preparing this record, it should be written in such a manner as to set forth truly and impressively the ravages of war and the sufferings it occasions both to victors and vanquished. In order to do this, I will address myself directly to my Chelsea friends and readers, and ask what they would think of the following proceedings. Suppose that ten thousand men of all arms should enter the streets of our quiet city late some sabbath afternoon, after having been four days in marching, as I judge about forty-five miles, and that during the last of these days many of them had fought a closely contested action of nearly three hours' duration in Revere or Everett, in which they have lost heavily. Eight men out of every ten are infantry, who have carried the weight of *thirty-five pounds*, at the lowest estimate, on their persons. Their boots have been ground in sand and water until they are as leaky as sieves, and it is an open question with the wearers whether or not they are not more of a burden than a benefit to the feet they were designed to protect. Those same feet, it being understood, in many cases are as much worn and chafed as the boots.

These men, it should be stated, have marched, most of the way, at the top of their speed, with but brief opportunities

for rest, often double-quicking in order to close up gaps in the column, halting usually late in the evening. Many of them have performed extra labor during the nights, — of guard, fatigue, or pioneer duty. Their food has been of the plainest kind, — salt beef, hard tack, and coffee, varied somewhat with sweet potatoes. The beef has become so monotonous and stale, that the stomach loathes it; and the longing for soft and palatable food has set many of them, for the first time in their lives, into involuntary dreams during the day concerning what they shall eat and what they shall drink; the visions which float pleasantly in airy fancies through their minds being of well-spread tables at which they used formerly to sit, but which are now so impossible of fulfilment as to tantalize them. Their beds have been so hard, their fatigue so extreme, and they so crowded for room as they have lain, that, after the first nap of an hour or two, a heavy, troubled doze is the nearest approach they can make to their usual quiet sleep at home. The days are hot; but the night air is so cold, that the ice must be broken by shaking their canteens before drinking. These conditions of the march are about an average experience, the most irksome and exhaustive of them all being the enormous burden carried. This I will itemize: 1st, the gun, eight pounds; 2d, one hundred rounds of ball-cartridges, another eight or ten pounds (I weighed them all at the time, but have not the exact figures now); then, in about the following order, the haversack, canteen, belts and plates, cap-box, and, slung over the shoulder, the rubber and woollen blankets, worse than all the rest, because so bulky. All these must be carried, besides extra socks, and any personal articles needed. A five-gallon can of kerosene weighs about twenty-eight pounds; so that nearly ten pounds in addition would be required to fill out the list I have given. All this, it should be kept in mind, must be carried over narrow roads rutted deeply by artillery, and in the midst of a crowding, hustling mob of weary soldiers, often surly to the men of any other regiment than their own, as you will soon learn, if, from any cause, you press on or lag behind.

Do you doubt, or fail to realize, dear reader, what this means? If so, I wish that you would just take the aforesaid can, or some other article equally heavy,—say a large-sized full coal-hod,—leaving off all the rest, and start for Boston with it some fine morning, across the bridge: you can soon find out in this way what soldiering means. You will understand that you can change the can from one hand to the other, or set it on the ground and rest, but please observe that the soldier cannot do this. All his luggage must be fastened to his person: his arms and hands must be free to use his weapon at any moment. Theoretically, of course, his traps can be taken off as they were put on; but practically his situation is such that he can only readily relieve himself of his blankets. When once put on in the morning, his other equipments must remain on. Every soldier can recall the convulsive throb or jerk by which the sorely jaded men struggled for a moment's relief by throwing their equipments upwards, thus easing the shoulders for an instant.

I have been writing of the burdens of war as experienced by the soldiers of a conquering column, as ours was. They are terrible. I dare not speak of individual instances of suffering in our own company which I saw; but I must generalize.

I saw the men of the Forty-fifth, which was as fine a regiment as any in the service, fall out by the dozen on the morning of the day before the battle of Kinston. The road on either side was lined with them; and it did not require a second look to satisfy the observer that they were not shirks or cowards, for extreme suffering was marked upon every line of their faces. What a condition the wounded of their number must have been in to pass under the surgeon's hands the next day! If these were the trials of the victors, what must be the situation of the vanquished! And how are the communities treated who have the ill fortune to be ground between the upper and the nether millstones of contending armies! I should state here, that the line-officers of an infantry regiment are, to a large extent, fellow-sufferers with their subordinates. They march on foot, as the soldiers do,

and they are, in addition, so burdened with mental responsibilities that their vital powers are heavily drawn upon. It is next to impossible for them to look sharply after all that is going on, and maintain strict or even reasonable discipline; and much of the irregular proceedings of victorious troops when entering towns or cities originates from this cause.

I have supposed the entrance of such a column as this into Chelsea; their faces so blackened by powder and camp-fires, and their clothing so grimed by mud, that the intimate friends of the members of Company H would not have been able at once to recognize us. I saw during the march some of the most dashing line-officers of the regiment with their boots slung on their swords, and the sword on their shoulder, their legs being bare.

The artillery and cavalry halt in the squares and wider streets: the infantry occupy the narrow ones from one end to the other, — Division, Cherry, Poplar, and Ash, from Williams Street to Washington Avenue. To make the illustration compare as near as possible with the circumstances at Kinston, we will take it for granted that there are no dwellings on these streets, but that they are simply the back-yards of the houses on the wide streets.

The next thing that will follow is this: the instant that the soldiers are dismissed from the ranks, all the fences and out-buildings are levelled to the ground, and roaring fires are kindled with the material. The next step is to enter the houses, asking for cooking-utensils, and taking them if they are not voluntarily yielded. Then, after eating supper, boards are placed upon the earth, the houses are entered again, and all the bedding is brought out and laid upon the boards for the use of the most footsore and exhausted. All desirable conveniences come with them as a matter of course, — stuffed chairs, washing-utensils, mirrors, and other things too numerous to mention. In one case that I know of, a party entered a house in this way, and found themselves in the nick of time to sit down to a hearty meal prepared for the inmates, who stood by and saw it rapidly disappear without remonstrance. The houses are ransacked from cellar to gar-

ret: articles of no possible use to the takers, such as ladies' silk dresses, are appropriated, to be thrown away the next day. In one sense, a reign of terror exists. Yet I should leave the reader with a wrong impression, if I did not further state that there was little or no violence used. Most of the residents had left, and this fact largely accounts for these proceedings. Those who remained had the sense to see that we were not ugly, and, where they used fair speech, they escaped the worst of the license of the soldiery.

There was a large fire in the town during the night, and some plundering of tobacco warehouses; but of these things as an eye-witness I cannot make any report. Some time in the evening I lay down alone on the sidewalk; and the last thing that I remember hearing above the din and confusion was the sweet notes of the band of the Forty-fifth, which lulled me to sleep. The night was warm, the only comfortable one we had on the march, and I slept soundly till morning, — the first and last full night's rest during the march.

In making the comparison between the two localities, I should have stated that I reckon Kinston to have been, at that time, a place of perhaps two thousand inhabitants, and about the dimensions of Chelsea before it included Caryville. You may judge, Mr. Editor, what a fine column of local items "The Kinston Pioneer" for the next week must have had. If I have not succeeded in impressing upon my readers the fearful havoc of war, as seen in some of the least of its evils, all that I could further do, as a last desperate resource, would be to improvise something in the same vein as Dibdin's famous sea-song, "Ye gentlemen of England who live at home at ease," set it to music for the piano, and during its rehearsal in the pleasant homes of Chestnut and other Chelsea streets, I should suggest perambulating the household, taking an inventory of personal goods and chattels, with an occasional look at the back-yards and fences.

I think I hear some one inquiring, "If you Massachusetts men, just from home, 'cut up' in this manner, pray tell us what the rebels would have done here?" The answer is at hand. In the autumn of 1862, to quote from Carleton's "Four Years of Fighting," —

"The centre column of the rebels moved upon Frankfort, Ky., gathering up cattle, horses, goods of all kinds, cloths, clothes, boots, shoes, grain, and every thing which could minister to their comfort as they came. At Frankfort they *invited* the merchants to open their stores, made princely purchases of goods, paying liberally in the *legal currency of the Confederacy*, sending off long lines of wagons toward the South, laden with supplies."

This, be it understood, was the way they dealt with their *friends*. If they had come into Chelsea, every store would have been gutted at once without the pretence of payment, the private residences treated far worse than we did those of Kinston, and in addition the city would have been mulcted in a fine of money as large as could be squeezed out of us. For proof of what I am saying, the inquirer is referred to the conduct of the rebel army in Pennsylvania just before the battle of Gettysburg.

In an allusion a short distance above, I have set the distance we had marched at about forty-five miles. By a direct line it is but thirty; but we had made a long *détour* to the westward for strategic purposes. "Harper's Review," for December, 1864, contains an article entitled "Heroic Deeds of Heroic Men," from the pen of J. S. C. Abbott, giving a history of military movements in North Carolina up to that date. It has a map which locates our camp on Saturday night far to the north-west of Trenton, — too far, in my opinion, for accuracy, as we could not have reached, from that point, the battle-field at Kinston so early on sabbath morning as we did. There is no doubt, however, that our route was very circuitous.

On Monday morning, Dec. 15, we were up bright and early, and on the road, retracing our steps. We passed again over the bridge, which was burned some time during the forenoon, after all of the troops had recrossed the river. This brought us directly upon the battle-field. The first thing that we noticed was a church, — a forlorn, unpainted, barn-like structure, standing directly in the line of our fire. Its appearance may be imagined. It had escaped the most ruinous effects of shell; but its weather-worn and shrivelled

walls and roof were so perforated by musket-balls and small fragments of shell, that scarcely a hand-breadth of uninjured surface remained. As we marched on over the dark and bloody grounds so recently the scene of deadly strife, we passed occasionally the corpse of a Union soldier, the limbs composed in the decencies of death, and the cap drawn over the face, concealing the features as they had taken their last look at the King of Terrors, and received the impression of his awful visage. At our left, a short distance, the greater portion of our fallen heroes lay, enranked in death as they had marched and fought in life; the sad sight being somewhat alleviated to the outward sense by the thick undergrowth which covered the ground, partially enveloping their bodies, as if Nature herself yearned to take them tenderly to her bosom. Marching rapidly on, with many a sorrowful remark to each other, we came upon the ground which intervened between the contending forces; and here one of the most impressive of sights met our view. It was, as already stated, thickly wooded with trees of all sizes, from an inch up to a foot or more in diameter. The bark was literally all of it scraped from the trunks up as high in the air as thirty feet. Some of the largest-sized trees were cut completely off by the explosion of shells at the instant they struck; great branches were torn from them, and, generally speaking, the view was one of horrid desolation.

I saw no earthworks which might have sheltered the enemy; and it is almost inconceivable to me how five thousand men could have resisted, so long as they did, such a fire as we directed against them, or how our own forces, engaged at such short range, could have escaped without even heavier loss than occurred. The enemy were commanded by Gen. Evans of Ball's Bluff fame. We captured six hundred men and several cannon. It is said that many were killed, and their corpses thrown into the river to conceal their loss.

I judge that every soldier of intelligence and character comes out of his first battle with an internal experience which tells upon all of his future military life. It was so at least with me; for I passed on with a buoyant step as we

countermarched over the very ground upon which, only twenty-four hours before, I had been heavily burdened from a moral cause. Among the sharp corners which I had to turn as I passed the anxious hour before entering the recruiting-tent in Winnisimmet Square, the most acute angle presented itself in the shape of a large personal development of that remarkable growth of modern times called "humanitarianism," which I define sufficiently clearly for present purposes as the indisposition or moral inability to inflict or even to witness pain. Obliged by the nature of my calling to be an occasional observer of shocking accidents from machinery, falling from aloft, etc., I confess I was compelled to ask myself some very pointed questions on this subject. If your sympathies are so strong that you cannot witness, without extreme suffering, these exposures of civil life, are you not mistaken in the idea that you are called to perform a soldier's duty? The question was not answered to my satisfaction until I had passed through the scenes of Kinston: there the burden was lifted from my mind. Singularly enough, although I had little in this respect to test me on that field, I came off from it thoroughly assured that I need not carry any weight from that cause in future, and my experience afterward confirmed the correctness of my conclusion.

Our ambulance corps was well organized; and the conditions of the fight at Kinston enabled them to care immediately for the wounded, bringing them off the field in closed vehicles. Although but a short distance from them, we were not near enough to hear their moans. The few dead that I saw as we pressed forward, were covered with blankets; so that I do not recall a single instance of the repulsive sight of wounds and blood, deathly faces, or agonizing groans such as I afterwards witnessed and heard at Whitehall, and later on, in the spring of 1863, at Blount's Creek. Yet, as I have said, I passed through an internal experience which gave me confidence in myself. Much to my surprise, the heavy discharges of artillery elevated my mental and moral energies, instead of depressing them. If I had realized in

Chelsea under what conditions of extreme exhaustion I should go into battle, I should have said at once, " I can never withstand these moral weaknesses with such depression of the physical energies." To my great astonishment, I was taken up into the realm of profound emotion: a solemn awe possessed my soul as the momentous conditions of life and death under which we are living in our earthly relations moved upon me. I do not say that I was entirely freed from apprehension or mental suffering; but I was delivered from the dread anticipation, which had haunted me for months, of loss of self-control.

We marched on rapidly all that day. The course of the column might have been traced by the tobacco that was thrown away by the boys, after lugging it until they were tired of the extra burden. There was much suffering from sore feet and fatigue; but we had received a new impulse, to which our spirits rose. At the outset we had swept so far to the westward, that our anticipations had begun to look toward Wilmington as our destination: this was dissipated as we turned in the direction of Kinston when we neared that point. The gossip of the column then took the course of an advance of our base from Newbern to Kinston; the gunboats, as we supposed, being on the move with ourselves to open the navigation of the Neuse. These theories had all disappeared with our onward march to the west and the burning of the bridge at Kinston. Truly something " was up," as the veterans said at starting. We knew so little of the country and of the situation, that there was ample room for imaginative exercise of our wits. Some would have it that we were bound to Goldsborough, that is, to stay there: others were not satisfied with any thing short of Raleigh.

We were reckoning without our host. On Saturday night before the fight at Kinston, after three days of unsuccessful struggle around Fredericksburg, Burnside's army ceased their efforts. On Tuesday night they retreated across the Rappahannock; and Gen. Lee was free, if he had thought us worth the pains, to put enough men into North Carolina to capture the whole of our force. That this was not done is due, as I

suppose, to the extraordinary celerity of our movements, the
good judgment of Gen. Foster, and the success that attended
all our efforts. We were much less annoyed by guerillas than
we had been on the other side of Kinston. The country was
more elevated, and there were fewer houses; but those that
we saw were larger. One of these plantations, where we
halted for the night, was large enough for a township. We
went into camp near its centre; and our cavalry, who skirmished around its outer limits, appeared like pygmies, the
weeds were so high, and they were so distant. It had an
immense tree centrally located, with seats under it for summer recreation. These large properties, with their conspicuous cotton-press with extended arms, their negro-quarters,
— log-houses almost under the eaves of the grand old-fashioned mansion of the proprietors, — were something different from any thing we had ever seen. Every thing about
them savored of aristocratic power. These men are charged
with having carried the State out of the Union against the
wishes of the upper counties. On one occasion we were
welcomed in a most enthusiastic manner by a considerable
body of colored people. I shall not attempt to delineate the
emotiveness of the African as we heard it at this time: we
laughed until the tears came in our eyes.

We had a sad reminder of the nature of our journey in
an occasional grave by the roadside. Our ambulances gave
up their dead as the poor wounded men within them ceased
from suffering. The circumstances of the march did not
admit of sending back to Newbern after the first night out;
so that the wounded of all the engagements were carried to
Goldsborough, some of the worst cases, however, remaining
at Kinston; and from there, on the return march, they were
placed on vessels which came up the Neuse as far as it was
open: it was closed at a certain point by torpedoes. Chaplain Manning, writing from Camp Rogers, gives us a glimpse
of what was passing in these mournful appendages to our
column, in the following letter to "The Boston Journal,"
sent soon after our return: —

CAMP ROGERS, Jan. 6, 1863.

It was a singular yet to me a most affecting funeral. Following that plain coffin through the rain, every thing about us so lonely and bleak, I could but think of the afternoon when its occupant, Fuller Morton, was brought to us wounded at Spring Bank, of the patience with which he bore the pain of surgical operation, and of that long, sad train of ambulances with us on our return from Goldsborough, full of the suffering and dying, and in one of which, brought back only to die, was this young and buoyant soldier. And we thank thee, O Father, that the mournful and horrible sights which we have been compelled to witness here are veiled from the eyes of our wives and little ones.

We continued our march on Tuesday morning, the 16th, until ten o'clock A.M., when our second engagement, the battle of Whitehall, began.

CHAPTER IV.

WHITEHALL AND GOLDSBOROUGH.

THE Forty-third was very near the head of the column. We were moving through the narrow forest-road, with "route step," "arms at will," in the usual military "go-as-you-please" manner of long marches, when we heard a few rifle-cracks, followed almost instantly by the boom of one of the brass Napoleons sending its terrific echoes up the road, and through the forest.

We knew at once that the ball had opened again. An involuntary emotional throb vibrated through the column, as, silently, without formal orders, we found our places as we marched, and pressed forward.

It was but a few moments before we came out from the forest, and began the descent into the valley of Whitehall. Gen. Foster and his staff had halted at the edge of the forest while the column passed on. Looking down the road about an eighth of a mile, I noticed something in flames, the bridge, as I suppose; and in its vicinity a signal-man was vigorously waving his flag, communicating with the staff.

I also saw for an instant the left flank of a regiment moving on the double-quick at right angles to the road. This was probably the Twenty-third Regiment. It was, I judge, about a fourth of a mile across the valley, and its centre was some thirty feet or more lower than the outside. The left or southern side was quite clear of trees or undergrowth, while on the right the reverse was the case. On this open space of the left side the batteries of artillery were going into position in plain sight, one after the other, as they came upon the field. The Ninth New-Jersey, the Twenty-third

and the Seventeenth Massachusetts Infantry Regiments, had already deployed as skirmishers among the trees and thickets at the bottom of the valley on the right of the road, and were making a sharp and continuous roll of musketry, which was soon followed by the deep and awful uproar of the artillery, as gun after gun unlimbered, and opened its fire.

The Confederates were posted in a thick forest on the north-western side of the valley. The Neuse River rolled between us and them, but, as at Kinston, it was entirely out of sight; and but few of us knew of its existence at that point. Our regiment passed on down the road, meeting, as we went, an irregular but quite continuous procession of wounded men coming up on foot from the line of skirmishers. All of these were struck somewhere upon the upper part of the body: an arm was shattered, or, in most cases, the head, neck, or shoulders had been hit by rifle-balls. Streams of blood were trickling, in some instances, down their faces, upon many of which a deathly pallor sat. Some were so faint as to require the help of a comrade on each side; but most of them walked alone with trembling and uncertain step. The expression which marked the countenances of all was of deep seriousness. They were silent; but, as we exchanged glances, it seemed as though they pitied us as much as we did them. We were marching down into the fire which was fast swallowing up the line of skirmishers they had deployed. They knew, better than we did, what our compacted line of battle would meet in a few moments.

We kept steadily on, and soon became conscious of being again under fire. There was no music about it, however. We met this time not only the aim of the enemy, but the direction of the road and the situation of our own batteries was such, that we were really under a double fire, and, inasmuch as our own forces were firing shells at very short range, we were in danger from their premature explosion. Fuzes are cut at the moment of use, and it is quite a nice point to decide with accuracy, in the excitement of action, the precise time and place at which the shell shall burst. Down we marched, however, until we had reached the bottom or centre

of the valley, when we were halted, facing to the right,
towards the enemy. Of them, however, we saw nothing.
Before us was a comparatively open space, occupied partially
by undergrowth, scattered trees, etc.; then the Neuse, narrow
at this point, fringed with the tangled vines and shrubbery
of these regions, and entirely out, as I have said, of our
knowledge as well as our sight; then, beyond that, a forest-
crowned hill, or what passed for such in North Carolina: and
on this rise of land, beneath its trees, and completely hidden,
from us at least, in the luxuriant low brushwood, was a busy
and defiant enemy. This we soon learned; for, the moment
that we halted, we became conscious of being the subjects of
a continuous and tolerably well-directed infantry-fire, mainly,
as I judged, of smooth-bores. Our opponents could not have
been more than a few hundred feet from us, — not more than
half as far as from the square to the ferry. That we did not
instantly begin to fall in large numbers was due to the fact
that we were slightly overshot. The air just over our heads
seemed to be full of musket-balls. They struck the trees in
our vicinity repeatedly; and in a few moments the word was
passed along the company line, that Edwin Benner was killed.
This the most of us believed to be true, till after the action,
when we were informed that a ball had glanced from a tree,
and passed between his arm and body with sufficient force to
cut his clothes, and slightly wound his side. He was not
disposed to leave the company; but his comrades, seeing the
torn clothing, insisted on conducting him to the field-hospital.
When his garments were removed, the ball dropped to the
ground, upon which he immediately returned to his place in
the ranks.

The battalion stood in line in this position somewhere from
five to fifteen minutes. There were at least fifteen hundred
men from the three skirmishing regiments just in front of
us; but not a soul was visible, and the noise of their fire was
drowned in the tremendous concussion of the artillery. No
order came for us to fire, or for any other action. The inward prayer of every one of us, I have no doubt, if expressed,
would have been, "For God's sake give us something to do!"

The suspense of such moments is terrible, and each moment seems an age. I doubt if the nerves of Marshal Ney himself would not have wavered, if the men detailed to shoot him had amused themselves by repeated volleys aimed just over his head. It needed only a single word from our colonel to have instantly changed our situation from extreme depression to the most vehemently pleasurable excitement of the soldier's avocation, — that of returning the fire of the enemy. But the word did not come, and it is well that it did not. We were so nearly on the same level as our skirmishers, and so close to them, that they would have been more likely to have been hit than the rebels; and besides, in our standing position, so near the enemy and in plain sight, we should have drawn the fire of the rebel artillerists, who would have quickly made a long list of "casualties" to tack on to our record, while they were so concealed that we could not have returned the compliment.

Finally, just at the moment when our patience was about failing us, the order came "Right face!" to the rear, on the road by which we had come on to the field. We moved back a little more than the length of the regiment, which brought us partially under the cover of trees and bushes on the right hand as we had entered the valley. Into this cover, by orders, we passed, and lay upon our faces. The battery of Napoleons (Morrison's) had filed to the extreme right of our line, close to the river, and were making themselves generally useful in an obstreperous sort of a way. Their fire was directed nearly at right angles with the batteries on our extreme left, and they were evidently disposed to make the most of their opportunities. Our position in the woods brought us somewhat in their rear, and the copious smoke of their discharges drifted over us; so that our exposures here were limited to the general and promiscuous firing of the enemy: this, however, was sufficiently vigorous to keep us in quite close contact with mother-earth.

We lay in this manner some time, perhaps a half-hour. My position was close to the road up which the sad procession of the wounded and the dead was continually passing.

I have very distinct recollections of the deathly groans of poor wounded men, lying upon the stretchers, borne along the pathway only a foot or two above my head. It was not very enlivening; but the moral forces which had been evoked by my experiences at Kinston were in the ascendant, and I recall a strange, weird-like kind of complacency in the awful scenes which were happening around me. While lying here, I saw Chaplain Manning go down the road to succor the wounded, unarmed, on foot, and alone, with the visor of his cap drawn down upon his face; and a comrade tells me that he noticed Chaplain A. L. Stone of the Forty-fifth, about the same time, engaged as one of the bearers of a stretcher on which a soldier lay.

The next thing that happened was an order from the colonel to "fall in with fixed bayonets." This startled us; for it looked like a charge either on our own part, or on that of the rebels. Repeated by the captains and their subordinates along the whole line, it penetrated our ears in spite of the thunder of our artillery. We rose promptly to our feet, took to the road, and instantly formed in line, facing to the south. We then responded to the order, "Battalion! Right face! Forward! March!" and proceeded again directly down into the valley. On reaching a spot a little in advance of where we had formerly stood, we found that the Massachusetts Seventeenth was just in front of us, and that they were moving along the road on their hands and knees. The precise length of time that it took us, officers and men, to copy their example, was so short that it was not appreciable. Down we went, every mother's son of us, except Col. Whiton, into a creeping posture. The cause was as follows: it was not the fire of the enemy which appalled us, but that of our own guns. They were arranged on the outer edge of a circle, into the centre of which our advance had taken us. The converging fire of thirty-six pieces of artillery was pouring over our heads, apparently not more than ten or fifteen feet above us. I say apparently: I might as well put it evidently, for we were not altogether dependent on our ears. I thought at the time, and I believe now, that the air was phosphores-

cent with the light of the burning fuzes of the shells. A pale, pearly lustre overshadowed us, although it was mid-day, with a bright sun overhead. I have not the slightest doubt but that, if it had been in the night, we should have appeared as though covered with a sheet of fire. The wind of the batteries and the ammunition, for we were near enough to feel the effects of both, was like a gale: to tell the truth, we could hardly keep our feet.

We passed along the road a few minutes in this manner, wondering what it could mean, when all at once we heard from a distance in our rear the cry of "Halt!" feebly at first, obtruding itself, as it were, between momentary intervals in the firing, but becoming more distinct as the officer who uttered it approached at full speed on horseback, waving his sword. As he drew nearer to the line of fire, he halted in order to keep his head on his shoulders, and asked with great earnestness the very question we had been putting to ourselves: "Where do you think you are going?" In short, we were "about faced" *instanter*, taken back to our old shelter, and again lay upon the ground. The whole proceeding had arisen from some misconception of orders, quite likely unavoidable under the extreme difficulty of giving and receiving them in such circumstances.

It so happened, that, when we fell in, Col. Holbrook was abreast of the left flank or rear of the battalion, and the mistake by which we had made the needless advance I have spoken of was corrected in season for him to hold the three rear companies on the ground where the line was formed. Lieut.-Col. Whiton was at the head of the regiment. When we retreated, our company lay, for the most part, a little farther from the road than we had done at first. In a short time two artillery caissons in one team came down toward us at a high speed, halting suddenly at the point where Company H was lying. The drivers called out in stentorian tones to us to get out of their way: we complied, and they turned abruptly to the right, and passed over the ground upon which we had been lying in order to reach the battery in our rear.

The valley between the spot where we were and the river

was full of small trees, and the soil was soft. As soon as the
artillerists lost their descending momentum, the obstacles
that they met brought them to a standstill, and they began
to cry out lustily to our battalion for aid. They were but a
short distance from us; but their voices sounded, such was
the noise of the firing, as if at the bottom of a well or at the
end of a long tunnel. For a few moments, only a few of the
more adventurous spirits among us rose to their feet; but
a most vigorous appeal from our captain for volunteers soon
sent a large group of us to their assistance. They had managed
to interlock their wheels with trees of several inches in
diameter, so that they could neither advance nor retreat.
Our men got under the axle, and lifted on the wheels of the
rear caisson until all parties were convinced that the labor
was useless; then the artillerists got out their axes, and
began to cut their way clear, while we returned to our places.

Shortly after this, as I have reason to believe, though I
did not know of it at the time, private Isaac Y. Smith of
Orleans, Mass., a member of Company E, was shot through
the body as he lay upon the ground, and instantly killed;
those nearest to him only noticing a slight tremor or convulsion
as he passed away. In the confused way in which we
were lying, he was surrounded by the men of our company.
A number of casualties happened along our line about this
time, which possibly led to another movement. We were
taken across the road over into the field or hillside on the
left, and placed in front of a battery, about a hundred feet
or more in advance of it. The battery was diligently firing
twelve-pound rifled shell. Here we lay until the battle was
ended, — an hour at least, so far as my memory informs me.

It seems almost incredible, but I am certain of the fact,
that while in this situation I slept soundly for some time;
how long I cannot tell, as all that I recall is the fact that I
became conscious of waking from a condition of absolute insensibility
to all earthly concerns. A man must be very tired
when he can lie on the hard ground and fall asleep, with the
horrid screech of a continuous passage of rifled shells just
over his head. But I did it. We were not sensible at the

time of any special attention from the rebels; but the Forty-fifth, lying in a similar position, just at our left, lost some of their men, their color-bearer, Parkman, being among the number. Somewhere from two to three hours had passed since we entered the valley. During the noon-hour the firing on our part ceased, and on the part of the rebels it had dwindled to occasional discharges from sharpshooters. Our regiment was withdrawn from the field to the rear, and, after an hour's delay, was put in charge of the baggage-train for the rest of the day. While we were waiting, we got our dinners as well as we could: I think without any thing warm. There was a mutual and joyful exchange of congratulations among us, that we had escaped with so little loss, though there were some marked exposures. I saw one man lift his cartridge-box from his thigh, and show where a ball had passed between it and his body, tearing the leather into fragments, without cutting his clothes. Months afterwards I made the acquaintance of a member of the Dedham company, who told me that he carried a large fragment of shell all the afternoon in his haversack, knowing nothing of its presence there until he ate his supper. Something like a dozen of such incidents as these occurred, involving injury to blankets, clothes, and equipments, without bodily harm. It is astonishing that we passed through such exposures with such slight loss.

Chaplain Manning's letter, already quoted, makes the following interesting statements: —

"On Tuesday morning, soon after breaking camp, the roar of cannon in the advance told us that a battle was at hand. We were now near Whitehall, where the rebels made a desperate stand; and for several hours we knew not whether life or death, defeat or victory, was to be our lot. The firing of our own batteries was terrific; and those of the enemy replied with much spirit, ploughing up the ground about us, and cutting down now and then a tree some few rods to our rear. Under this cross-fire our regiment and some others lay during the battle. The wounded and dead were constantly passing us borne on stretchers or in blankets, by persons detailed for that purpose. The volleys of musketry in the

edge of the woods to our front were nearly continuous, where we could see the flitting forms of the rebels; and the incessant discharges of artillery made the heavens shake. Many of our men were hit by bullets and fragments of shell, and several were slightly hurt; but only one was killed outright. A shell carried away the arm, and tore away the vitals, of Isaac Y. Smith, a private from Cape Cod in Company E, killing him instantly. The hospital was in a hollow, sheltered by trees, near the entrance to the field of battle. I visited it several times during the fight, where the scenes of the previous Sunday were repeated, only I saw no rebels there. But the same ghastly wounds, unmurmuring submission to painful operations, the same image of death, — *plurima mortis imago*, — was around me; and though I could not account for the fact, and it was contrary to all my impressions, the sufferers lay perfectly still, hardly a groan or complaint escaping.

"After the battle, we had time to bring away the body of our slain comrade, and lay him, wrapped in his soldier-garments, in a neatly prepared grave. Caps were removed, and tears stood in many eyes, while, surrounding his lowly resting-place, we joined in a simple prayer. And there we left him. . . . The color-bearer of the Forty-fifth, Parkman, slain in the same battle, sleeps near him, laid carefully down by his thoughtful comrades, 'his martial cloak wrapped around him.' . . .

"My letter must close abruptly; but it will accomplish its purpose, if it strengthens the belief in the hearts of the people of Massachusetts, that the men who have gone forth to uphold her honor are worthy of the renown of our ancient Commonwealth; worthy of the sacred cause which calls them from their peaceful homes to the wasting ills of the camp, fatigues of the march, and horrors and perils of battle."

Our situation in this fight cannot be fully understood without a statement of what took place on the skirmish line, for which purpose I will quote a part of the official report of the Twenty-third Massachusetts Regiment: —

"On the 16th, our brigade having the advance, we came upon the enemy at Whitehall: they were strongly intrenched on the right bank, the river being quite narrow at this point. A gunboat, partly built, at this place was destroyed. The Twenty-third was immediately ordered forward to support the Seventeenth Massa-

chusetts and the Ninth New-Jersey, who were in advance, and
had engaged the enemy. The line being formed, we moved forward to the woods and up to the bank of the river, where the enemy
poured the lead and iron into us like rain. We opened fire when
they were within ten yards of us. Separated by the narrow stream,
which was so deep that it was impossible to charge across, it was
provoking to the boys to stand there and not be able to give them
the 'steel;' but a steady fire from our men made them seek shelter
behind the trees. The regiment remained under fire about two
hours, when it was ordered to the rear. We lost in the engagement thirteen killed and fifty-four wounded; total, sixty-seven.
We were obliged to leave some of our dead and wounded on the
field, on account of the rebel sharpshooters on the right bank of
the river."

We learned, as we passed on, that there had been no halt
of the column. Six regiments besides our own, the Fortyfourth and Fifty-first Massachusetts Regiments in addition
to those already named, were all that entered the valley: all
the rest of the forces, to their extreme surprise, had turned to
the left, and passing to the rear of our batteries, being somewhat sheltered from fire by the crest of the hill, had continued their march without cessation. On a part of the
ground which was too steep to admit of the passage of the
baggage-train, a road had been graded by our pioneers during
the fight by a deep cut on one of its sides for several hundred feet. Along this road we passed, still hearing the fire
of the rebel sharpshooters. It semed so insignificant, however, after what we had just seen and heard, that we paid
but little attention to it until we became conscious, as a turn
in the road brought us nearer the other side of the river, that
we were ourselves the direct object of the fire. It was a
long shot, however. Occasionally a ball would whiz past or
overhead, and through the rail fence we could see the dirt
fly as they struck the ground. There was some consultation
among us, not even a corporal being in sight, in respect to
the feasibility of replying; but we could see nothing to aim
at, so we desisted, and soon passed beyond the reach of our
persistent friends across the river.

As a fitting close to this account I will relate an incident which happened to me early in the afternoon. As I trudged along by the side of the wagon to which I was detailed, I noticed walking near me a little runty, oldish-appearing soldier of the Ninth New-Jersey. He was one of those tough, wiry men, made of steel, who seem to unite the qualities of the lower orders of creation with a fair share of the distinctively human traits. We had some conversation together, and I remember that in the course of it he held out his gun, which was smutty from firing, in front of him, in a kind of informal, off-hand "Present arms," slapping the stock, as he did so, in the usual manner of the manual, but with an evident and peculiar affection, and remarking at the same time as follows: —

"I *know* that I have killed three rebels with this to-day." These words were uttered with an earnestness and intensity of feeling which would have done credit to John Brown. There was nothing, however, of malignity in them, nothing any way ferocious. There was a patriotic fervor about the man that made it apparent to me that it was not individual hate which actuated him, but a whole-hearted devotion of soul to his calling as a defender of the Union. The incident did not make much of an impression on me at the time: I felt no repugnance to him, and I have often thought of it as proving what a wonderful power of adaptation to circumstances our race possesses.

The baggage-train was composed of four-horse, covered wagons. We marched three abreast of each side of the wagons all the afternoon, until camp was reached, when we were excused, to our extreme satisfaction, for the wagons were driven much of the time faster than we could travel, faster even than the rapid pace we had been accustomed to. If we could have clung to their rear end with one hand, it would have aided us sufficiently to keep up; but we found a group of men attached to each one of them, — men who had fallen to the rear, put their guns into the teams, and were holding on for dear life. They all protested that they were so exhausted that they could not yield their places for an

instant. The road at this point was very heavy. I found that the teamsters were obliging us not only to "double quick," which is fast travelling, but to "run," which is much faster, to keep up with them. Sensible that I could endure such rough usage as this but a short time, I gave my driver fair warning that he must not depend on us for protection, and resumed my usual pace. I soon fell, of course, to the rear, and was not alone in doing so. This made me quite anxious for a time, as I knew we must be near the rear of the column.

After a while, however, the train having closed up the gap in the column, which had been open, slowed down somewhat, and we managed, by effort, to retain our places near the wagons.

This experience was a brief one; but it was very suggestive to me. Those teamsters were practically a part of the army; their protection was essential to the safety of the whole force; we might as well have lost our artillery as to have lost them: but virtually they were a discordant element among us. Their demeanor and conduct was indifferent and selfish to the last degree. No one appeared to be in authority over them, and they acted as though they would cast loose from the wagons, get on to their horses and run, on the least appearance of danger. We of the guard were really at the mercy of those whom we were detailed to protect. There was no concert of action between us and them, and the desperate efforts we made to do our duty were exhaustive in the extreme. If we had been suddenly attacked, I do not see what we could have done to defend ourselves, much less our convoy. It was impossible for the three mounted field-officers of our regiment to exercise authority over so long and thin a line; and what was beyond the power of a man on horseback was, of course, impossible to weary line-officers, after a week of such marching as we had seen. The whole arrangement struck me as being open to the gravest criticism.

The teamsters, however, were not so much to blame as the system which deprives so large and important a body of men of the advantage of honorable organization. When the first

Napoleon planned his battalions of the train, he took a step which should be copied in every army. Those drivers should have been uniformed and armed, and they should also have been numerous enough to defend themselves, with the assistance of a small body of cavalry, against any ordinary attack, until infantry could be brought to their support. Such a corps as this could ride on their own wagons, or at least take turns with each other in doing so.

On Tuesday night we encamped as usual, without opposition. Resuming the march on Wednesday, we were told early in the forenoon that we were approaching Goldsborough. The pickets of the enemy gave warning to their side of our presence by large fires sending thick black columns of smoke high up into the air. Here the regiment was detached from the main column, placed under the charge of a staff-officer, Major Gourard, and sent several miles to the right, to a place called Spring-Bank Bridge. We were accompanied by a section (two guns) of artillery (Ransom's Battery, Twenty-third New-York) and a company of cavalry (Third New-York). The rebels burned the bridge as we approached it. The regiment halted on a small plantation about a quarter of a mile from the river, Company H remaining with them. Two companies, under Major Lane, were sent to the river with the artillery, and afterwards re-enforced with two more. These companies skirmished with the enemy across the river all day, losing one killed (Corporal Sparrow of Company I) and one mortally wounded (Corporal Fuller Morton of Company E). The body of Corporal Sparrow was necessarily abandoned, as the enemy fired persistently at all who made the effort to approach it.

Our company lay through the day in our camp in a condition of suspense and expectation. We heard an occasional cannon-shot from up the river, at Goldsborough, whither the main army had gone; but no intelligence came to us. Our interest was heightened just at nightfall by rapid artillery-firing at the front. This firing was sustained for about half an hour, and then suddenly ceased. We, of course, in our isolated situation, were intensely interested to learn its cause

and consequences. Our consumption of ammunition had been very great, particularly at Whitehall. We felt that the struggle, whatever it was, must have been forced upon Gen. Foster, as we could not account in any other way for the late hour at which it happened, and we knew that there must have been urgent reasons for such a free use of powder so far from our base of supply.

As the evening drew on, and no word came to us, it became manifest that we must prepare to pass the night where we were. Guards were stationed at short distances into the forest, and the usual fires were built for warmth. The honorable position intrusted to us impressed us deeply with a sense of responsibility. We knew, that, if the rebels forded the river, we must fight with the utmost determination in order to protect the flank and rear of our forces at Goldsborough. Under these circumstances it is not to be wondered at that we were thoughtful as the darkness closed in upon us in the centre of the little plantation. Just as we were retiring, Capt. Hanover came to me, and, after alluding to the exposures of our position, he spoke with deep feeling of the wonderful preservation of life in our regiment, and asked me to lead the company in thanksgiving to the Almighty. I consented at once, for I felt as he did, as I remembered how we had skirted the edge of battle at Kinston without harm, had plunged into its vortex at Whitehall, almost to the line of skirmishers, with slight loss, and now, here at Goldsborough, had so far escaped wholly as a company, and partially as a regiment.

After the men were called together, the captain spoke briefly, and led in singing a hymn. I then knelt upon my knees at the camp-fire, and read the Hundred and Twelfth Psalm, selected very hastily, which I will here quote by its most appropriate verses.

1. Praise ye the Lord. Blessed is the man that feareth the Lord, that delighteth greatly in his commandments.

4. Unto the upright there ariseth light in the darkness: he is gracious, and full of compassion, and righteous.

6. Surely he shall not be moved forever: the righteous shall be in everlasting remembrance.

7. He shall not be afraid of evil tidings: his heart is fixed.

8. His heart is established; he shall not be afraid until he see his desire upon his enemies.

9. He hath dispersed, he hath given to the poor; his righteousness endureth forever; his horn shall be exalted with honor.

10. The wicked shall see it, and be grieved; he shall gnash with his teeth, and melt away: the desire of the wicked shall perish.

This was followed by a standing devotional exercise, of which I can only dimly recall the emotions of gratitude for the past, and supplication for the future; our dear country, our friends, our homes, ourselves, and our remarkable preservation, presenting themselves as fit themes for naming with thanksgiving and intercession in the Divine presence.

The members of other companies pressed around, and joined quietly and reverently in the exercises. I have been in thousands of religious meetings during my life; but of them all I think that was the most sincere and heartfelt. Capt. Hanover wrote of it in a private letter, of which the following paragraph found its way to "The Pioneer" of Jan. 31, 1863:—

"After the battles of Kinston and Whitehall, while our regiment, with a battery and cavalry force, were away from the main army, to look after the rebels this side of Goldsborough, I felt that I could not lay down to sleep, nor that my men ought to do so, without an acknowledgment to God for our almost miraculous preservation from death and wounds. I mentioned my feelings to privates ——, ——, who heartily sympathized with me. I called my company together, and told them in brief how I felt, and asked their attention to Mr. ——, who had very kindly and promptly responded to my invitation to read from the Psalms, and offer a prayer. I need not say with what attention the men listened to him, nor how many eyes were moistened, nor how much better we all felt after the exercises were over."

We retired to rest, and lay until after midnight, when an officer came from Gen. Foster with orders for our force to fall in, and rejoin the main body of the army on its return to Newbern. We were instructed by our officers to act quickly

and quietly. We did not wait for a second invitation, but were soon in line, after throwing all our remaining rails on the fires. We then proceeded out into the road, and were halted at the point at which we had come upon the place.

At first we were at a loss to understand this. We had learned from our companies, which had been skirmishing on the bank of the river, but had now returned, that the enemy appeared to be gathering on the other side in force, and we had reason to believe that matters would be lively in that vicinity if we remained till daylight. But still we waited. It was cold, and we were quite impatient, until we learned that the officers of the guard had a very trying job on their hands in calling-in the sentries, under somewhat peculiar circumstances.

They had been obliged to post them, on the evening before, in obscure pathways in the forest, and to give them orders to fire upon any thing approaching from outside the camp. The difficulty lay in finding all the guards in the darkness, without going outside of them and drawing their fire. The circumstances did not allow of shouting, so that they were obliged to move slowly and with great caution; but they finally accomplished their object.

The sentries themselves, it should be said, were somewhat mystified, and so were put upon their guard. They were not so far into the forest but that some of them could see all that took place in camp. They noticed the muster of the regiment, and finally saw it moving off without them; and some were for a time sorely perplexed. But an hour's waiting brought all things out right, and we moved on with an alert step; for the mystery as to our destination, which had hitherto enveloped us as a cloud, had been removed. We had a new, and, it must be confessed, a delightful sensation. We were to return to Newbern.

But there was hanging over two of our number, even at this moment of joy, an experience, — that of losing their way, — which they both declare will abide until their dying day. And it was the two of all others whom we should have missed the most, both in respect to their official position and the

manner in which those positions were filled by them. Just after starting, Capt. Hanover spoke to Orderly Edmunds, telling him that he felt miserably sick, and desired him to wait a few moments with him. They fell out, together with the captain's colored boy, a young lad named familiarly "Jim." Their halt was but for a few moments, and, while they waited, Major Lane came along, and advised them earnestly to hurry up, as they were behind every thing else. They endeavored to do so, although the captain was very weak. As they passed along, having no apprehension at all, all at once they were involved in anxious doubt, which was not altogether dispelled until they reached the main column on the evening of the next day, after fifteen hours of terrible fatigue and apprehension.

In a few moments after they resumed their march, they came to a divergent road, and in the darkness could not tell which was the right one. One went up hill; the other turned toward the right, and was more level. They were so unfortunate as to take it; and every step thereafter led them towards Goldsborough, instead of Newbern. Our army had already begun its return march when we heard the firing in the early evening, and its front had passed far toward our left, as we were heading southward, when our friends were lost. In quoting from a recent note of Capt. Hanover concerning the affair, I will say, that, perhaps of all the members of our company, they were the least prepared to wander about all those weary hours. They had both suffered so terribly from sore feet, that their condition in this respect was known to all of us, and had excited the liveliest sympathy on our part.

"But in time," he says, after describing his attack of sickness, "we started on after the boys, as we thought, although the sandy road prevented our hearing them, and the darkness our seeing them. Yes, we travelled miles and miles, only to learn ultimately that all those weary miles and all those weary hours were taking us directly from them, and towards the enemy. When daylight came, we still continued our course, until, upon consultation, we decided to take the back track,

which proved to be the right one for Newbern, as we learned, after walking many more miles, from a sign-post, at the foot of which we lay down to rest our weary limbs, and which said, pointing the way we were going, 'Sixty miles to Newbern.' Well, it was a satisfaction to have our route indorsed, as we had been 'going it blind' so long."

Mr. Edmunds says that at first they avoided houses and men, dodging into the forest to hide when danger was apprehended. They made up their minds that they would not be taken prisoners by civilians, nor by any one, except by a number of armed opponents. But finally, as the day wore on, they became desperate, and were obliged to ask their way. To their surprise, they were met civilly at least, if not cordially. The most minute directions were given them, and they found roads and localities as described. Every thing appeared quiet as they passed along: no one molested them, or asked any questions.

As they travelled during the afternoon, they came across an army cracker-box, the first definite information they had that they were on our track. and finally struck the column some distance in the rear of our regiment, which they regained, much to their own and our satisfaction, about eight o'clock on Thursday evening.

Singular as it may appear, we had not been specially anxious in their behalf. We did not dream of their being lost. They were supposed to be with the column, and their absence from the company we ascribed to their footsore and exhausted condition. It is very difficult, as I have hinted before, for individuals to march faster than those in whose immediate presence they find themselves. If it is persisted in, it is necessary to crowd and jostle parties, who, many of them, are already jaded, and cross with fatigue. If it is light, they see at once by your regimental number that you are out of place, and in their surly mood they jump at the conclusion that you have no good reason for falling to the rear, and give you a piece of their mind. This being the case, it becomes quite difficult to get up to a regiment which has passed on towards the front, as we many of us knew; and our friends had the same experience.

As the regiment, with our companions of the cavalry and artillery, marched on, which we did for at least three hours before reaching the main army, we were interested by the first sight we had of what afterwards became quite a common thing with us; that is a forest-fire. It was the custom for our cavalry to ride rapidly several miles in advance of the infantry, and set fire to the trees on the sides of the road. Sometimes this was done on side-roads for strategic purposes; but usually they only anticipated the presence of the column, its use, in this case, being to deceive the enemy in respect to the size and position of our forces. In certain conditions of weather, etc., these fires spread rapidly, and burned with great fury. The sight was very imposing from a distance, the sky for miles in our front being brilliantly illuminated; and as we came up, and entered upon the roads which had been fired, the scenes we witnessed were impressive with the gloomy grandeur of desolation. We were enveloped in smoke, as when we lay before the flaming muzzles of our cannon during the actions. Now and then a tall tree would come crashing to the ground with a deafening noise; and sometimes we halted, and watched our chance to creep warily past some monarch of the forest, fast tending to its fall.

What with fatigue, wakefulness, and unsuitable food, my imagination was taken captive by the scenes of destruction which I had for a week been witnessing, and, although perfectly level in my conversation on all ordinary themes, my mind wandered as we marched on in the darkness of the early morning, prolonged, as it was, by the smoke, somewhat into the day. I fancied that I was in the streets of a great city during a conflagration. The trees, many of which were on fire to their tops, a hundred feet or more in height, answered readily to the draught my disordered mind made upon them to represent steeples and chimneys. The burning forest, having been so far complaisant to my wavering whims, moulded itself still further into roofless gables and open windows, with long serpent-like tongues of fire flashing through them; while the bronzed faces of my comrades, peering into the strange scene around us, answered for the crowd of spectators. The

ponderous engines of war which rolled and rumbled along
the road, with the artillerists upon their seats, filed, without
any disturbing incongruity, into the avenues of my involuntary mystical experiences as the organized force of firemen
and the imposing machines with which our great cities fight
their most terrible enemy.

As we marched away from the fire, and came out to the
clear sky and broad daylight, these sickly and gloomy fancies
ceased. My condition was such, mentally and physically,
that I had virtually seen a mirage revealing itself in the
forest-fire, although it was almost entirely subjective. The
imagination, for a time, got the better of the senses, and prevented them from exercising their usual functions.

I fancy that the trees and waving foliage, the fleecy clouds
and rippling lakes, which sometimes float before the eyes of
weary and thirsty travellers in the desert, owe much of their
power to the disordered cravings of the mind to be relieved
of its repulsive surroundings.

There had been a short halt after we joined the column;
and, while we waited, we ate our breakfast, after which, some
of our lads dispersed themselves among the other regiments
to learn what had happened during the day. The railroad
had been torn up, and a covered bridge, on which it crossed
the Neuse, had been burnt.

The artillery-firing which we had heard at sunset was in
consequence of a most resolute and determined effort, on the
part of the enemy, to capture a part of our artillery which
remained upon the field while our troops were retiring. They
were repulsed with great loss. Their advance was as heroic,
and as disastrous to them, as their grand charge at Gettysburg, and they made no further effort to annoy us; but we
completed our return to Newbern without opposition of any
sort. I copy below a full and most interesting account of
what happened at this time, from "Wearing the Blue," by
Major Denny of Worcester; the book being a graphic history
of the Twenty-fifth Massachusetts Regiment.

" The army commenced to retire, Lee's brigade being directed

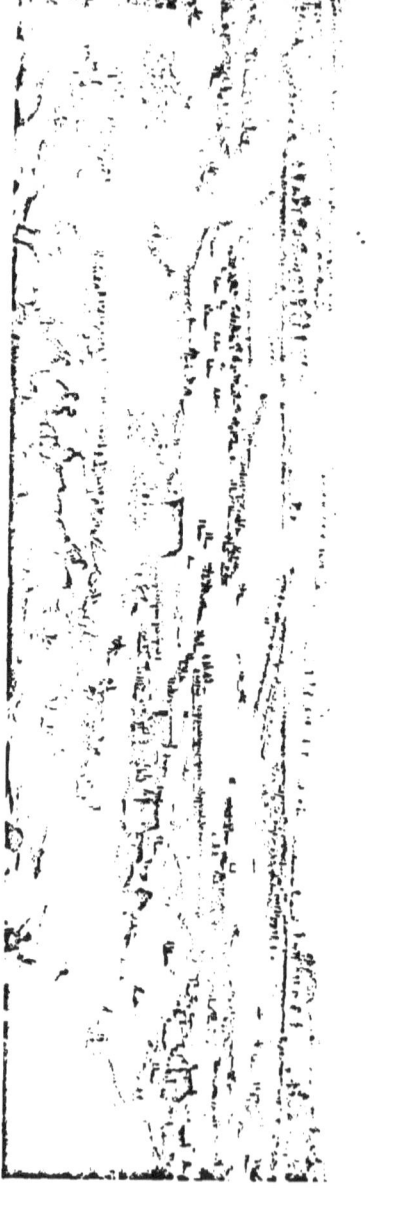

BATTLE OF GOLDSBOROUGH.

to cover the march in retreat; and so we waited by the roadside
until late in the afternoon, — quite late; for the earth was

'Bathed in the rays of the great setting flame.'

And not until then was the main body of troops in motion. The
Twenty-fifth was awaiting the 'Attention!' of Pickett; while on
the knoll in our immediate front Belger and Morrison with their
batteries, and Mix with his cavalry, awaited with us the orders to
move. We were feeling tired, and easy as to the future, for in a
few moments we would be turned towards home. In an instant,
on the knoll in our front, every living thing seemed to shake off
the inertia which had possessed them. Even the horses, that had
stood with their wearied heads drooping, curved their necks, and
pricked up their ears, as if they knew that *something* was coming,
as if they scented danger in the rustling branches of the trees.
Startled by the change, we had barely time to note it, before every
man of the batteries had sprung to their places. The cavalry,
vaulting into saddles, drew up in line; and in the clear sunlight on
that crest we caught the gleam of their sabres as they drew them,
and came to a 'carry.' Men came running back to the fence
from every direction as the infantry straightened out into line of
battle. There might have been a dozen (cannon) shots, so rapid
they could not be counted; and the smoke rolled back under gun
and caisson, and over men and horses, until they all stood in dense
clouds. The yells, momentarily smothered, broke out between the
rapid discharges of cannon, and were answered by the cheers of
our cavalry, as in that evening's sunset they swung their glittering
sabres over their heads, and defied the coming storm. This was a
new experience to the men of the nine-months regiments at the
fence; and Belger, feeling a little nervous, sent back to the lane
for one of the old regiments. The Twenty-fifth started off at
double-quick, rapidly passing down the short lane, across the brook,
into the field, and lay down in close column by division. We
were close up to Belger's battery, and flattened ourselves out as
well as we could in the sand; for one cannot well be too small or
too thin on such occasions. Three rebel lines of battle came
charging across the railroad over the ditches, sweeping on through
the low land, and around the base of the little hill. They gained
the slope, and were coming directly for the batteries. They
wavered, for a moment checked, but on again with fearful persist-
ency. The colors in the first line fall, but are again gathered up.

Belger sights his right gun himself, and a great puff rolls out. Men in the advancing line throw up their hands, while headless and mangled men are rolled together,—a horrid snarl of mutilated humanity. The firing was repeated, and groups of gray disappeared; but the gaps were filled, and they struggled on. The brow of the little hill was all aglow with flame. The smoke-drifts rolled in, but in a moment faded away, revealing the long line nearer than ever. 'Steady there!' 'Don't fire too fast!' 'Make every shot tell!' shouted Belger. His orderly sergeant limped to our ranks, smartly stung by a passing shot, but, after rubbing his leg a moment, thought he was not much hurt, and went back. 'Give 'em grape double shotted!' rings out from the battery. 'All out!' the disheartening response. 'Give 'em shrapnel!' — 'Not another round left, captain!' — 'Give 'em shell, then!' cried the chief; which we knew well was the last resort. We strained our eyes into the cloud of smoke, expecting every moment to see the enemy sweep over the guns. Farther in front, Belger saw more than we could see. Wrought up to the highest pitch of excitement at the thought that his guns were in danger, the impetuous artilleryman spurred his steed out of those foggy folds, and, pointing to his pieces, cried in the agony of the moment, as he turned to the men of the Twenty-fifth, 'Boys, don't let them have those guns!' We must have looked our answer; for back he went, and was again lost to sight. On our right front the battery horses moaned in terror and in pain, tossing their heads as the fierce rain of lead and iron tore through their flesh, and furrowed the earth beneath their feet.

"From one of the enemy's field-pieces aimed at our colors, kept steadily in sight by Sergeant James O'Neill, the shots spun through our ranks with loud hums, or buried themselves with deadly thuds in sand and living men. . . . The crisis was soon passed, however. A few moments of surging to and fro around the batteries, and the decimated and demoralized rebel brigade was hurled back into the meadow, and over the railroad whence they had emerged.

"After this defeat of the rebel onslaught, our left flank was seriously threatened; but two guns from our position were trained upon the flanking column, and to our left rear two thirty-twos enfiladed the enemy just as the Twenty-seventh Massachusetts wheeled into line to meet them. Lyman shouted, 'By file, commence firing!' The solitary cracks were soon merged into one

irregular rattle; and a roar of musketry smothered every other sound.

"The enemy again fell back into the depth of the forest; the fire of the rebel batteries slackened; our own batteries went to the rear, and opened again, firing over our heads. Some of our regiments, that had moved off the field before the rebel attack, had faced about, and joined in the defence; but now they again marched off the field. Our brigade followed quickly.

"Oh the weariness of that night's march! — who can tell it? who can remember it. but with pain? Tired, wretched, and sore; chafed and fretted by the sand which had filtered into our shoes; galled by our cartridge-boxes, which had fairly worn a place for themselves into our flesh, — we dragged our aching bodies over the rough and uneven roads, neither knowing nor caring where we went. Near midnight we turned into a cornfield, and sank down to uninterrupted rest.

"E. T. WITHERBY."

Some time previous to reaching Goldsborough, a strong cavalry force had been detached, and sent to Mount Olive, — a station on the Wilmington railroad, twenty miles to the south. They had succeeded in destroying the track in that vicinity, so as to insure our safety from any forces which might otherwise have been brought from Wilmington, and had returned without loss.

Our boys brought back an item which first fell upon my ears about as follows: "What do you think? Those New-York fellows over there are all talking about the Seventeenth and Barney Mann."

Inasmuch as our city had a strong representation among the officers and men of the Seventeenth, there is no occasion for any apology for a slight digression at this point, in order that they may speak for themselves through the official report of Col. Fellows to the adjutant-general of the State. This report is written with an unobtrusive reticence as to the real exposures and services of the regiment, so much so, that the ordinary reader will hardly realize how spontaneous and well-deserved the cheers were with which they were rewarded for their gallant deeds by their associates of the march. I make a few insertions between brackets.

"The main object of the expedition was to burn a railroad-bridge, destroy the track, and cut off communication. We pushed onward with skirmishers deployed, and gained the railroad, driving the enemy before us. I was then ordered to approach the bridge [it was necessary to march a mile on the track to do this], leaving the skirmishers to watch the enemy; but on doing this we were opened upon by a heavy fire of artillery.[on the railroad] in front of us, and musketry from the woods on both sides. We continued to advance, and arrived within ten feet of the bridge, using the banks of the road as a temporary shelter. Morrison's battery came up, and took position near our flag, on the right flank. I pointed out to the captain the bridge and the depot beyond, where a train had just arrived with re-enforcements for the enemy. Giving his orders with coolness and judgment, he planted a shell directly among them, and kept up a steady fire in that direction. Meanwhile the shot and shell from the enemy's artillery came thick and fast among us, yet not a man quailed; and my orders were obeyed with as much coolness as they are upon battalion-drill. I sheltered the men in a hollow directly in the rear of the artillery, and was then notified that two men from each of the two regiments were to be sent to fire the bridge. I called for volunteers; and Barney Mann, our late adjutant, offered to find them. A short time after, I saw him wounded, and then learned that he had gone himself, with another man, for the purpose. The two from the Ninth New-Jersey were also there; and the bridge was fired [it was a fine, covered structure, several hundred feet in length]. I was then notified that the object of the expedition was accomplished, and that Gen. Foster gave the credit of it to the two regiments. When the batteries withdrew, I formed upon the right of the Ninth New-Jersey, according to orders; and the regiment was received with three rousing cheers by the army all around us. Our escape with such slight loss — one killed, and eighteen wounded — seems little short of a miracle. Other regiments have suffered more severely than this. I think a commander, however, should base his reputation upon doing the most work with little loss of men; and a timely order to lie down, when nothing else could be done, has saved many lives."

From an interesting account in "Soldiering in North Carolina," by "one of the Seventeenth," I take the following extract in further statement of the facts: —

"Col. Fellows was continually going up and down the line, encouraging his men, and showing them by his example a pattern of the most fearless bravery."

Previous to the call for volunteers from the Seventeenth to burn the bridge, Capt. Graham, an officer of Gen. Foster's staff, a young man of the most conspicuous bravery, had made an ineffectual attempt to the same end, but was repulsed by the storm of bullets which fell around him.

"Lieut. Barnabas N. Mann then came forward, with a bundle of prepared combustibles in his hands, and called for two volunteers to accompany him to the bridge to operate with another party in an endeavor to fire the same. The men were instantly forthcoming, of course; and the trio started on their dangerous errand. We watched them with anxiety, and saw them gain the bridge amid a perfect death-shower of bullets, one of which unfortunately hit our brave Lieut. Mann on the plate of his belt, causing a severe contused wound. They returned with the wounded officer, reporting that they did not succeed in their enterprise. But in this they were mistaken, as will be seen presently. The enemy's fire began to slacken, and, just as another attempt was about to be made to burn the bridge, smoke could be seen issuing from it; and soon the whole structure was wrapped in flames."

Our return march was unmolested, as before stated. A short halt took place below Kinston, as we supposed, to place our wounded on vessels; and late on sabbath morning, the 21st, we reached our camp.

CHAPTER V.

REVIEW OF THE GOLDSBOROUGH MARCH.

A PARTIAL review of the Goldsborough march is needed to complete its record. Gen. Amory, our commanding officer, made the following report of the loss in his brigade: —

	KILLED.	WOUNDED.
Seventeenth Massachusetts	1	29
Twenty-third Massachusetts	15	52
Forty-third Massachusetts	2	1
Forty-fifth Massachusetts	17	60
Fifty-first Massachusetts	—	2

Of our regiment it should be further stated, that our wounded comrade died, and one perished of exhaustion, — C. W. Hutchins, an exemplary young man of Company K; making a total of four deaths, besides one missing, from our own company, — Hiram Judkins, a non-resident, who fell in some unexplained manner into the enemy's hands, and was by them passed into the Union lines on the Potomac. We did not see him again. He is recorded as having been discharged for disability, March 8, 1863.

Gen. Foster's report of the killed, wounded, and missing of the whole army, is as follows (it is quoted from Moore's "Rebellion Record," vol. vi. p. 256), 90 killed, 478 wounded, 9 missing.

We must have marched at least a hundred and sixty miles. We were favored with pleasant weather during the whole time, and suffered but little for lack of drinking-water. I have previously given Gen. Foster a brief introduction to the reader, and, inasmuch as we had become quite familiarly acquainted with him during the march, some further notice seems appropriate. He was a man about forty-five, portly,

and physically robust, with the exception of a slight weakness in one of his legs from a wound received in the Mexican war. He was affable to the verge of familiarity, and prepossessing in appearance, uniting the highest qualities of the civilian and the soldier. He was stationed at Boston for several years soon after the war, and was always accessible to his old comrades of all grades in the Eighteenth Corps. He died at Nashua, N.H., of consumption, Sept. 2, 1874. His obituary in one of the Boston papers contained the following paragraph: —

"In the death of Gen. Foster a noble and gallant heart is stilled. He is remembered with especial regard, and something of fondness, by the many Massachusetts troops who were under his command in North Carolina. Many of them will pleasantly recall to mind his commanding form and beaming face as he was wont to ride along the weary marching column, and drop words of compliment and cheer."

His conduct of the expedition impressed us deeply with a sense of his strategic ability. It was severely criticised at the time in one respect; namely, the rapid manner in which we were obliged to march. It was said that the column should have been halted after crossing the streams (for such they were, some of them), to save the men in the rear from the exhaustion of double-quicking to close the gap in front of them. But I apprehend that there would have been danger of disastrous delay in following this course. The safety and success of such a movement as ours was, lays, in great part, in its rapidity of motion. Delays, in such circumstances, are, in the highest and most emphatic sense, not only dangerous, but likely to be fatal. The renowned hero Stonewall Jackson owed much of his celebrity to the success with which he planned and executed daring assaults of this kind. Early in the war, in May, 1862, he took a column across the Alleghanies into West Virginia. By the merest piece of good luck, his coming was ascertained before he had a chance to "rush things" in his usual style. He halted a short time, and our forces, under Gen. Milroy, went out instantly to

meet him, instead of waiting to be attacked; and handled him so roughly during an afternoon fight, that he quietly took himself back again the next morning, although he had already marched seven days. It was said by those who knew him best, that allusions to his raid into West Virginia were very distasteful to him. He reported a loss of seventy-one killed (of whom there were three colonels and two majors) and three hundred and ninety wounded, among whom was Gen. Edward Johnston.

The points which impressed us the most, as we afterwards discussed them in our camp by the Trent, were the manner in which the rebel earthworks were flanked at South-west Creek; the long *détour* to the west, by which our flanking march was extended in such a manner as to deceive even ourselves as to our destination; then the vigorous blow at Kinston, struck so quickly by the rapid turn of our force to the north-east, that we met only a small number of the rebels; the temporary passage across the river of so large a portion of our army, leaving the enemy for some hours in doubt whether we were to stop there, or go still farther to the north of the Neuse, repeating the previous march to Tarborough. These movements were all of them masterpieces of military wisdom, so far as we were capable of judging. To understand them fully, it should be known that the enemy held uninterrupted control of the railroad (Atlantic and North-Carolina) running east and west, on the north bank of the Neuse, between Goldsborough and Kinston; and they could easily, by this means, have had a much larger number at Kinston to oppose us, if our course could have been known sooner, or even readily inferred. Then the courageous confidence in his own resources, which enabled him to fight at Whitehall without halting his whole column, was a continuation of the same firmness and self-command which was again exercised at Goldsborough, where the rebels were kept on the move all day, on a line reaching from the point the Forty-third occupied at Spring-Bank Bridge, to the fords, several miles above the town, where they finally crossed to attack him in the assault on the artillery. This he did by

such a disposition of his force as to leave the enemy for some hours in doubt whether or not his attack on the railroad was a feint designed to cover his real purpose to capture the town. We were also exposed to an attack from the rebels, who could easily have come up from the south on the Wilmington and Weldon Railroad; but this liability was provided for by the raid of the cavalry regiment to Mount Olive, where they tore up the track, and effectually covered our left flank.

His wife was a true helpmeet to such a man. She was in a high degree courageous, active, and philanthropic. She was not with the column; but we heard of her, during our term of service, wherever it was possible for her to go in helpful and consoling ministrations to the wounded or sick of our number. It made no difference whether her duties were performed in the wards of Stanley Hospital at Newbern, or whether she was engaged in looking after some unnoticed or otherwise neglected private on board a transport, her energy and faithfulness were the same. We all heard of her beneficent deeds, and held her in grateful estimation.

Always, while on the march, Gen. Foster was associated with a tall and finely built man, whom we came to know as our guide. He was in the dress of a citizen, and, I think, entirely unarmed. As he rode by the general's side, his appearance and bearing was such as to command the deep interest of every thoughtful soldier. His demeanor was in full accordance with a countenance as composed and dignified as that of Washington. The rebels would have riddled him with bullets, or hung him with short shrift to the nearest tree, if he had fallen into their hands; yet he had committed no crime, except that of loving his whole country better than a small part of it.

When we reached Newbern, on our return, we learned of the disaster at Fredericksburg. The effect upon our minds was depressing; but it was only the first of a series of influences of the same character, which lasted during our whole term of service, and compelled us, much against our will, to the conclusion that the end to which we had looked hopefully

forward when we enlisted — a speedy conclusion of the war — was not to be expected.

In reviewing the march and its results, I feel warranted in bringing to light one of its incidents which later events proved to have been of greater consequence than we supposed at the time. The Third New-York Cavalry had approached Whitehall on the evening before the battle; and a private of their number, by the name of Butler, had plunged into the wintry stream, and swam across, in order to burn a gunboat which was on the stocks. His effort was ineffectual, as he was discovered, and driven back under a shower of bullets. What he failed to accomplish with the torch, we did on the next day with our cannon. This gunboat was to have been an iron-clad. It seems almost ridiculous! but that insignificant hamlet far up in the forest was really a naval station. No more, certainly no less. If the craft had been completed, the chances are, that we might have had livelier times at Newbern than we actually experienced. This impression derives its force from the fact that the rebels succeeded in finishing a vessel of this description on the Roanoke in the spring of 1864. They descended the river with it, and sunk one of the gunboats which were at Plymouth at the time, driving the others away. This placed the garrison there at the mercy of a large force, under Gen. Hoke, who made a fierce assault, capturing the whole garrison, composed of the Eighty-fifth New-York Regiment, the Hundred and First, and Hundred and Third Regiments of Pennsylvania Infantry of Gen. Wessel's brigade, the Sixteenth Connecticut Infantry, Twenty-fourth New-York Battery, two companies of the Second Massachusetts Heavy Artillery, and a company of the Twelfth New-York Cavalry. The first three of these regiments were with us in the march. They were taken to Andersonville, and many of them perished miserably in that infernal den. The sharpness of the sufferings of the Pennsylvania men was aggravated by the fact, that, at the moment of their capture, they were waiting transportation home, having re-enlisted, and been furloughed for a visit to their friends. A full account of this most ter-

rible disaster to the department of North Carolina may be found in "John McElroy's Experience of a Private Soldier at Andersonville," etc. (Bates Hall Library, 4220 a, 64), — a book in which the revolting treatment of the Union prisoners is delineated in a manner in which grace of style and force are remarkably united.

To those who may ask for more definite statements than have been given concerning "the pomp and circumstance of glorious war," as observed by us, I am obliged to confess my inability to meet their wishes, mainly for lack of the raw material to work up into acceptable forms. The only music that I heard during the whole march has been already alluded to in the account of the occurrences at Kinston. All our regular musicians were in the ambulance-corps. Not a note did we hear from fife, bugle, or drum. Now and then Gen. Foster was cheered by the veterans as he rode through the column. As we came out of Kinston on Monday morning, we met our friends of the Fifth Regiment with cheers; the City Guard of Charlestown being with them. They had held the bridge during the night against the attempts of guerillas to burn it. The appearance of the column in crossing the streams was very picturesque, in spite of our sombre coats of blue and the irregular manner in which we marched. The glittering polish of our muskets flashing in the sunlight, as we descended into the gullies, balanced ourselves upon the bridges by the side of the road, or struggled in the water, and then rose on the other side, was quite impressive to the sight. The artillery, in particular, made a fine appearance in this respect as the four magnificent horses (always of the largest size) galloped at full speed across the water with their gun and its caisson; every thing upon which an artillerist could sit being crowded with men. For myself, I will say that the most exultant emotion of patriotic feeling which I experienced was at the moment of reaching the banks of the Trent River, opposite our camp, on the sabbath morning of our return. As we came out of the forest, Newbern and the Rivers Trent and Neuse opened suddenly upon our sight, and an unexpected pleasure was ours. Both rivers were full

of our gunboats, — light-draught steamers adapted to the navigation of the shoal waters of the sounds of North Carolina. They were anchored in line, astern of each other, at short distances apart, all the way from the upper Trent bridge, around the peninsula on which Newbern stands, up into the Neuse on the north side of the town. Their colors were set, and to me it was a most heart-cheering and really magnificent sight, reminding me, as it did, of the immensity of the power of the government as manifested in the effectiveness of the blockade of the whole Southern coast. This work was almost Titanic in its character; yet it was so thoroughly done, that the rebels themselves, as well as their sympathizers in England, were obliged to admit the fact. It is well known that they were troubled to get surgical instruments, not for lack of money, but because their ports were closed. We were ourselves urgently solicited on our march for common salt by destitute families. It is almost needless to say that these gunboats came in immediately on our departure to assure the safety of the place during our absence.

I should feel that an omission of a marked character would be chargeable to me, if I should fail to record an interesting incident of our marches, as follows: they were often prolonged until as late as ten P.M.; and, during the hours of darkness, our spirits rose readily into the realms of poetry and song. Some one would start a patriotic ode or hymn: it would be taken up by all who could sing, and a new and elevated impulse imparted to our heavy footsteps. Whatever else was sung, the martyr hero who pioneered our great conflict was sure to be remembered. "The soul of John Brown went marching on" with us, as with every armed column which penetrated Secessia. We all sang it in our hearts, if not with our voices. All shades of politics and all nationalities, all personal opinions and peculiarities, merged themselves in a deep and universal conviction that the grand old man, who came as near as mortal could to "making the gallows as glorious as the cross," was really right, though technically wrong.

In making this reference to our singing, a fact which is so

ethereal in its nature that many writers would only use it rhetorically. I do it with a full conviction that it was an indication of the character and motives of the army of the North, which was really finally decisive of the great contest. The rebels had no songs which went so deep into the ideal and religious nature of man as ours did: they were all characterized by a sensuous localism. During the war the Richmond correspondent of "The London Times" wrote, and, what is more remarkable still, the Thunderer printed, the following ingenuous admission: —

"No one who has been conversant with the Northern States during the last two and a half years can have failed to notice with astonishment the faith, stronger than death, which the Northerners have exhibited in their manifest destiny, their religion, their Alpha and Omega, their dream of dominion from sea to sea, and, to quote Mr. Everett's own words, 'from the icy pole to the flaming belt of the equator.' The successes of the South have altogether failed to inspire them with a tithe of that confidence in themselves which neither defeat, nor hope deferred, nor illusions dispelled, have ever shaken out of the Northerners. Deny it who may, there is something sublime in this shadowy earnestness and misty magnificence of Northern faith and self-reliance."

I cannot resist the temptation to give here two poetic illustrations of the widely differing characteristics of the North and the South. The first is the *only* spirit-stirring song that I thought worth copying, out of several hundred Southern war-songs which are to be found in a scrap-book at the Boston Public Library. The second will speak for itself in confirming my statements.

STONEWALL JACKSON'S WAY.

FOUND ON A CONFEDERATE SERGEANT OF JACKSON'S BRIGADE, TAKEN AT WINCHESTER, VA.

Come, stack arms, men! Pile on the rails,
   Stir up the camp-fire bright;
No matter if the canteen fails,
   We'll make a rousing night:
Here Shenandoah brawls along,
   And burly Blue Ridge echoes strong,
To swell our brigade's rousing song
   Of "Stonewall Jackson's way."

We see him now, — the old slouched hat
  Cocked o'er his eye askew,
The shrewd, dry smile, the speech so pat,
  So calm, so blunt, so true.
The "Blue Light Elder" his foe knows well:
  Says he, "That's Banks; he don't like shell —
Lord,[1] save his soul! — we'll give him — well,"
  That's "Stonewall Jackson's way."

Silence! ground arms! kneel all! caps off!
  Old "Blue-Light's" going to pray:
Strangle the fool that dares to scoff.
  Attention! It's his way!
Appealing from his native sod
  In forma pauperis to God,
Say, "Bare thine arm, stretch forth thy rod,
  Amen!" That's "Stonewall Jackson's way."

He's in the saddle now. Fall in!
  Steady, the whole brigade:
Hill's at the ford, cut off: we'll win
  His way out, ball and blade!
What matter if our shoes *are* worn!
  What matter if our feet *are* torn!
Quickstep! we're with him ere the dawn:
  That's "Stonewall Jackson's way."

The sun's bright lances rout the mists
  Of morning; and, by George!
Here's Longstreet struggling in the lists,
  Hemmed in an ugly gorge.
Pope and his Yankees fierce before,
  Bayonets and grape! Hear Stonewall roar
"Charge, Stewart! and pay off Ashby's score"
  In "Stonewall Jackson's way."

Ah, maiden! wait and watch and yearn
  For news of Jackson's band;
Ah, widow! view with eyes that burn
  That ring upon the hand;
Ah, wife! sew on, pray on, hope on,
  Thy life shall not be all forlorn:
The foe had better ne'er been born
  Than get in "Stonewall's way.".

MARTINSBURG, Sept. 13, 1862.

[1] Original manuscript, —

  "Lord, save his soul, we'll give him hell!
  In 'Stonewall Jackson's way.'"

BATTLE-HYMN OF THE REPUBLIC.

MRS. JULIA WARD HOWE.

Mine eyes have seen the glory of the coming of the Lord;
He is trampling out the vintage where the grapes of wrath are stored;
He hath loosed the fateful lightning of his terrible, swift sword:
        His truth is marching on.

I have seen him in the watch-fires of a hundred circling camps;
They have builded him an altar in the evening dews and damps;
I have read his righteous sentence by the dim and flaring lamps:
        His day is marching on.

I have read a fiery gospel writ in burnished rows of steel:
" As ye deal with my contemners, so with you my grace shall deal: "
Let the hero born of woman crush the serpent with his heel,
        Since God is marching on.

He has sounded forth the trumpet that shall never call retreat;
He is sifting out the hearts of men before his judgment-seat:
Oh, be swift, my soul, to answer him! be jubilant, my feet!
        Our God is marching on.

In the beauty of the lilies Christ was born across the sea,
With a glory in his bosom that transfigures you and me:
As he died to make men holy, let us die to make men free,
        While God is marching on.
                CHORUS — " Glory, glory, hallelujah! "

Two more allusions remain, and the Great March will cease to occupy our attention.

Living as I have all my days in the vicinity of a large seaport, I have often had occasion to look with profound interest upon the gatherings upon the decks of shipping, as the religious exercises appropriate to the departure of missionaries for foreign lands are held. I have long been of opinion that the scenes there witnessed are prompted by the highest motives which can actuate human beings, that they are in fact a practical rebuke, of the most searching character, of by far the larger portion of the lives of those of us who profess to be actuated by the same motives as our friends who go abroad, and make their residence in unhealthy climates and among uncongenial people and associations.

I had supposed that such scenes were exceptional in their nature, and that nothing like them was to be expected elsewhere. But I was to live long enough to see an illustration, not necessarily religious in its character, of sacrifice, which, in my judgment, elevates every man who complies cheerfully with its terms as far beyond the usual limits of our ordinary life as the self-abnegation of the Christian missionary raises him above the prevailing standard of discipleship. I refer to the obligation which rests upon every colonel or commanding officer of a regiment to hazard his own life, that those intrusted to his authority may be as far as possible shielded from the terrible exposures of war; this duty on his part, of course, involving the corresponding obligation on the men to be equally ready to risk or to sacrifice themselves, if necessary, in defence of the nation.

The direct form that this obligation takes calls upon the colonel to remain standing while under fire, after all the men, even his associates the lieutenant-colonel and major, are comparatively sheltered by lying down, or in some other way. The manner in which a sense of common danger and sacrifice in a great cause develops itself on the field of action forms one of the most interesting of my recollections. There is familiarity between officers and men without disrespect: a marked and impressive sociality rules the moments as they fly. No one knows but what at any instant the brittle thread of life may be shockingly sundered, and the possibility is sufficiently probable to impress even the most superficial with a certain unwonted elevation of demeanor. Col. Holbrook walked with the utmost coolness up and down the road the whole length of the regiment, or in front of the battery which we supported, during the whole of the action at Whitehall. He must have been in plain sight, during most of the time, to the enemy. He was in frequent communication with us, and we with him. We had considered him cold and unsympathetic; but these opinions were permanently reversed by his conduct. Naturally somewhat undemonstrative in his nature, he rose into the kindest interest in our welfare, expressed more in manner than in words, but not lacking in the last respect.

It would be useless to attempt to recall the details of this intercourse: it is sufficient to say that language which would appear utterly commonplace in print was really impressive in the highest degree, both in tone and manner, when uttered in such circumstances as those by which we were surrounded.

It should be said, that, in a less degree, this same obligation of self-sacrifice rests upon the officers of the line also. We had the evidence at Whitehall that its terms would be honorably and faithfully met. Lieutenants Colesworthy of our company, and Nickerson of Company E, were upon their feet at once when private Smith was killed. It was thought at first that his injury was only to the arm, and they proceeded to obtain a tourniquet. But it proved that the missile had not only cut off his arm, but had gone also through his body, and buried itself in the ground, so that he had passed beyond mortal aid.

The final allusion that I wish to make is to the freedmen, as they were beginning to be called at that time; for the Emancipation Proclamation was soon to bring its blessings, and make its claims upon them.

One of the last sights that I saw, as I looked back over my shoulder, when we entered the gloomy recesses of the swamp at Kinston, was a line of black faces behind us, out of the range of shot, making a good show for a battalion, at least. They were officers' servants and camp-followers, attached in various ways to the column. They were not at that time supposed to possess sufficient courage to fight. But time works changes; and in war it often does it quite rapidly. Four months afterward, Gen. Wild came into North Carolina, and formed the First Brigade of United-States colored troops among these same men. They were the pioneers of two hundred thousand Africans who were enrolled before the end of the war.

Very pitiable was the scene which I often witnessed as I sat or reclined by myself during the night by the camp-fires. These poor people were but slightly provided, and, for the most part, not provided at all, with blankets, or even coats. After they thought the men were all asleep, they would

swarm in around the fires, shivering with the cold, pinched and cramped in their whole being, as the flies are in early autumn. The soldiers lay with their feet as near the fire as was allowable on account of the exposure of their blankets to the heat. Perhaps there was eighteen inches (half a yard) of space open. No white man could stop longer than a few moments in this opening, so intense was the heat of the blazing Southern pine; but into these narrow limits many of them would go without the least hesitation, and not only stretch themselves out at full length on the ground, but lay there quietly for hours. At first I did not interfere, thinking that they would not be able to endure the heat for any length of time; but the men soon began to notice the cessation of warmth at their feet, and in some cases drove them away. Whenever I observed this, I prevented them from returning to that particular spot, holding them where I was myself, at the end of the rails in the vacant place of a few feet between the fires.

I have never heard or seen any statement in respect to the number of colored people who accompanied us on our return. It must have been quite large, if there were as many scattered along the route as there were that marched by the side of our battalion. Those in the vicinity of Company H were of a high character. Whole families were together. The parents carried the young children in their arms or upon their shoulders. I noticed that they were quite reserved. It was not easy to draw them out in conversation. This was a general peculiarity of the time, quite possibly owing to the rude chaffing which they often experienced.

CHAPTER VI.

THE TRENTON MARCH.

FOR three days after returning, we did nothing but rest: the ordinary duty of guarding the camp was all that was required. Many of us could only walk with difficulty for a week. Quite a number of the irrepressibles of the regiment found themselves without clothing and guns; and they were obliged to wait for a new outfit at their own expense. This happened through their indiscretion in attempting to combine pleasure with duty. Two or three youngsters would get together, and camp by themselves at a distance from others: they would all fall asleep around a blazing fire to be waked up suddenly by its spreading in the furze and dry weeds around them. It was said that some barely escaped with their lives, for the flames got such headway as to burn the black-walnut stocks of their guns to cinders. They were the subjects of the ridicule of their comrades, as they flitted, ghostlike, about the camp in their underclothes, while waiting for their new uniforms.

Christmas Day was made a scene of festivity and fun, so far as our means allowed. For a short time, our officers of all grades were supposed to have resigned their positions, which passed into the hands of the rank and file of the regiment. Wooden swords and other strangely bombastic proceedings were the order of the hour. Orderly Edmunds gave his roll of the company into the hands of a worthy comrade ordinarily known as "Billy," and supposed to be a person of sufficient education and address for the place; but the first thing that he did was to insist on calling the names of the company wrong end to, beginning at the bottom, instead of at the top, of the list. The men were so unaccus-

tomed to this, or for some other reason, that they responded very disrespectfully, or not at all, and finally went tumultuously on to the parade-ground under the charge of another worthy private acting as captain, whom I shall call "Hop." His vigorous efforts to induce his command to "keep the cadence of the step," and other semi-military injunctions to which we were accustomed, signally failed to enforce discipline. The dress-parade under the command of a young corporal of Company B, whom I may with propriety designate as Col. Harum Scarum, was disorderly and ridiculous to a high degree; his utmost efforts to prevail upon the men to "keep their hands down," and comply with the ordinary obligations of the exercise in other respects, being derided to his face.

These comic proceedings finally came to an end by natural limitations, and we returned to the settled order of the camp. I deem it appropriate here to pass to the other extreme, and give a view of the moral and religious condition and privileges of the regiment, as delineated in an interesting letter from our chaplain to "The Boston Journal:"—

CAMP ROGERS, Dec. 30, 1862.

While sharing somewhat in the evils common to all regiments, the Forty-third has given many cheering evidences of a moral and religious soundness much exceeding the average in this department. Its soldiers are, for the most part, of mature age: the plant of self-respect has had time to gain a certain deep-rooted steadiness within them, which renders them superior to the opinions of "veterans," and which disinclines them to be imitators, or influenced without good and patent reasons. Steps were taken at the outset to provide a chapel tent (the gift of the Old South Church, at a cost of seven hundred dollars). The influence for good this secured cannot be overestimated. It gives us, wherever we pitch our camp, one consecrated spot, one broad and white covering, — the holy and beautiful tabernacle of our God, — lifting itself ever into the view of the soldier when he goes out and comes in while parading and drilling, and as he busies himself with the almost numberless occupations of the camp. Into this place of sacred solemnities we come on the sabbath morning at the very hour when our wives and

mothers are worshipping God in more costly sanctuaries, and we feel, that, while going through our service there, that we commune with multitudes of the honored and beloved who are far away.

We have an excellent choir, and they sing the old standard hymns and tunes, for the most part; and many of the soldiers who have had hymn-books furnished them help to swell the voice of praise. I have seldom heard better "congregational singing" than within this "amiable" tabernacle of God: I certainly have heard far poorer, of which parishes in Massachusetts were becomingly proud. At the opening of our service we repeat the Lord's Prayer audibly in concert, very many of the soldiers, I am happy to say, devoutly joining. The Scriptures are read (always one or more of the Psalms) responsively; the preacher beginning, and the soldiers reading in concert the alternate verses. After service, the soldiers linger for reading matter, which is always furnished upon a table in the centre of the tent, of such quantity and quality as the discreet generosity of friends at home has placed within our reach.

In regard to our religious service on Sunday, we differ from many regiments around us, adopting neither the *compulsory* nor the purely *optional* plan. The chaplain cannot be too grateful for the aid and co-operation which he has had from his fellow-officers in managing this most delicate and difficult point. All, from the colonel down, have, I believe, both by precept and example, impressed it upon their commands that it is neither soldierly, nor loyal to the spirit of our government, to neglect the culture of the soul. This descending and surrounding influence, not amounting to a necessity, but hardly leaving the will of the soldier to the "liberty of indifference," bears very wholesome fruits. Our chapel is well filled; and the preacher has the comfort of knowing that he speaks to an assembly gathered from desire, and not by sheer military authority.

Having in our regiment several officers and men of the Masonic order, the chapel is assigned for their meetings two evenings each week. They have covered the ground of the tent with a beautiful white sand, which lights up most brilliantly in the evening, and is as dry and soft to the tread as a tapestry carpet. They have also provided a stove, and fitted up certain desks and benches, all covered with a dark-red cambric, giving to the whole tent a very homelike and inviting appearance. [Comfortable seats were afterwards added.]

The evening meetings of a strictly religious character held here are much the same as at home,—a prayer and conference meeting on Sunday evening, and one on Thursday evening, at both of which the chaplain presides. There is also a meeting for practice in singing every Saturday night. Recently a literary society has been organized, with most promising auspices, which will probably occupy the chapel the two remaining evenings of the week. I have learned with great satisfaction, that beside these more general meetings,—all tending directly or indirectly to the moral elevation of the soldier,—company prayer-meetings are held regularly and frequently in some of the streets; and in some of the tents, at the suggestion of men not professedly pious, there is Scripture-reading and prayer by some pious comrade before retiring. There was an unusual degree of interest and solemnity in the meeting of last Sunday evening; the chapel being nearly full, and many eager to pray and speak, with a fervency and humility not often witnessed under any circumstances.

Our company was second to none in the regiment in respect to character and intelligence, and contributed its due share to all the above developments. I will say, in addition, that, during the early spring, considerable numbers of the religious men of the regiment went to Newbern on the sabbath to teach in the colored schools. This was at the request of the colonel and chaplain. The presence of the rebel column put a stop to this.

We found ourselves associated with two somewhat remarkable religious characters, each one of them being sufficiently peculiar to draw attention outside of the company, and so connecting themselves with its history as to call for allusion. One was that of a man in middle life, decorous and upright in his relation to all the proprieties and moralities, fluent, also, and outspoken in advocacy of religion, but who failed entirely to command the respect of his comrades, for the following cause. Concealment is impossible in a camp. All sides of a man's character come to light in its searching and comprehensive trials. Men who are acting habitually on the highest lines of natural sacrifice in the constant surrender of individual desires and preferences to the common good

(and all soldiers are in some sense called upon to do this) are not inclined to regard with favor a religious man who is always on the outlook for his own interests, making himself unpleasantly conspicuous by the constant assertion, at all times and in all circumstances, of an offensively selfish individualism.

The other case was far less objectionable morally, but even more marked with eccentricity. We had among us one whose countenance was deeply impressed with a strong religious cast, — one of those faces which carry demonstrative evidence, to all shrewd observers, of the utmost sincerity. Strange to say, this worthy man found himself under arrest one day, — held to answer before the highest regimental authority for no less an offence than this; namely, knocking down a sentry. The circumstances were as follows: —

The peculiar mental and spiritual condition of our worthy associate was such, that the government issue of rations was entirely inadequate to his sustenance. It was really a necessity with him to obtain, in solitary devotion, a daily supply of that "living bread" which is sent evermore from heaven to replenish the wasting energies of the soul. He was in the habit of going out of camp for this purpose; and being too straightforward to use any artifice about it, and finding himself opposed by one of the guard, he incontinently struck out from the shoulder with such force as to knock the man heels over head.

The colonel found he had a case before him somewhat out of the usual line of culprits. The simplicity and earnestness of the man were too evident to be rudely repressed. Our friend escaped with a gentle admonition to "go and sin no more;" and the affair had a happy ending. By the exercise of a little discretion he managed thereafter to find occasions for private devotion; the case being so well understood throughout the regiment, that even Catholic sentries came to a common understanding, with the rest of us, in respect to the Protestant "saint" in Company H, and took good care not to see too much when he was in the neighborhood.

From my own letter of the date already quoted, and others

following, I make the following selections, to indicate the course of our experiences at this time: —

CAMP ROGERS, Jan. 1, 1863.

... Rumor is quite rife as to the destination of our regiment. If the unreliable dame is to be believed, we shall shortly be on the wing. How this will be, I cannot, of course, tell; but the indications are, that we shall not accompany the expedition which another batch of reports from the same delusive source say is slowly fitting out against Wilmington. All that I can do in these matters is to give you the atmosphere, as I may say, of the camp at the moment, or for a few days previous to, writing.

I cannot say too much in praise of the winter climate of North Carolina. It is truly delightful. We have as yet seen nothing colder (in the daytime) than we had in Readville, and not steady cold at that. Just now it is a little sharp; but we have had no ice over a quarter of an inch thick. There have not been more than three or four days when the sky has had that gloomy, leaden aspect so peculiar to it in our Northern homes at this season of the year. The clouds are warm and rosy in their character, and appearances of rain are soon dispelled. We have had but two continuous rain-storms since our arrival, though it is said that there will be a change for the worse in this respect as the season advances. I find it very difficult to realize your situation in Chelsea in respect to weather, and also to believe that this is New-Year's Day.

CAMP ROGERS, Jan. 5, 1863.

We have had two quite interesting occurrences in camp lately, — one public, the other private, in its character. The first was the appearance among us of Mr. Bond, who is associated with Mayor Fay in kind efforts to relieve the necessities of the soldiers. He is a merchant who has two sons in the Forty-fifth, and he was sent out by Gov. Andrew immediately on hearing that we were on a march. He was present at Chapel Tent service last Sunday a week ago, and, although no orator, he made a very feeling address to us, assuring us of the interest and influence of the State government and people in our behalf. What made it peculiarly pleasant to me and to others of Company H who were present was the fact that he was very complimentary and pointed in his remarks concerning Chelsea and her citizen soldiers. It was the most pleasing address of a public character that I have heard since I

volunteered. At its close he invited us to come to him with any request that we had, or any parcel to deliver to our friends. I had the satisfaction of shaking hands with him.

I had almost forgotten to say that about a fortnight ago, while I was busy sewing the string on to the flap of our tent, who should walk into our street, but Charlie Farnum, the former carpenter of the ferry, and Capt. Dale, who used to run the coaches. They are now on the United-States steamer "Maple Leaf." I should not have been more surprised if the "Trimountain" had thrust her bow round the sergeant's tent into Company H's street. They left Chelsea in September; but their faces were as welcome to us as if they had just come from home. You had better believe that I made a pump-handle of Charlie's right arm for a spell, and there were enough to serve the captain the same way.

. . . I can well imagine how desirous you are to hear from us; and as I read your letters last night, only five days from home, I could not but rejoice in the facilities for rapid intercourse now existing. As I wrote you in my last, there seems every indication that Amory's Brigade, including, of course, ourselves, will remain for the defence of Newbern. This, of course, is not certainly known, and, even if it is the present intention of our general, he might very suddenly alter his mind. It is now, however, thought probable, by those who desired and expected to go, that we shall remain here. So far as I can ascertain, re-enforcements have been pouring in upon us to such an extent that our general can well afford the necessary number to hold Newbern while he makes the advance on Wilmington. [All this gossip about Wilmington was finally dissipated by the ultimate direction of the force to Charleston, S.C.]

MONDAY, A.M., Jan. 12, 1863.

It is some time since the above was written; but no mails have left Newbern in the interim, as is supposed on account of the preparations for the great expedition, which it is desirable to conceal as far as is possible. I am in complete ignorance as to when this will go, though I shall keep it open until the last moment before our departure, of which you will probably hear before you have the reading of this letter. Last night, orders were read to cook three days' rations, and to take two days' in addition, and to be prepared to march within forty-eight hours. Our three companies have been called in, though one, Company I of Cambridge, was

sent out yesterday. So far as we are informed, this order only extends to three regiments of our brigade, — the Forty-third, Forty-fifth, and Fifty-first. We have the impression, from the shortness of the time covered by our rations, from the fact that our knapsacks are not to leave our tents, and from some words that would seem to have come from the officer who brought the order, that we are the only infantry who are to go just at this particular time; that we are not destined to Wilmington, but that this is a *reconnoissance* to ascertain, before the main army starts, whether the enemy are in force in our vicinity.

Capt. Hanover's feet were still in such a condition that the surgeon detained him in camp. Lieut. Bradbury had assumed the direction of the pioneers of the regiment; so that we went under the command of Lieut. Colesworthy. Four pieces of artillery were with us, and a battalion of cavalry.

The march proved, in fact, to be mainly for the purpose of burning mills, which were used to supply the rebel army with food, and in other incidental ways — such as stampeding the slaves. etc. — to render the territory lying between us and the Wilmington and Weldon road unserviceable to the enemy. The presence of our forces in the State actually accomplished this, as had already been evident to us; for we had found the large plantations overrun with weeds, the slaves either having made their escape to the seacoast, or been removed by their owners to the interior.

Our departure on the march was delayed by threatening and rainy weather until the morning of the 17th, when we started for Trenton, a small town on the river upon whose banks our camp was located: it was twenty-five miles distant in a north westerly direction. We marched across Brice's Creek, and on the south side of the Trent, by an entirely different route from our former one. For the greater part of the way the land was low, and heavy with the recent rain. We were not hurried, however, and the distance was so short, that the trials of the Great March were not to any extent repeated. We had dispensed with boots, and had substituted army shoes in their places. As we approached Trenton, we were nearly to our ankles in sticky mud, and we strained the

cords of our legs severely, besides chafing the soles of our feet. The ground was frozen for several hours during the mornings; and the army shoes were so thin as to be but little protection against this exposure. We also suffered from the lack of the support which a boot gives to the instep and ankle. If the march had been as long as the other, I do not think we should have been any better off: but there is one point in favor of the shoe which decides the opinion of soldiers almost unanimously; namely, it can be taken off at any moment, and replaced with but little trouble. This is not true of the boot: it is next to impossible to adjust swollen feet and wet boots to each other while burdened with the equipments of the march. The refreshing easement which comes from an occasional wringing of the wet stocking, and cleansing of the muddy skin, is out of the question where boots are worn.

Those of our number who were observant of natural scenery had an exquisite pleasure of a mystical character, which is thus graphically described by our chaplain in one of his letters, the freedmen and women sharing also his notice: —

"Near Trenton we passed a striking specimen of the Southern swamp. The imagination of Dante could not picture a scene more ghostly and dismal. The black noisome pool spreading away through the leafless forest; the trunks of the trees rising cone-shaped out of the miry depths, like dumb and motionless sentinels of lost spirits below; the unearthly stillness; the cold twilight; the long branches covered and festooned with the pendent and swaying gray moss, — the effect of these sights on our unaccustomed minds was dreary and startling in the extreme. I could understand the remark of Buckle, 'that superstition loves the vicinity of the gloomy and terrible in nature.' It would hardly have surprised me had I seen Charon's boat pushing off from the shore, beating back crowds of shadows pressing in vain for a passage over the Styx-like waters, heedless of the pleas of unburied Palinurus, gliding with his spectral freight beneath the spectral trees, away into recesses fit only for the habitations of spectres. For myself, I must confess a strange fascination in this spot. I left it reluctantly,

and would walk miles to spend one lonely hour amid the weird fancies it calls up.

". . . There followed in our train some hundreds of the doomed children of Africa; not the strong and robust of early manhood, but the aged, the infirm, the women and their little ones, crowded into ox-carts, riding donkeys, hobbling on foot, imperfectly and picturesquely apparelled, — a motley and laughable, yet, at the same time, piteous and affecting company, glad that the 1st of January, 1863, had at length shed its sacred beams of freedom upon them; listening, as though there were celestial enchantment in the sound, to the trumpet-blast of the proclamation summoning them forth from their long captivity to the awful probation of self-government."

Shortly after passing through the swamp, an incident of an interesting nature happened. It was so peculiar that it could hardly have occurred to any marching column, except in a civil war, between those of the same language and faith. It was noticeable on all our routes that all travel except our own was for the time suspended, or diverted, at the head of the column, to other roads. We met no one but those who were in arms to oppose us, except in the solitary instance about to be related.

We were halted a few moments, and while standing in loose order, at such ease as could be taken in that form, we were surprised and gladdened by the passage through our ranks of an intelligent and prepossessing lad of some nine or ten years of age, coming from the opposite direction. He was childlike, yet self-possessed in his bearing. Too young to have a share in the fierce passions of the conflict, "exceeding peace had made him bold." He was so winning that we all wanted to have something to say to him; and he answered us pleasantly, as he flitted by with a charming freedom of manner which won our hearts.

In reply to inquiries as to his coming and destination, he gave the singular return that "he came from his aunt Hannah's, and was going to Paradise." The innocent little fellow was not, however, expecting immediate translation. His rather startling reply was due to the fact that there was

a village of that name in the vicinity, to which he was going. Circumstances sometimes set words, like "apples of gold, in pictures of silver;" their power of association in this instance was such, that one at least, in that body of armed men, instantly thought of Him who said of little children, that "their angels do always behold the face of my Father." There were averted faces as he passed on. I mistrust that some eyes were moistened as this impressive reminiscence of home and heaven vanished from our sight.

It was only a month since we met the enemy at Kinston on just such a beautiful sabbath morning as this was: our apprehensions were naturally raised to a high pitch. None of us could tell what would happen before night at Trenton. As we contrasted the sweet countenance of the child with the infuriated faces that we had seen while passing through the country during the previous march, we leaned to the hopeful side, and we were not disappointed.

We were expecting to surprise certain irregular armed forces which were supposed to make Trenton their headquarters. To this end, orders were passed along the ranks to cease talking, and on no account to straggle or to fire our pieces. This order was not heard by all of our number. A worthy citizen of Chelsea, attached to another company, and detailed from that to the pioneers, was not aware that it had been promulgated. Tempted by the sight of a fine hog, he fired, and killed it: this upset the whole programme. He was put instantly under arrest, was sharply reprimanded, and would have been punished, had it not been evident to all that his fault was mainly one of inadvertence.

Shortly afterwards we came to an opening in the forest occupied by a very neat little chapel, from which it was apparent that we had frightened the worshippers. The windows were open, and the hymn-books were lying in such a manner as to indicate sudden flight.

We entered the town (on the 18th inst.) without violence, encamped as usual in a field, and remained until the next morning. The birds that we were after had flown.

On the march out, when somewhere well on our way to

Trenton, our feet, all at once and for a few paces only, struck, with a strange sensation, on a ledge of rock. We were descending a gully at the time. The experience was entirely unexpected by me, as we had seen no rocks in place before, nor did we afterwards. The ledge in question was the shelly limestone of which the public buildings in Newbern are constructed: its color is a rich gray. It is, I presume, the same stone which is found in Florida, and used there for the same purpose. Its appearance is very agreeable. If it resists the action of frost, its use in the North would be desirable. Leaving the town by a different road from the one by which we had entered, we soon came to a place where we were obliged to follow a narrow path on the top of a mill-dam, all three of the regiments passing through a small grist-mill built upon the dam. I recollect seeing, as our company went through, a group of soldiers busily engaged in lifting a new run of stones out of their places, with the intention of plunging them into the water below. But what attracted our attention the most was the fact that the dam itself had been mined by the rebels, or, rather, cut across at right angles with its course. An opening had been made, of at least a foot in width, reaching far down below the top of the water in the pond: this opening was packed with weeds and loose brushwood, so skilfully adjusted as just barely to resist the pressure of the water, yet so arranged as to give way, perhaps, with the pulling of a string, thus letting the whole mill-pond down into the road below. They had played this trick upon our troops at Goldsborough, just as we were leaving the field, and came near drowning some of the short men on the left flank of companies; but our officers were too wide awake for them in this instance, and, by taking us over on top of the dam, we avoided the risk of marching on the road.

There was some, but not much, plundering in Trenton by the uncontrollables of the column. There seems to be an itching among soldiers to possess some article of property as a trophy. The following ludicrous connections associate themselves with these transactions. Company A, which pre-

ceded us in the regimental line, was ably commanded by one of our own citizens, Capt. Henry J. Hallgreen. Its other officers, both commissioned and non-commissioned, were of a high character. The same might be said of quite a number of the privates, several of whom were our own townsmen. The company, however, was burdened with some injurious social influences; and of some of its members who were unavoidably under our observation as we marched, I am afraid that there could not much be written approvingly; and one of the number "entertained" us for several miles after leaving Trenton in the following manner. He had entered a doctor's office, and appropriated a human skeleton: this he slung over his shoulder, and took along with him for the distance I have named. It is hardly necessary to say that the good-for-nothing "spalpeen" was amply supplied with the peculiar style of wit with which the Green Isle provides her children, and he made fun enough to keep us all wide awake while it lasted. The skeleton was headless, so that we lost the bland expression so characteristic of the superior portion of the human frame; but I got an excellent object-lesson as I gazed upon the massive spinal column which was marching along a few feet in front of me. I had no previous idea how liberally Nature has furnished us with "backbone." In spite of the ghastliness of the sight, it was ridiculous in the extreme. The way in which the leg-bones dangled after their bearer, swinging, pendulum-like, against his shins, every step that was taken, is still present to my memory. Was there ever such a "file-closer" before? Oh, happy family of Company A! if you did not have a good time, it was not for lack of the disposition. When our lively friend got tired of his burden, he set it on the top of a worm-fence, astride of the angle next to the road, propping it in an erect position, and left it.

We had marched, on our passage out, through a village called Pollocksville: when we reached it on our return, on the 19th, Company H and the rest of the regiment, except two companies, F and G, halted, and hutted ourselves. The two companies, under the command of Col. Whiton, made a lengthy *détour* to the south, accompanied by the cavalry,

which had a successful skirmish with the enemy. The two other regiments went also, leaving us to guard the train and the roads. I shall here avail myself again of the pen of our chaplain in describing incidents which I did not witness.

"On Tuesday a detachment of our men, together with certain other troops, was sent about eight miles in a southerly direction, into the vicinity of White Oak Creek, and encamped soon after mid-day, having marched at a moderate pace, and through frequent showers, to a place called 'Young's Cross-Roads.' Our detachment was in command of Lieut.-Col. Whiton, an officer who has a wonderful faculty of getting a great deal of work out of his men, and yet doing it all in so good-natured a way that they rarely think of complaining. We were a jolly company here; our surgeon, as ever, full of accommodation, and the adjutant voting 'G. Young a brick' repeatedly; and insisting that his name, whatever became of Whitehall and Goldsborough, ought, by all means, to be inscribed in the very biggest sort of gold letters on our regimental banner. Well was it for us that we happened to be in such capital humor, since we had abundant use for all our mirthfulness before morning. Toward night the rain began to fall, so that we found great difficulty in providing a little forage for our unsheltered horses, and erecting a kind of nondescript covering under which to huddle in our rubber blankets. Again and again the rain showed a persistent determination to put out our campfire; and only by very vigilant and unremitting efforts to the contrary did we succeed in baffling its intention. Toward midnight the men became, for the most part, 'drowned out,' and resorted in dripping and shivering crowds to our solitary fire. Among them were two or three cavalry soldiers worn out by long riding through the mud and darkness, and chilled and drenched to the skin by the rain-storm. From them we learned that they had been southward near Onslow, on the New River; that they had fired on several parties of rebels, lost two men, taken one or two prisoners, and either burned, or found burned on their arrival, certain bridges possessing a military importance. In the morning, having dried our blankets and clothes as well as we could, and the pickets being drawn in, we were allowed, after considerable waiting for orders, to march back to Pollocksville. Here, without even halting, we were joined by our comrades; and so, returning by the way we came, we pressed toward Camp Rogers."

We also had a drenching rain at Pollocksville, and it was my fortune to have my first experience on picket in the height of the storm. It was one of the two darkest nights that I ever saw. It was impossible to see the back of my hand held at arm's-length: the palm, being lighter colored, was barely visible. I was on a road about half a mile from camp, with two associates,— men with whom I was entirely unacquainted, and both of them so illiterate, that it was difficult to understand what they said.

Our instructions were as usual in respect to challenging, and receiving the countersign, etc.; but we were to fire instantly at any party approaching through the forest on either side of the road. I went upon duty first; and while pacing a short space abreast of our hut, constructed of rails laid against a bank of earth, I was surprised by the sudden appearance of an intruder coming in upon me from a direction which would have warranted me in firing at him. It proved to be one of my comrades, however; but the pitchy darkness and his thick tongue, together with his inexperience, and lack of appreciation of his duties, made it quite difficult at first to account for his conduct.

Our hut was situated in a pocket, or bay, at the side of the road, made by the removal of earth for purposes of construction. In complying with a natural call my blundering associate had stepped out from it without saying a word to me, had gone some distance to the front, entered the woods, and came in upon me, when he returned, in the manner described. He should have gone to the rear, with a word of caution as he went.

On the morning of the 21st we started for our camp at Newbern in season to reach it during the afternoon. We found the country, for several miles, covered with water from six inches to three feet in depth. Most of it was up to our knees. We were homeward bound, however, and cheerful. The Forty-third had the advance; and I think I never saw such rapid marching. It seemed almost as if we flew. The Forty-fifth was next to us, and they did their best to keep up, but finally gave out. We got into our camp nearly an hour

ahead of them. It was really amusing, when they came along, to see with what sublime indifference they went past. Some of us were out on the parade-ground, trying to get a recognition from our personal friends in their ranks; but it was no use. No one would have dreamed that they knew any thing about any such regiment as ours.

This march had an excellent effect upon us. We saw that we were trusted. The three regiments were all nine-months men, and, besides this, our minds were so affected by its comparatively peaceful character, that a natural and healthful re-action from the profound experiences of the previous march took place. We had met with such a stern resistance on that occasion, that, when ordered out again, we naturally expected, with so small a force, to meet with vigorous opposition. The result was so different from our apprehensions, that we easily, thereafter, adjusted ourselves to the exigencies of our soldier-life, and met danger with a certain indifference which distinguishes veterans from new troops.

It afterwards became a camp witticism, among us of the Forty-third, to ask each other, with a tone and accent well understood among ourselves, "Were you on the Trenton march? were you at Pollocksville?" the point of the joke lying in the contrast between our actual experience and what we expected; the humorous assumption being also understood, that any comrade who was able to answer affirmatively did thereby fully establish his reputation as a soldier.

CHAPTER VII.

THE CAMP AT NEWBERN.

THE time that intervened between our return from Trenton and the active operations which began about the middle of March was the most quiet period of our service, and it seems the most appropriate interval to devote to such descriptive incidents and circumstances as may best set forth the experiences of the citizen soldier in the camp. Camp Rogers was a square of not less than eight hundred feet on each of its sides, — about as large as the enclosure between Broadway and Walnut, Fourth and Fifth Streets. Its symmetry, however, was slightly broken at the angle where it was bounded by the Trent. On its southerly border it rested on the road by which we marched to Trenton. At the central point of this side, three guard-tents were located, and this was the recognized official entrance to the camp. Directly opposite these tents, across the parade-ground which occupied the whole front of the camp, and was at least one hundred and fifty feet wide, was the company street of H, the central street of nine others. This street was nearly the same length as the depth of the parade-ground; that is, about one hundred and fifty feet. Our company was sheltered in six Sibley tents of a conical shape, sixteen feet in diameter at their bases, and about the same height, an opening of a foot being left at the top, with a cover over it for smoke and ventilation. These tents were of thick duck, and, after we became accustomed to their care, were really much more comfortable dwellings than would be supposed.

They had one singular exposure, however: in some of our heaviest rains they would suddenly begin to leak for a foot or two upwards from their base. The rain dropped upon our

faces as we lay asleep, and obliged us to have recourse to a peculiar expedient to relieve ourselves. When we found that we had got to do it, and not till then, we would fumble round in the dark for the thinnest newspaper we could find (and you know, Mr. Editor, that some newspapers are very "thin"), put our rubber blanket over us, and then rush out in the rain, and paste the paper on the spot just over where our heads would come. Surprising as it may appear, this was a sure remedy. The paper would adhere to the cloth as closely as if placed there by a "bill-sticker;" but we had to work lively to do it. Sixteen of us were allotted to each tent: the tallest men, having the same number in each tent as the shortest, were, of course, much more straitened for room. Many of the regiments stockaded the tents; that is, piles or stakes were driven into the ground in a circle of the same diameter as the tents, and the canvas was stretched on top of them about four feet above the ground. These stakes were so open, however, to the cold night air, that it was necessary to bank the earth against them, and this precaution brought with it an exposure which was so marked, that our surgeon set his face against their use. It had been found that the earth embankment was of the nature of a cellar: it predisposed the tent to dampness, besides sheltering rats. We thought the doctor was hard on us at first; but we afterward learned to respect his authority in all sanitary measures.

Passing through the company street, we come at its head to the cook-house: this was a hut composed of boards torn from a neighboring house. And at this point we reach the street occupied on its farther or northern side by the wall tents of the line-officers. This street ran parallel with the road to Trenton, from east to west, the whole width of the camp. Another street was beyond it, also parallel, occupied by the field-officers and by the chapel tent, the regimental flagstaff being conspicuous. In the rear of the field-officers' tents were the stables for their horses, leaving an unoccupied space beyond.

On the sides of the camp, as we enter at the guard-tents, we notice the regimental "sinks," or privies, shielded from

view by a screen of shrubbery, and on the westerly side two tents and a log building, which are devoted to the pioneers; while the sutler's tent, of good size, and a small one by the armorer of the regiment, Mr. C. R. Fisher of Company H, and the private accommodations of the officers, just to the right of the passage to the river, fill out the outline. The camp was located on a slight rise of ground, making drainage easy, and when decorated with trees, which were placed at suitable intervals in the streets, it was really beautiful. We took pains to replace these trees — mostly pine and holly — as they lost their verdure, and, as the weather became hot, extended their shade by arbors between the tents. During the winter, our water-supply from a spring just outside of our lines was sufficient; as the season changed, wells were dug at the head of the streets, which answered our purposes, with some help from a spring on the river-side, which was copious enough to force its way up from the bottom through the water of the river.

Extracts from two letters written at this time will introduce the reader to some of the every-day details of our situation.

CAMP ROGERS, Jan. 30, 1863.

We are having more of a season of rest, both mental and bodily, than has been the case at any one time since our arrival here, and it is peculiarly refreshing to me, as the state of excitement in which we lived while our destination was uncertain was very unpleasant. The chief business of many seemed to be to hear and tell some new thing; in fact, some made themselves appear offensively foolish; but the wind is now all out of their sails, and we have peace.

Our colonel told the officers, as they gathered around him at dress-parade yesterday, that Stonewall Jackson had sent word that he was coming to dine with us to-day. This, on the face, looked a little alarming; but as our officers told it to us in our streets, after coming in, we concluded that it was intended as a joke on us for the liberal supply of boxes which our friends had recently sent (some 275 in the regiment). . . .

I am writing this page in a high wind and cloudy sky, the ground is white with snow from a squall, — the first we have seen since we left Boston Harbor.

Feb. 11, 1863.

You can hardly form an idea of what delightful weather we have had all winter. My mittens have not been on my hands more than three or four times, and we are fast falling into the practice of eating our meals out of doors : in fact, there have been a number of days lately when it was too hot to eat outside with safety at noon. . . . We are now raising a tall flagstaff, which has employed our pioneers at intervals for some six weeks. It is eighty feet in height, and it is surmounted with a double-headed tiger carved in very fine style by one of the members of our company, Samuel W. Johnson of Weston, Mass. In addition to this, we commenced to-day extensive grading operations in our company streets, which it is proposed, if we remain here, to extend to the whole camp, even the parade-ground. . . .

We are engaged in making ourselves as safe, as comfortable, and as ornamental as is possible. The safety refers to the building of earthworks, of which, in addition to three small ones which our brigade has made across the Trent, we are to construct a large one close to our camp; the comfortable, to hosts of little things which New-Englanders will gather around themselves; and the ornamental, to the pines and hollies, with their beautiful red berries, with which our streets are lined, making it look as leafy as though we had been here ten years at least.

In describing our company street and the life we lived in it, our oven, located near the cook-house, in line with the tents, deserves notice, if for nothing more than its connection with our weekly dish of baked beans, which we had as regular as if we had been at home. It was made of bricks set in clay.

Our rations as a whole were excellent in quality, and ample in quantity. I have only one qualification to make, and that is, that much of our bread (hard tack) was made of doctored flour. It was not baked in the department, so that I feel free to expose its deficiencies. Every soldier remembers the difference between a flesh-colored cake, aërated clear through by yeast, flaky, and as brittle as was consistent with its preservation and transportation, and the kind mixed with them, — white in color, hard as a rock, not even porous, impervious to moisture, resisting all our efforts to

soak them in our coffee. Verily, I believe that the issue of these "stones" to us soldiers, the wards of the nation, when we asked for "bread," was as fatal to thousands of brave men as the shot of the enemy. Constipation is the ever-present sanitary foe of the soldier, and the road to it was paved with "doctored" hard tack. Every dollar that was accumulated in this way is costing the nation ten in pensions for "disability."

To the praise of the government, it should be said that it made laudable efforts to get ahead of the contractors in this matter. It had an extensive bakery at Newbern; and half our rations of bread were issued in large, nice loaves, freshly baked. A half of one of the loaves was given to each one of us every week. Fresh beef, just killed at Newbern, was issued in the same liberal manner. It was really an interesting and even laughable sight to see the great plates of it,— three days' rations,—all cooked, which were passed to us. It only required ordinary economy to make it last the full time. We had boxes sunk in the ground on the outer circle of the tents, near our heads as we lay. These were our "cellars;" and our eatables were deposited in them.

Not the least among the officials of our company was our worthy cook, William B. Bryant. To our extreme regret he passed away in 1866. We shall all remember him as long as we recall any of the circumstances of our unwonted life in North Carolina. Of course, everybody grumbles at the cook, — that is, nearly all, — and the man that can live it all down, and fairly stop the mouths of the querulous, is no common character. He must have the endurance of the ox in incessant labor, and the hide of the rhinoceros to ward off the flying shafts of the petulant and the particular. Our friend combined in an odd yet happy manner some excellent and kindly traits of character, with sufficient force to command respect. When his patience was exhausted by complaints, he could make it as squally as he pleased all around the cook-house, and, after the atmosphere had cleared, would call the grumblers back in a deprecating tone, and give them a little more or a little less fat, etc., with as acceptable grace

as if he had only his youthful brood at home to care for, instead of a hundred men.

Next in order to the culinary department of the regiment comes the sutler's tent. Mr. James Q. Gilmore of our city supplied our needs in this respect in a satisfactory manner. I can readily imagine that a low-bred and avaricious sutler can be a most efficient instrument of evil in a camp; but I know nothing about it, as the personal influence of the friend who filled this post in our battalion was the reverse of all this.

A sutler's tent is a country store, with all that relates absolutely and entirely to the feminine element of society left out. Mr. Gilmore was well supported by his help, most of whom were disabled soldiers of the Potomac army. We were uniformly as well treated as if there had been a rival "store" over on the other corner.

I will here supplement the statement of our chaplain concerning our moral and religious status, with some further details. I think that we escaped almost entirely the lowering influences of gambling. Nothing of this was public, at least. Those who were free from this demoralizing vice when they joined the regiment must have remained so. I do not know how deeply our armies were infected with this insidious moral malaria; but I heard and saw more of it in North Carolina than I like to record. I was startled and confounded, on one occasion, to see a regiment at an outpost, under circumstances where they might at any moment have been called into action, engaged in play. The paymaster was in camp; and, just as quick as the officers and men got their money, they extemporized gaming-tables in the broad light of day, on stumps of trees, drums, knapsacks, etc., and the whole regiment went into the fearfully demoralizing excitement, piles of greenbacks being everywhere visible. The exposures and temptations of the officers and men of the regular army in isolated posts must be terrible. The practice should be as sternly prohibited among them as duelling is.

Another exposure of the soldier we did not so fully escape. In the extensive details from the brigade which were made

to build earthworks. I am sorry to be obliged to say that the
government took the place of the tempter by its issue of a
whiskey ration. There was not the slightest reason for it.
The labor was not hard; the day's work was short; and we
were not driven. It was entirely optional with us whether
to work or not. The principal reason for doing it, besides
getting the drink, was to escape the *ennui* of drills: these,
however, were seldom over five hours and a half per day. In
my judgment, there is not sufficient reason for the issue of
liquor by the government, except at the suggestion of the
surgeon, and then, only under extraordinary circumstances,
when warm coffee or tea cannot be supplied.

These remarks are not to be understood as implying the
prevalence of drunkenness among us: on the contrary, we were
as free from it as from gambling. Our surgeon, Dr. Webber,
was entirely opposed to the liquor ration. It was not issued
in the regiment. We had none on the severest marches we
made. Our camp was an outpost with very restricted relations to the rest of the world. Visits to Newbern were few,
and far between. Martial law was supreme in the department, and it is practically prohibitory of the sale of liquor.

The great plain upon which we were located was the
Champ de Mars of Newbern. Our drills at first took the
impressive form of the sham battle, during which exercises
the brigade went through the evolutions and firing appropriate to warfare in the open field. After the first month or
two, however, firing was omitted, the drill of the brigade
became merely mechanical, and was tedious in the extreme;
the only movement which I recall as relieving our *ennui*
being that which for the moment transforms the three to five
thousand men of the brigade into a disorderly mob; for this
is, apparently, the effect of a certain order. In an instant of
time every man starts on the double-quick, so far as the un-
practised observer can see, without any reference to any one
but himself. The scene is a surprising one. The men seem
struck with a panic, and to be doing their best to get off from
the field in a vehement access of terror; but really every
man knows his duty, and place, and is held to it by a fine

social instinct moulded into military forms. The movement takes several minutes; and at its completion every soldier locates himself without the slightest hesitation or confusion, and each regiment forms part of a compacted line of battle entirely different from the original one. The scene, as the men moved over the undulations of the plain, was beautiful in the extreme.

These evolutions took their highest form in a grand review (on Feb. 25), for which I am indebted, for a full and interesting account, to the anonymous author of "The Campaign of the Forty-fifth."

"It was a beautiful sight to watch the long line of troops which filed over the bridge, their bayonets flashing in the sunlight, as regiment after regiment came up, and took its place in line. The line was formed in brigades, four regiments deep, in the order of the brigades, our brigade holding the right, the artillery and cavalry occupying the extreme left.

"The thunder of the artillery announced the arrival of our gallant commander, Major-Gen. Foster; and soon he appeared at our front, finely mounted, and attended by his full staff. Drums are ruffled, and arms presented, while the band plays 'Hail to the Chief,' as he dashes along in his inspection of each regiment, the music continuing while he is passing through the brigade, then the next band takes up the strain.

"After a long rest, and a lunch by all who had been prudent enough to bring a supply of hard tack in their pockets, our turn came for an active part in the proceedings of the day. Gen. Foster had taken his station on a slight eminence, and sat facing the centre of the line, which, brigade deep, extended for full a mile. Surrounded by his staff, he was the object of attraction of a crowd of spectators who thronged about him, — from Mrs. Foster and her brilliant staff of ladies, down to the most ragged contraband in all that motley assembly.

"As we wheeled by platoons, and marched in review, the sight which greeted us was one long to be remembered for its grandeur and beauty. Line upon line of unbroken ranks stretched on as far as the eye could reach. Over each regiment waved our beautiful flag, its colors glowing with unwonted richness in the warm winter's sun, the bayonets throwing back flashes of light, and the

artillery and cavalry relieving the scene from all monotony, while the Neuse, sparkling in the sunlight, and its distant bank covered with the forest evergreen, formed a perfect background for this gorgeous picture. Then there was the long row of spectators, some seated in vehicles of all sorts and descriptions, others mounted on animals ranging from the finest charger to the scrubbiest donkey; while on foot was a crowd composed of every age, sex, and color. In their midst sat our commander, patiently awaiting our approach.

"As we drew near, the band filed off to the left, and took its position directly opposite the general, where it continued playing till our brigade had all passed, when it was relieved by the next band, and once more took its place in line. As each platoon passed, the general saluted, while he honored the colors by removing his hat, the band also giving the customary salute. Battalion after battalion, battery after battery, troop after troop, they came, till the first battalion, making the complete circuit, came upon the rear of the last troop, thus forming an unbroken circle. As each regiment reached the place of starting, it halted until the long glittering array was once more in position; then again the artillery thundered forth the salute, and the grand review was over."

During the winter the distinctive form of the drills of the companies during the mornings was that of skirmishing, and toward the close of our term we were practised in streetfiring, with an ominous forecast of the July riots.

When we arrived at Newbern, we found a parapet earthwork located on the plain, close to the upper bridge across the Trent. It was armed with eight-inch cannon, and was called Fort Gaston. Its gunners kept themselves in practice by occasionally shelling the plain. Stakes were set at recorded distances, say a thousand feet away, etc.; and experience in cutting fuzes was acquired by close observation of the point at which the shells exploded.

These occasions would call us all from our tents; and, after they were over, the experts in eluding the guards would go out, and bring in the fragments of iron. Terrible things they were, some of them, to be burst in the midst of human beings. I had supposed that cast iron would break with a clean,

square fracture; but I found, to my surprise, all sorts of diabolical angles and spear-like forms in the specimens which the boys brought in. We passed them round the tents with various comments and grim jokes, something, as I apprehend, like those with which Artemus Ward's stage-driver beguiled the time as they were riding along the edge of the precipices in the Sierras of California; that is, in telling about those who had been killed by them.

Some of the most necessary avocations of life are carried on with tolerable freedom in a camp. There is little or no difficulty in getting the services of a barber. Such jobs as the repairs of shoes or clothing, which require more time in the execution, are readily done in the intervals of duty. Carpentering, or other work calling for large or costly tools, is not so easily accomplished; but needs in that direction are met, in a rough way, by requisitions on the pioneers or cooks for planes, axes, knives, etc. Artistic work, like that of the dentist, is more difficult to obtain. We were favored, however, by the presence of "the doctor" (S. R. Adams) among our number, whose well-earned reputation extended throughout the department, and brought many a poor sufferer with an aching jaw from distant regiments, into our street, to depart a happier man.

Generally speaking, however, a camp of Yankees is a jackknife paradise. We skilled workers in wood and iron could do nothing for lack of our accustomed tools. The amount of brierwood pipes, and various "bric-a-brac" articles made out of beef-bones and the horns of cattle, to say nothing about silver coin converted into medals, was enormous. Justice compels me to say that much of our work was of a high order. Many a memento of Camp Rogers is in existence in some of these forms, and they will go worthily down to posterity as pleasant memorials of the days which tested the highest qualities of manhood.

My next chapter will begin with a letter written two days after the one with which I shall close. Gen. Foster had evidently been warned that a large force, composed of Longstreet's best troops, was on their way to North Carolina, and

he was on the alert to give them a suitable reception. The notice came none too soon; for, in ten days after its arrival, it thundered and lightened all around Newbern, and from that time to the end of our term there was no lack of interesting events and stirring excitement.

CAMP ROGERS, NEWBERN, March 3, 1863.

I visited Newbern yesterday for the second time since I was here; the first being on the 9th of December, when I happened to light upon just the moment that it was all astir with the preparations for the march on Goldsborough, and there was altogether too much excitement for me to enjoy myself. But yesterday it was quite the reverse. My eyes were delighted with sights to which for four months they have been almost entire strangers. I found myself walking the streets among citizens, — women and children, — heard gentle voices, and saw them engaged in shopping, gardening, etc. I felt myself moved with gratitude to God, that hitherto he had preserved me, and now, with submission to his will, allowed me to begin, with the opening of the beautiful spring, — for nature here is all astir, — to look forward to a glad re-union to the home circle. . . . How tremendous the crisis in our national affairs! It seems to me that if I could have foreseen, when I volunteered, the disasters that have happened, my faith would have failed me. Of one thing, however, I feel assured, — however this great contest may end, the North is to be freed from its complicity with the curse of slavery. If there is a shade of doubt in these remarks respecting the success of our efforts to preserve the Union, you must not look upon it as a settled or willing conclusion on my part, but to my narrowness of perception, surrounded as I am by influences so forbidding as the present are in some important respects. We seem as a nation to be brought to the brink of the Red Sea. If the Almighty by his providence calls us to go forward, *we must*, trusting to him to heap the waters so that they overwhelm us not.

CHAPTER VIII.

ATTACK ON NEWBERN.

CAMP ROGERS, March 5, 1863.

A MAIL for the North closes at seven, and, as our circumstances are a little unusual, I thought I had better drop a few lines to you. To-day, at noon, we received verbal orders, or, rather, word, to be ready at an hour's notice to march in light order, and for the cooks to be prepared to cook three days' rations. We were given reason to suppose that we should receive definite orders on dress-parade, but they did not come; and we are told instead to keep ourselves in readiness to march at any moment. The rations, however, have not been issued to the cooks; and when Lieut. Bradbury, who has a large force of pioneers at work on a road, went to Gen. Foster this afternoon to know if his men were to go, the general told him that the Forty-third had no orders yet, and of course he had not, and so sent him about his business.

Nothing of special interest occurred for a week, and we were beginning to wonder what the warning meant, when occurrences transpired sufficiently impressive to quicken the dullest comprehension among us.

CAMP ROGERS, March 18, 1863.

Last Friday afternoon, the 13th, just after supper, we were startled by a dozen or more artillery-discharges, fired with such rapidity as to indicate the extreme of danger, — very different from the slow shelling of the woods which we have been accustomed to hear on our marches, or the artillery-practice of the forts, which has been going on more or less since the expedition to Charleston went off.

This firing appeared to be out on the Kinston road, some miles to the north of us. It appears that Gen. Foster had proposed something on the next day, the 14th, in the shape of a celebra-

tion of the capture of Newbern; for during the evening we received orders to be ready to march into town in the morning in our dress-coats; but we were told to take forty rounds of ammunition with us, as our pickets on the Kinston road had been driven in two miles, and it was uncertain what the developments of the day might be.

During the night, about one o'clock, there were unusual noises and moving about in camp, rousing us from sleep. The long roll was beaten, and we soon learned that it was in connection with fresh orders to have our breakfast at three o'clock, and march immediately after with one day's ration.

We got off about daylight, and went across the Trent by the upper bridge, going over to the Kinston road, and striking it about a mile to the north of Newbern. As we approached the road, we came out of the forest, bringing Newbern into view about two miles off on our right. We found that Fort Totten was actively engaged in firing. We supposed it was a salute to the day, but were mystified to observe the frequent explosion of shells close to the fort itself, and we were still further confused, as we marched out away from the town, to hear that the firing continued.

[This was one of the finest sights that we saw; but it came so unexpectedly that we did not realize it at the time. The fort was nearly hidden by the dense volumes of smoke from its own guns: they were heavy pieces, aimed directly at the enemy; and the *animus* with which they were being worked was entirely different from what we supposed. The great white cloudy rings from the bursting shells in the air above, strangely mingled with the lightning-like flashes which were vomited from the black folds of smoke below, with the national colors defiantly waving from a tall staff over them all, were impressive in the highest degree.]

We had gone about three miles from Newbern when we suddenly received countermanding orders, and were marched back to our camp by the same road we came. The firing at Newbern continued until noon, and we also heard, about eleven, rapid firing again out on the Kinston road. At three in the afternoon, at ten minutes' notice, we again fell in, resuming our march in the same direction, but reaching, this time, a place about six miles out, relieving the regiment which had been attacked, — the Massachusetts Twenty-fifth.

I should here state that we learned during the forenoon that the

enemy were trying to shell Newbern from the north bank of the Neuse. The river is so wide, however,— two miles at this point, — and the gunboats were so active, that they did not accomplish much. Those that we saw bursting over Fort Totten came from this source.

As we marched out, we met returning soldiers, who all agreed in their statements that the enemy were in force a short distance ahead; but on we pushed, reaching our camping-ground about seven, with the understanding that at least two brigades of the enemy were only two miles off. We could see their camp-fires burning brightly across the plantation.

We were put for the night into a narrow gully through which a brook ran, and told to kindle small fires low down toward the water, so as not to draw the fire of the enemy. The Twenty-fifth soon withdrew, marching back to Newbern, leaving us with one company of cavalry and two pieces of artillery. We composed ourselves to sleep — those of us who could. I made a poor piece of work of it, as my pillow was a stump of a tree just as the woodman left it standing in the ground; and the gully was so steep, that my lower limbs were literally "two feet" lower than my head. Those of us who were awake had the pleasure of seeing our old "Merrimac" friends of the Forty-sixth file in on the other side of the brook about eleven o'clock. We were glad enough to meet them.

Our cavalry scouts assured us the next morning that the enemy had retreated. We lay in camp until about three o'clock P.M., expecting orders to return. But this was not to be; for two brigadiers, Amory and Potter, came out to us, and we marched on till after dark, again encamping, and posting our pickets. As soon as we could see, on Monday morning, we were off again, as silent as if we had been so many thieves. This time we went as far as our first camp-ground on the Great March, — some fifteen miles from Newbern, and nearly half-way in a direct line to Kinston. We saw evidence all along the road that a large force had just preceded us; and when we halted we formed in line of battle across the road, with our cannon pointing down into Deep Gully. We waited here an hour, not knowing but that any moment might begin an action, as the place was one of the most defensible on the whole road. During this time the cavalry advanced cautiously some miles ahead, accompanied by Gen. Amory, and returned

with the report that the enemy had really disappeared; whereat we turned our faces joyfully homewards about nine A.M., leaving a few companies of the Forty-sixth at the picket-posts, and reaching Camp Rogers about four in the afternoon of Monday the 16th, having marched over twenty miles that day.

We found that the invalid guard had been badly frightened during our absence, as it was so definitely reported, as almost to compel belief, that the enemy were out in force to the south and west of us; that they had captured and burned the posts on the railroad between here and Beaufort, and torn up the road, — all of which proved afterward to be wholly untrue. In short, it was a time of excitement and alarm. But all is well that ends well, and we feel as reasonably assured as ever that Newbern cannot be retaken, except by a large force.

There were some incidents of interest which came under my notice as we were going out. I happened to be close to Chaplain James of the Twenty-fifth just as he was describing the heroic valor with which the rebels charged upon and captured a Quaker cannon, to find out at their leisure that it was a pine stick charred black by fire. The chaplain could hardly sit on his horse for laughter. This little affair has pleased us all. Just after we had passed him, and got well out toward our Saturday night's camp by the brook, who should we meet but a charming lady on horseback in company with several officers of high rank. Some said she was an officer's daughter; others, that she was a fast woman from Baltimore: of this I do not know, but it was a most unusual sight.

This was the only time that we were brought into direct relations with the brave Twenty-fifth Regiment. It originated in the city of Worcester, in social and military circles familiar with the struggle in Kansas which preceded the war. No record can be found more heroic than its history. Some of its experiences in the last campaign in Virginia demonstrate that truth is stranger than fiction.

The Forty-third stood in line opposite to them, a few moments, in a narrow road and in darkness, on the evening that we relieved them: they had been under fire all day. The trees gave evidence, as we passed the spot the next morning, of the accuracy of the rebel aim. Their spirits had risen

to the occasion: they were bound to resist the rebel advance till the last moment, and our presence was welcomed with gratitude and patriotic affection. As I stood in my place in the line, I heard a soldier right opposite to me, but whose face I could not see, break out, in a subdued yet impressive manner, with Scripture words of salutation and thanks to us. I am sorry that I preserved no note of them; but the tone and spirit was that of Isaiah, "How beautiful upon the mountains are the feet of those that bring good tidings!" To the credit of our own regiment, I will say that there were no rude or unseemly comments in reply.

In explanation of the preceding letters, it should be stated that Fort Totten, which we found enveloped in smoke from its own guns, as well as from the bursting shells of the enemy, was the central and largest earthwork of the defences of Newbern: these fortifications extended at least five miles, — from Fort Anderson on the north bank of the Neuse, to what was known as the "Block House," at Brice's Creek, near Camp Rogers, south of the Trent.

Fort Totten had a peculiarity which made it quite a conspicuous object in the level scenery of North Carolina. Inside of the work, a few feet in the rear of the guns, a high palisade was erected. It was composed of large trees set close to each other, in two rows a number of feet apart. The space between the rows was filled with earth. The palisade must have been at least thirty feet or more in height.

It was erected, as I judge, to protect the gunners from a fire in the rear, to which they would have been much exposed if the enemy had obtained possession of the plain on the south of the Trent, upon which our regiment, with others, was encamped.

Major C. O. Rogers of Boston, who was on a visit to the regiment at the time of this march, accompanied by several friends also from home, rode out from camp with us, — I think in the morning, — stopping a mile or two out. We cheered them lustily as we marched past their buggy where it had halted. The incident was an uncommon and a very pleasant one. We were not usually cheered on in our marches

by well-dressed civilians in carriages. We were reminded of home and the loyal millions of the North by their cordial manners. Out of the deep places of my inner being I had an unexpected experience as I left them and pressed on with my comrades to the perils of the expected encounter. Dana has graphically described, in his "Two Years before the Mast," the supreme satisfaction he had, while aloft upon the yardarm of the ship, in looking down upon a seasick passenger on deck. A similar feeling of conscious power took possession of me, as I thought of the weak and almost imbecile appearance and situation of non-combatants amid warlike scenes. We were at home: they were not. Our individuality had been merged in each other until every man felt, in some respects, as though he had the strength of a thousand. One of the greatest mysteries of our being was forcing itself upon my attention by the trivial circumstance of two or three unarmed gentlemen taking themselves very discreetly out of harm's way.

I owe a word to the memory of this large-hearted and unfortunate man. Lieut. Turner, our quartermaster, informs me that Major Rogers met him, on his return from Newbern in charge of the sick of the regiment, and inquired with great earnestness whether all had come. He further authorized him, with the utmost frankness and good-will, to draw upon him for any amount that was needed to secure the immediate return to their homes of all the invalids of the regiment.

While we waited in our camp, during the alarm of the first day, we noticed that the national colors were set, for the first and only time during our stay, on the highest church-steeple in Newbern. It was understood that they were placed there by special orders from Foster, so that the rebel column across the Neuse might be assured that their friends whom we baffled on the Kinston road had not succeeded in taking the town.

Gen. Foster served his country with zeal. I was reminded by his conduct, on many occasions, of a reminiscence of Davy Crockett, the Kentucky pioneer, who was represented, in

some rude Western literature which tickled my untrained boyish fancy, as taking refuge for the night in the hollow of a fallen tree. While he lay in sound sleep in this helpless situation, one of his bitter enemies came by, and attempted to pay off some old scores by punching his head with a stick. Crockett was fearfully enraged, as well he might be, at this unfair advantage; but he could not resist until he got out of the tree, when he at once proceeded to business. It always seemed to me as if it would have been a good thing for the country, if the whole force which was confined in Sumter during that memorable winter of 1861 had been promoted to major-generals on their liberation, as Foster was.

We had a fortnight's respite after the events which have been related, when we were again put upon the alert by orders, on April 1, to be ready to march at a moment's notice; and on Saturday, April 4, we were reviewed by Gens. Palmer and Amory. I was struck with the searching scrutiny with which Gen. Palmer and his staff subjected us to examination. I don't think that they cared a copper in respect to the details of our dress or equipments. They appeared to look altogether at our faces, as they rode slowly by, looking with great earnestness at every individual. This surprised me, it was so different from the usual formal and external character of inspections; but we ascertained a few days after what it meant. We had not known much personally about Palmer as our division officer, and quite likely he knew as little about us. When we took, with our friends of the Seventeenth, the lead of a column of ten thousand men, a few days afterward, we knew at once what that searching inquiry into our *morale* meant.

During the week that ensued after the first of the month, we were in a state of expectation connected with events which were transpiring about Little Washington. The ground actually trembled under us, as we lay in our tents, from the firing of heavy artillery, at a distance of twenty-six miles, during the siege which had begun at that place. The following extract from the report of the Massachusetts Twenty-seventh Infantry gives a detail of the circumstances of the investment: —

"The duty at Washington was unmarked by any incidents of interest until the latter part of March. The many rumors and threats of an attack, that had been heard for some weeks, finally culminated on the 30th of March by the driving-in of our advance pickets. Gen. Foster, being then in Washington on a visit, took command of the garrison, at that time consisting of the Twenty-seventh Massachusetts Infantry, eight companies; Forty-fourth Massachusetts Infantry, eight companies; First North-Carolina Infantry, two companies; Third New-York Cavalry, one company; Third New-York Artillery, one battery; having in all, on land and gunboats, twenty-eight pieces of artillery, heavy and light.

"The enemy's force was commanded by Major-Gen. D. H. Hill, and consisted of Daniel's Brigade of Infantry, five regiments; Garnett's Brigade of Infantry, six regiments; Pettigrew's Brigade of Infantry, six regiments; Robertson's Brigade of Cavalry, three regiments; which force, with forty pieces of artillery, and some independent battalions not brigaded, brought up the enemy's force to about fifteen thousand." — *Adjutant-General's Report of 1863.*

The following extracts from letters indicate the course of affairs which immediately followed: —

CAMP ROGERS, April 3, 1863.

We are being disquieted again this week, having received orders on Monday noon to be ready to march at a moment's notice, — orders which have not as yet been countermanded. We have been hearing heavy distant firing at intervals, sometimes all day, ever since then; and the statements are, that Gen. Foster with the Twenty-seventh and Forty-fourth is shut in at Little Washington, some distance north of here, by the occupation of an earthwork, on the river below them, by the rebels. We suppose that the firing is from the heavy guns of our vessels endeavoring to dislodge them. The statement also is, that re-enforcements have been sent for from Fortress Monroe, and that a considerable number have been drawn out of Newbern.

It is said that Gen. Amory, our brigadier, is in command at Newbern. Such orders as we received on Monday are issued, it is said, to all the regiments, so as to keep all in a state of watchfulness, and preparation for whatever may happen. I notice, by a "New-York Herald" of the 27th ult., that the rebels attempted recently a similar game at Plymouth, and that help came from Suffolk, driving them out.

CAMP ROGERS, April 7, 1863,
Ten o'clock P.M.

I had, as I supposed, finished up for the night, and had lain down to sleep, when the long roll was beaten, word was passed to "fall in," and we must be off. It is said that we go on transports to Little Washington. I had supposed that business was settled up; but it seems not. This is all that I have time to write. I hope it will not be long before you hear good news again.

The "transports" on which we were to go proved to be small stern-wheel gunboats, on which we embarked, and were carried across the Neuse. Here we lay all night and all the next afternoon, when we started, about ten thousand men of all arms having come across during the night and forenoon. The Seventeenth took the advance; and we followed, marching until nine P.M., going perhaps, eleven miles. I got a good night's rest, having slept but little on the previous night. We supposed the whole column was in camp with us, but found in the morning that all but three regiments and some cavalry and artillery had halted some miles back, while, as a feint to deceive the enemy by our camp-fires, we had advanced by a different road from the ultimate design of our commander. After marching some four miles back in the morning of the 9th, we rejoined our forces, and turned into a road leading toward Washington, but more to the eastward, and kept on, still in the advance. About noon we began to hear firing from our cavalry vedettes and the skirmishers of the Seventeenth, which continued at intervals until four P.M., when a heavy volley of musketry, followed by the shouts of the rebels, admonished us of the proximity of the enemy. We were near enough to distinguish individual voices in the cheer we heard; but the road was circuitous, and it took us some minutes to come up. We found two pieces of our artillery engaged with the enemy across a narrow creek, the musketry on both sides having ceased. The men of the Seventeenth had lain down in line on the right side of the road, and as we came up we did the same, the two cannon being abreast of us. The enemy had a better knowledge of the ground than we. They killed several of our horses at the outset, (?) and badly wounded Capt. Belger of the battery in the thigh. Part of the artillerists were new recruits, and some of the younger of them behaved badly. After three-quarters of an hour of vigorous firing on both sides, our guns stopped, and we supposed we were to be ordered across the bridge; but, instead of this, we were about faced, and

to our great surprise we marched, and marched back on our tracks until half-past nine P.M.

After an uncomfortable night, it being extremely damp and chilly, we marched to Newbern. I had a most intensely interesting experience as we lay under fire. All the wounded men passed me; and I was near enough to the highest officers to hear much that was said. Our present impression is, that Gen. Spinola, who was in command, made a botch of the affair; that he should not have attacked so violently without meaning to sustain us. We have marched and countermarched about fifty miles in three days, toward, but not to, Little Washington, and have returned home apparently as wise as we went. We supposed we were to help Gen. Foster out of his limbo; but, instead of that, we very unexpectedly returned to Newbern, and Washington seems as far from relief as ever.

These allusions to the interesting incidents of the artillery duel at Blount's Creek, as they came directly under my own observation, call for further remarks. Such occurrences were happening every day at some point on our extended lines between the Atlantic and the Mississippi. They might have been numbered, undoubtedly, by thousands, during the four years of fighting; but they were so insignificant in comparison with the greater events which were transpiring, that they are usually dismissed with a line in the military reports and histories. After the novelty of fighting had worn off, the press gave them scant notice; and domestic letters, from the participants in them, to the home-circle, were, for obvious reasons, guarded and vague in their statements of repulsive details. Many of these petty fights, however, tested the stamina of officers and men quite as effectively as if they had been parts of an action miles in extent, destined to pass into history, and to be transmitted to posterity with an honored name.

Having these conditions in my mind, I shall endeavor to transfer to paper some very vivid recollections, which may serve to give more prominence to the feelings of individuals who were present than is usual in adventures of this sort. In doing this, I recall the fact, that our regiment was ani-

mated, as we approached the enemy, by a strong personal motive, — a feeling of which we had not been conscious during any of the previous engagements. We had acquired an interest in Gen. Foster, which went deeper than respect. Our sympathetic emotions were in full activity, and we heartily co-operated with our officers in the effort to rescue him. There were also strong personal ties of friendship between many of us and our friends in the Forty-fourth, which quickened our interest in them; but their Newbern camp was remote, and they were in a different brigade, so that we had not made acquaintance with them as a regiment.

Our surgeon halted at a suitable place to pitch the field-hospital tent, — a short distance to the rear of the spot where the fight occurred. He was a man of few but well-chosen words; and he was not disposed to flatter. As we went by him almost on the double-quick, in our eagerness to be at work, he remarked that "he did not believe that there was a coward in the regiment."

We were so near the enemy, that the artillerists whom we supported were more than usually solicitous in respect to their protectors. Spinola was from New York; but he had some very inefficient drafted men under his command, from the poorest material which Pennsylvania sent to the war. We heard the men of the battery inquiring what regiment was with them; and, when the answer was made that it was the Forty-third Massachusetts, it was to our supreme satisfaction that the comment followed at once, without the least hesitation, "All right. We are satisfied."

We had been driving the enemy's pickets before us for a mile. Whenever there was an opening, the skirmishers of the Seventeenth were in plain sight in the field. The natural language of the cautionary faculties was vividly impressed upon their bearing. One of the Confederates dropped his cap, and was in too much of a hurry to stop to pick it up. It was taken in charge by our leading company, and passed from hand to hand to the rear along the column, after making many a vault through the air, as it was thrown to outstretched arms. It was neat and jaunty in a marked degree, with hori-

zontal visor, and stylish appearance, contrasting strangely with the usual squalid outfit of the rebel rank and file as we had observed them.

When within a short distance of the point where we finally halted, we found two of the skirmishers of the Seventeenth — fine, intelligent men, both of them — standing by the side of the road, endeavoring as best they might to answer the questions which our men were putting to them as we came along. They were so out of breath from the scare they had had, and from being obliged to repeat their story so often, that it was with difficulty that they could talk at all; but they pointed down the road a short distance, and said, "Just there — where the road curves — we received the fire — of a whole regiment — as we crept round the sweep. The air was alive with balls, — but we escaped." Passing one or two hundred feet farther on, we found the Seventeenth lying on the ground, as near the curve as they could go without being in sight of the enemy; and we piled in in the same manner, our two guns unlimbering at the same time, and beginning their fire diagonally over toward the right or northerly side of the road. Nothing was visible; and I have the impression that they were guided in their aim entirely by the sound of the enemy's artillery, which was by this time wide awake. The ground upon which we lay rose several feet above the road, and it was thickly covered by trees and undergrowth. As we ranged ourselves, we left two openings or gaps in our line, through which the cannoneers delivered their fire; so that the impressive spectacle was presented of a sort of living parapet, composed of our bodies; while the openings represented the embrasures of the fortification, through which the jets of flame momentarily darted from the guns.

The next occurrences which I recall are in connection with the flesh-wound of Capt. Belger of the battery. It was on one of his legs, well up toward the body, and bled freely. His clothes were badly torn around the wound, and he was evidently a fit subject to go to the hospital. But he had no idea of any such thing. Something had occurred at the head of the column, which had greatly disturbed his serenity of

mind. His talk was any thing but pious. When I first saw
him, he was on foot in the road, close by us; but he ordered
his horse, and, although he was too weak to mount unaided,
he insisted on being helped into the saddle, and rode to the
rear to bring up more artillery, as I heard him say. His
officers quietly expostulated with him, but to no effect.
That was the last I saw of him; and I doubt very much
whether he got any farther to the rear than the field-hospital.
I incline to the opinion that the pain of his wound caused
him to lose control of his temper. I have never learned with
certainty what really took place to throw him off his balance.
It was currently reported among us at the time, that one of
his guns was carried so far along the road, that some of its
horses were killed, and the men were driven from the piece;
but I am not able to state this as a fact.

We soon became conscious, from our own observation and
the passage up the road of wounded men from the Seventeenth, that the rebels had our range. The first one that was
brought up was a large, fleshy private, on a stretcher. He
was apparently dead, in fact was thought to be so; but,
though wounded in the breast, he afterwards recovered. He
lay upon his back, grasping his gun firmly, with his arms
around it, his features, as nearly as we could see about ten
feet off, being fixed and deathly. He was so heavy, that the
bearers walked with an unsteady step, causing his body to
roll or vibrate from side to side, reminding me, by an incon-
gruous and very unpleasant association, of sights I had seen
about market-places, or at the autumnal killing in the country.

The next victim that passed up was a fine-appearing sergeant, who walked composedly to the rear, with one of his
arms dangling useless by his side from a wound above the
elbow. I have the impression that the surgeons treated him
so skilfully that the arm was saved.

The Seventeenth reports eight wounded during the half
or three-quarters of an hour we were under fire. The artillerists added enough to the number to keep our attention and
sympathies active as they passed by us. Two of these last

cases deeply excited my own interest. A caisson had halted in the road a few feet from where Company H was lying; and two boys were running back and forth to supply the guns, the nearest of which was about fifty feet from the caisson, with ammunition. I call them "boys;" for I think they must have been under the military age, which was eighteen. They would take a twelve-pound rifled shell in their hands, pressing it against the stomach or chest, and carry it in this manner to the guns. On his return to the caisson, one of them held out his hand towards us, and said that it had just been scraped by a flying fragment. I was not near enough to verify the statement; but his manner indicated truthfulness. Shortly after, another lad, close to me in the road, pointed to the bridge of his nose, just between the eyes, and I saw the flesh bleeding from the loss of a part of its substance. I had, in short, demonstrable evidence that he had escaped the loss of both his eyes, or his life even, by a hair's breadth. I endeavored to make his case known to my comrades; but the noise and the incessant occurrence of exciting incidents prevented me, and I have the impression that I was nearly alone in my observation of the occurrence.

That there were other details happening of which I did not myself become conscious, I am certain, from the fact that I have been recently told, by one in whom I have the fullest confidence, that the caisson itself, not ten feet off from us, was hit about this time.

The "boys" were pretty well frightened. They ceased work, and came and lay down with us. The lieutenant in charge of the guns soon missed them, and came to the caisson. At first he could not find them, as we did not like to expose them; but the red facing to their uniforms soon revealed them to his searching gaze, and he called them out, with some emphatic remarks concerning their conduct.

The lieutenant remained some time near the caisson, engaged in cutting fuzes, which he timed, as near as I can recollect, at less than a second. If the reader has any idea how far a twelve-pound Parrot shell can move in that time, he will know how far distant the rebels were from us, in the judgment of the officers.

The field-officers had all dismounted, and their horses were in charge of the grooms, a short distance to the rear. These men had as much as they could attend to. The horses were excessively frightened at the artillery discharges. I could see a nervous palpitation or vibration pervading their whole system at every explosion. They were held side by side with each other, with their heads to the front; and the exquisite sensibility of the noble animals would manifest itself first at the nostrils, and pass by a perceptible wave or shock along the whole body. It seemed as though they wanted to say, or to have some one say it for them, "What cruel wretches you are to drag us into your bloody quarrels!"

Col. Fellows was much under my observation as he passed back and forth. He appeared to be perfectly cool, but deeply moved with solicitude for his men. I recall his language, temperately expressed, yet with sufficient definiteness to assure me that the situation did not meet his approval. Our colonel was not with us, and our major was detailed to some special service just before we went into action; so that the care of the regiment devolved upon Lieut.-Col. Whiton. He remained nearly the whole time at the place of greatest danger, beyond the artillery, with the right-flank companies. I judged by his manner, as he passed occasionally along our line, that he felt the same dissatisfaction that we all did.

With regard to junior officers, it will show how closely we were pressed by the rebel fire to say, that in more than one instance, and without the least discredit to their courage, young men of spirit crept along the road past us, as we lay, on their hands and knees.

It should be said, in justice to Gen. Spinola, that the honor which was so suddenly thrust upon him by Foster's detention in Little Washington would probably have embarrassed all his associate major-generals. It was no small responsibility to step into the shoes of so able and experienced a man as our leader, commanding, as he did, our unlimited confidence. He probably felt obliged to do something, however, and so he "marched out with twice five thousand men, and then marched back again."

We judged afterwards that he did not mean any thing more than a feint. The main column was held back so far to the rear as to show that he did not intend to use them in coming on to the enemy's flank. When we got into Pamlico Sound afterwards, two of our number, Corporal C. T. Adams and private Benjamin Rackliff, made a reconnoissance of six or seven miles, after the rebel troops had left, over to the place where we were engaged. They ascertained, to their satisfaction, from the residents, that our opponents were much demoralized by our persistent fire. The rebels were veterans, and well qualified to judge of military probabilities, and they apparently inferred from our determined efforts, that we meant to hold their attention until they could be flanked by the main column, and taken prisoners. Our friends also learned the precise position of the rebel guns, and found that our fire had done no damage, except to tear up the trees in an inaccessible swamp.

The duel finally came to a close by orders to withdraw. Col. Fellows's men were so hard pressed, that he did not deem it best to attempt to form them where they were, but ordered them to disperse, and to form in the road in the rear of our regiment. The first knowledge that we had of the retreat was from the men of the Seventeenth, who came drifting over the slight elevation through the trees in front of us. Their faces showed plainly the stress of endurance which had been upon them. They had met it manfully, however.

Col. Whiton gave the order to us to form in the road; but the rebel guns were still active, though our own had ceased. Capt. Hanover observed this, and called out to him, in a pleasantly suggestive tone, to form line by companies, as being much more expedient and safer than to form by battalion. Col. Whiton assented, and we were taken hastily away from the scene of our afternoon's vivid experience.

While we were in process of forming our line as a company, Major Lane, who had come at full speed to his regiment as soon as his special duty was finished, rushed among us on foot, and received a welcome from Col. Whiton, which it did our hearts good to see. I think that both officers would have

been pleased to "waive ceremony," and have a hand-shake all round. I am sure that there would have been no lack of cordiality on our part.

The march that followed before we halted for the night was one of the most memorable that we made. There were intersecting roads which might have been availed of by the enemy to cut us off on our return, and it was necessary to move with great rapidity in order to prevent this. It seemed as though our cavalry had set the whole of Craven County on fire. I think we made no halt for supper, and we had no word in respect to the length of the march, which proved to be fifteen miles. What with hunger, the heat of the weather, the smoke and heat of the burning forest on all sides of us, we made quite a repetition of the experiences of the Great March, with some additional ones.

CHAPTER IX.

PAMLICO SOUND.

THE two letters which follow give the outlines of our further operations in the relief of Washington.

ON BOARD A TRANSPORT SCHOONER IN PAMLICO SOUND,
April 15, 1863.

Another strange mutation in our soldier-life brings me into the hold of a schooner, "The Anna M. Edwards," along with three companies of our regiment, G, I, and K; the rest of it being similarly situated in other schooners alongside. There are six of our gunboats here, besides some up at Little Washington. We can see, about three miles up the river, a strip of new earth, which is the rebel fortification; and there is said to be another one farther up the river. They are not very effective, however, as the passage of the river has been made by small schooners loaded with provisions and ammunition; and night before last a steamer, "The Escort," passed up with the Fifth Rhode-Island Regiment, so far as we know, without loss.

We are the only regiment in the river below the batteries, and thus far we have been of no use since our arrival here, on Sunday morning, except that volunteers from our number have been engaged in loading and running up the small schooners of which I have spoken. We don't know as yet what will be done with us. Yesterday, officers of Foster's staff came down, and one steamer was despatched to Newbern, and one to Plymouth; and, as we have the story, troops are to be brought from Suffolk, and also from Newbern, by land, to trap the rebs, or oblige them to run, as their position exposes them to a fire in the rear. We could do this ourselves from Newbern, if we were numerous enough. When I wrote you my letter of the 10th (begun April 7), I was too much fatigued to give particulars, and also too much pressed for time and the multiplied personal needs after so fatiguing a march as we had

had. It was fortunate that I took right hold of fixing myself up, as in twenty-four hours from our arrival in camp, at an hour's notice (April 11), we were off again. I had rested well, but thought I was terribly sore from a blister on the sole of my foot; but somehow or other the excitement cured it, for I have not had any pain from it since.

We were told that all must go who could crawl to Newbern, as we should not have any marching to do except that; and the promise has been kept, for we remained on board the steamer on which we came, "The Thomas Collier," until yesterday (the 14th), when she was wanted to go to Plymouth, and we were put into the schooner.

It is rainy, and we are obliged to keep below deck much of the time, and, of course, are much crowded; but we have suffered the fatigues of a march so recently, that the men are disposed to be contented.

THURSDAY, A.M., April 16.

This letter had been partly written, when "The Escort," to our extreme surprise, came alongside, and took three companies of the four on board, leaving us, and then went to the other two schooners, serving them in the same way, leaving the three largest companies of the regiment, H, C, and D, and returning to Newbern with the rest, as is understood to come out on another land-march, we will hope more successful than the last. It appears that we are to remain here for the present as a sort of marine guard for the fleet, under the command of Major Lane of Abington, a most estimable officer. In the event of a naval attack in connection with the land-forces, it is said we are to be distributed among the gunboats to act as sharpshooters.

"The Escort" reported that she passed up with perfect safety, not being hit at all; but, on coming alongside of our schooner, she bore sad evidence of the perils of her downward trip, having been hulled by cannon-shot several times, and losing her pilot by a musket-ball, and having one of her deck-hands badly wounded, besides a narrow escape from disabled machinery. The rebels built fires close by the river-bank, so as to make her a fair target, which accounts for the difference between her upward and downward trips.

A rebel deserter, an impressed Northerner, came on board one of the gunboats last night, and says the rebs are ready to leave at short notice; and if it is true, as is currently reported, that Foster

went down to Newbern yesterday on "The Escort," they are likely to have all the notice they want by a fire in the rear more effective than that the other day. His name is a tower of strength.

CAMP AT HILL'S POINT, April 19, 1863.

I am writing in a little coop constructed of old boards taken from an outhouse at a distance of a quarter of a mile. This coop or hut is located a few hundred feet in the rear of what was a formidable rebel battery. We landed here on Friday morning, the 17th. The earthwork is at the mouth of the Tar River, on its south side. Our hearts are swelling with joy at the news which Gen. Foster has brought this morning, that Rosecrans has won the greatest victory of the war in Tennessee, and also in our triumph, without much loss of life, over the recent rebel attack on Little Washington, which has kept us in motion all this month, but which seems now happily ended by the passage through from Newbern of our troops, under Gen. Foster; the Ninth New-Jersey and the Twenty-third Massachusetts Regiment being here in the same field with us, having come in this morning, both of them just from Hilton Head, S.C., by way of Newbern.

Yesterday the rest of our regiment passed up the river, on "The Escort," to Washington; and it is said that they went out immediately on a reconnoissance north of Washington, which is in plain sight about three miles off.

Three companies of the Forty-fourth, C, D, and I, landed here about the same time we did, and are doing duty with us. They are prolific in stories of their seventeen days' siege. They lost but few men; I think none killed, and but one or two mortally wounded, although under an artillery-fire from several directions. Their earthworks saved them. Our gunboats shelled the enemy away from their guns many times during the blockade; but the largest battery, this one where we are, was well provided with bomb-proofs, having been one of the original rebel defences of the place; so that they could not be dislodged without a land-force. The enemy had only twelve-pound field-guns in this earthwork; but these were sufficiently formidable to interrupt the usual navigation of the river, and even to make our gunboats rather cautious of coming to close quarters on account of the exposure of their boilers, the boats being of such light draught of water as to make them more liable in this respect than sea-going men-of-war. They are mostly New-York

ferry-boats, with their cabins shortened at both ends about a quarter of their length, and from three to five eight or nine inch guns at each end, and in two cases at least a hundred-pounder rifle pivot-gun. There are also three or four small propellers quite efficiently armed with Parrott rifles, and clad, about their upper works, with boiler-iron, as a shield against musketry.

The schooner referred to in the letter of April 15, upon which we finally found ourselves located, was about half full of "hard tack" in boxes. There was also a considerable number of bales of hay on deck: some of these we broke open, and spread upon the boxes in the hold, making our beds quite luxurious compared to what we had been accustomed to. We were fearfully exposed to fire from the matches or pipes of our smokers; but we resolved ourselves into a committee of the whole to watch each other in this respect. Drill was dispensed with. The small schooners we sent up the river in the night had been loaded from the steamer we came in, before we left her, and we had little or nothing to do. The east wind blew softly and warm up the Sound, and we were obliged to wait for whatever might turn up. The resources of the quartermaster's department were strained to the utmost to find food for us. Sergeant Thomas King, who attended to the victualling of our company, found himself obliged to itinerate among the gunboats for supplies of various sorts, not excepting tobacco, of which there was a famine among us. Ordinarily soldiers buy this of the sutler. When this resource failed them, the smokers made a desperate onslaught on our friend the commissary sergeant for relief. To the great surprise of those of us who did not use it, we all had "a hand" in the ration which was issued, whether we smoked or not. For the first and last time in my life I was an owner of the offensive weed.

Some notice is due the brave volunteers of Company E from the Cape, with some from the South-Shore companies, thirty in all, for their gallantry in running the blockade with provisions, guns, and ammunition. The cannons were lashed outside of the boats, so as to be cut loose in the event of their capture, and the boats were loaded to the gunwale. During

the passage up, they grounded, when they were so near the
rebels that their talk could be plainly heard. They were fired
upon at this time. A ball passed through the cap of one of
them, and another was severely wounded; but they succeeded
in getting through. They were highly complimented by Gen.
Foster for their skill and courage. After the excitement of
loading the schooners, and seeing "The Escort" off with the
Fifth Rhode-Island Regiment, was over, the little steamer
"Whitehead" went up within a mile of the rebel earthwork,
and signalled Little Washington for some time in vain, getting
no answer. We watched her motions with special interest,
as our lieutenant, Colesworthy, was on board as a volunteer,
and we supposed that she would be fired upon. The enemy
were silent, however. They may have suspected a trap to
get them into their works, and then open fire on them from
the gunboats near us.

In the daytime we could see a light haze, and in the night
a faint light, arising from a point in the forest some distance
to the rear of the fortification. When we landed, after they
left, a large camp was found about a half mile from the river,
the fires of which were still smouldering. They had used
hardwood altogether, so as not to draw the fire of our heavy
guns, as they would have been exposed to this, if their location had been well defined by the free use of pitch-pine.

The rebel artillery in the forest near us was part of the
same force which was engaged at Gettysburg a few weeks
later, and it would be a natural question to ask whether they
annoyed us any as we lay helpless in the schooner. One
day, while I was below deck, I heard the sudden discharge
of one of the eight-inch guns on board of the boat which
carried Commodore Flusser's flag, I think "The Miami." She
was close alongside, and she lay between us and the shore.
I jumped on deck as soon as I could; but I was not quick
enough to see the shell explode, though I could trace its
course by my ear, for it went through the air with a musical
whistle pitched upon a high key. My comrades pointed to a
large old-fashioned house close by the bank of the river, and
said that the shell burst just beyond the gable of that house.

I could myself see the colored people scampering away from the building in evident terror. I was also informed that a piece of artillery had been noticed from the deck as it passed a gap in the forest, moving down the river, apparently with the intention of finding a suitable position to open upon us. The connection between the above incidents, I presume, was something as follows : —

Flusser was as loyal, and as full of fight, as Foster was ; and the rebels knew it. The south bank of the sound was lined at short intervals with large plantation-houses. In directing the shell against the house, instead of the gun, he said in unmistakable language, "If you don't go back, I will open my broadside upon the buildings, and burn or destroy every one of them." At any rate we saw no more of the enemy.

One word here in respect to the clear, musical whistle of the shell, and the precision with which it burst just *beyond* the house. Fragments of shell are not supposed to fly backwards. The poor colored aunties, though terribly frightened, were not in much danger of being hurt. This accuracy was obtained by turning the shell, I might almost say by polishing it. If the ridge which the two sides of a mould leaves upon all castings had been allowed to remain, the shell would have made a whirring noise, and would have been deflected more or less from a straight line ; but our round shells for the heavy smooth-bore guns of the navy were placed in lathes, and all projections were turned off: the guns themselves were thus relieved from much injurious friction, in addition to the increased accuracy of aim.

"The Escort" presented an interesting sight to us as she ran alongside on her downward trip, after having passed the battery at Hill's Point. Foster was really on board, though he kept out of sight. I suppose he did not wish that we should know that he had escaped, as he hoped to surprise the rebels with a determined attack in the rear before they knew that he was at liberty. She ran past the battery just before daylight. Those who were on our deck knew that something was going on up the river. But a mist overhung us, and the guns were not heavy enough to attract attention at the dis-

tance (three miles) at which we lay. We soon saw her, however, as, after stopping a short time at a gunboat above us, she came alongside. She was well spattered with bullet-marks, and had been hulled several times by cannon-shot. Her pilot, who was at the helm when he was killed, lay upon the deck a corpse. Bales of hay were piled around the wheel-house, high enough to cover its windows, except just enough space to look out of; but the fatal bullet entered, nevertheless. The course of the channel was such, that, for a mile before she reached the battery, the boat must run directly head on. This would take at least five minutes, and would bring her under the fire of the battery not more than five hundred feet away: at this point she must turn sharply to the east, presenting her full broadside to a six-gun battery and the fire of infantry. During the terrible exposure, the vicinity all along the river-bank was illuininated by lighting fires prepared beforehand; so that she was probably as plainly in sight as if it had been in the daytime. Into this shower of lead and iron her fearless pilot guided her; and, when he dropped lifeless from her wheel, some one must have been ready to drag his corpse aside, and step with composure into his place.

She had a walking-beam; and the panel-work of the wheel-house extended aft, enclosing the machinery, as is customary in boats of that kind. I noticed that a three-inch ball had struck the pilot-house on its side, and passed aft, through the stiles of the doors and panel-work, at least twenty feet, gradually lowering until it reached the deck, which it hit at such an angle as to rebound overboard at the stern. This must have been done while the boat was running directly for the battery.

Capt. Graham, of Foster's staff, was the only officer who showed himself. His nerves were quite well braced; but it was difficult to realize that he had just passed through such an exacting experience. Some of our men grumbled at being left on board the schooner; but he told them, that, if they knew when they were well off, they had better keep still. And the event justified the hint he gave us, that we were

going to have an easy time, compared to those who went back to Newbern.

The above account is qualified by a member of the Fifth Rhode-Island Regiment who was in Little Washington at the time. He says that "The Escort" grounded shortly after she left the wharf, and was so much delayed, that it was broad daylight when she reached the battery.

Our last experience in the river was on the afternoon of the 16th. While we were lying listlessly about the deck, we saw one of the gunboats above us get up steam, and proceed slowly up the stream, frequently altering her course, as they moved cautiously onward, reconnoitring every suspicious locality. She met with no opposition, and finally disappeared in a bend of the river. The siege had ended!

This reconnoissance in force, of Longstreet, into North Carolina, and Suffolk in Virginia, is now supposed to have had very profound relations to the circumstances of the war at that time. The hopes of the rebels were at the highest. The army and the people were dazzled at what they regarded as the invincible prowess of Lee. The higher circles of society were elated at the growing disaffection in the North, and the rebel government felt sure of European mediation. Under certain circumstances which might have occurred, but which did not, a sudden assault on Norfolk, if successful, would have placed a seaport in the hands of the Confederacy. If there had happened to be a large Anglo-French fleet at hand, what then? We cannot tell; but we know that the blood poured out so freely at Gettysburg removed this bitter cup from our lips.

On the morning of the next day, the 17th, one of the gunboats brought down the three companies of the Forty-fourth, noticed in letter of April 19, to Hill's Point, the location of the rebel earthwork, and then came down to us, and towed our schooner to the same place.

When we landed at the battery we had an interesting study of the effects of heavy artillery. The gunboats had been firing a hundred-pound Parrott shell before our arrival. About a dozen of them had failed to explode, and they had

been collected by the enemy, and placed in a pond-hole in a deep depression just in the rear of the earthwork. Many of them had passed over the battery, and buried themselves in the opposite side of the valley. They had exploded in the ground, each one of them, making a hole large enough for a small cellar. I noticed that one of them had cut its way for quite a distance, diagonally, on top of the parapet, leaving an impression, or track, in the earth, resembling the furrow turned by a plough. The earthwork had not been injured in the least; or, if so, the damage had been repaired during the nights. The platform for the guns, inside of the parapet, was of earth, at least four feet deep, and it rested on hard-pine timbers as large as twelve inches square, and twenty feet long, which were placed close together, and they thus formed the roofs of the bomb-proofs under the guns, to which the artillerists retreated when driven from their pieces.

We saw no evidence anywhere of any loss of life on the part of the enemy, a single grave excepted, under a tree, close by the fort; the circumstances of its location being such as to favor the opinion that the occupant was instantly killed while in or about the fort. The epitaph was as follows:—

"To the memory of Henry Devinport, Co. C, 52 N. C. Regiment."

The earthwork of which I have been writing was built by the rebels as one of the original defences of Little Washington. It was a very grave error on our part to allow it to remain intact when the place was captured. Before we left it, we had the satisfaction of seeing the earth and timber of which it was composed "go up" at least sixty feet into the air; a cask of powder, as we understood it, being placed in each of its four or five chambers, so as to explode one after the other.

We were a few hundred feet in the rear at the time, and, after the first explosion, we were glad to lay as close to the ground as we could get.

The sight and the sound were awfully grand and impressive. It was as if we had been treated to an exhibition of live volcanoes springing suddenly, in rapid succession, out of

the ground. First a low, earthquake-like rumble, then an explosion so massive in its character as to rise entirely above a comparison with the heaviest artillery, and then the vehement extrusion of a great body of the reddest and most lurid flame, bearing large volumes of thick black smoke, as well as earth and heavy timber, aloft, to be followed with an instantaneous collapse and silence.

During the time we were here, we picketed the only road which led to the place. The men who were on our outer post fired during the early part of one night, and fell back to the barricade. This unsettled the guard somewhat, although we did not believe there was any real cause of alarm. Those who were on duty went out again, while the rest of us slept.

When the Confederates went off, they left a large forest-fire burning somewhere within a quarter or half mile of us. It illuminated the forest all round with a dim light, and we were near enough to it to hear a constant dull, furnace-like roar. My companions (six of them, I think), under command of acting Lieut. Edmunds, were supposed to be asleep in a small hut close to me, — the reserve post. I was in a sitting posture outside, near to them, dozing, but conscious. In an instant of time I was put upon my feet, wide awake, by one of the most tremendous crashes I ever heard. I suppose that the concussion of the falling buildings in our great November fire was no heavier than the shock with which I was thus suddenly assailed. Some great giant of the forest had gone down, and in its fall had dragged an acre or two of trees with it. I comprehended the situation at once, and was not, of course, thrown off my balance by it; but not so my comrades, every one of whom were naturally cool and brave men. I judge that they were really soundly asleep, yet with the monition upon their minds appropriate to the situation, and that the inward voice was more than ordinarily alert in consequence of the alarm we had already experienced. At any rate, they were for an instant or two scared out of their wits. I had never seen the hair actually rise on the heads of men, and their eyes look like saucers, but once in my life before, and that was under circumstances of extreme danger, on board

ship; but I saw it then. It was ludicrous in the highest
degree; and yet it was a fearful sight. For a few seconds I
thought they would get away from me, and go back to camp
on the dead run without their guns; but the tones of my
voice, as much as any thing I could say in such a situation,
soon calmed them, and then the laughter was as uncontrolled
as the terror had been. What a sight it must be to see a
brave regiment stampeded in the night, in a panic! It happened to such regiments in both armies, from less impressive
reasons than in this instance.

During the forenoon of April 24, the steamer "Long
Island" came down from Little Washington, with our regiment on board. We gladly rejoined them, having been separated eight days; the only detail of our company during our
connection with the regiment.

After we were on board, she proceeded down into the
Sound, and round to Newbern, reaching Camp Rogers the
next day at noon; our company having been absent two
weeks. The following letter details the exterior circumstances of the next call which was made upon the regiment.
This march was made in connection with the battle of Chan-
cellorsville. On this very day, our friends of H, First Regiment, received orders to have eight days' rations ready; and
they began their march on the next day, the 28th.

CAMP ROGERS, May 3, 1863.

When I wrote you last sabbath (the 26th ult.), we hoped, to
say the least, that we should be allowed to remain in camp long
enough to thoroughly recruit ourselves; which seemed a reasonable
desire, as there had only been an interval of ten days since the
first week in March, that we had been free from the discomfort of
marching orders. But at ten P.M. that night we were aroused
by Capt. Hanover coming to our tents, and telling us that we must
be ready to march at daylight on the 27th, with three days' rations
and one hundred rounds of ammunition. We composed ourselves
again to such sleep as we could get under the circumstances. When
we awoke, toward morning, we were told that our march had been
postponed until ten A.M., before which time we were in line, and
started, as we had come to understand from various sources, for
the depot in Newbern.

We found, as we got into Newbern, that two regiments of our own brigade, the Seventeenth and the Forty-fifth, were afoot, and also the Massachusetts Fifth and Twenty-seventh; and out on the railroad we were joined by a Pennsylvania regiment, the Fifty-eighth. After a listless and wearisome waiting of two or three hours in the streets of Newbern, which proved to be a foretaste of the most prominent peculiarity of the expedition, we got on to platform-cars, and started in the direction of Kinston. The train stopped at Bacheller's Creek, a fortified picket-station about eight miles from Newbern, which has been deemed the outer post in this direction, though I believe the road has been in working-order a few miles farther. Here a part of the force left the train, our own regiment being among them. About sundown we again took the cars, and rode some eight miles farther, encamping with the Seventeenth and Forty-fifth. Meanwhile the Fifty-eighth and Twenty-Seventh march off on a side-road, with the intention of getting in the rear of a rebel picket-post, which it is understood has been established within ten miles of this our last camp.

We remained in this camp two days. About eleven o'clock in the forenoon of the first day, the Forty-fifth, lying alongside of us, received orders to " fall in." Without their haversacks, they were marched out upon the railroad to the before-mentioned picket-post, and, with the aid of the regiments which had already gone out, drove off the rebels, — a force of perhaps three hundred men, — with the loss of two or three killed and a few wounded on our side.

The next night afterwards, our regiment received orders to be prepared to go out on the railroad as guard to the pioneers of our own and the Forty-fifth Regiments, who were engaged in rebuilding the road. We accordingly went out about four miles, encamping in the forest, and remaining there until ten A.M. the next day, which was Friday, the 1st of May, when we had orders to fall in for Newbern. Large bodies move slowly; and, although a single regiment is not much in these days, we had to wait nearly an hour before our pickets could be called in. Meantime some of the men had set fire to our huts and the trees about them, which burned very freely on account of having their bark taken off, for about one-third of the diameter and some fifteen feet high, to allow the sap to exude; and this, by the smoke and fierceness of the heat, drove us away from our first line, toward the railroad, where we

finally form, and march back on foot, hopping across the sleepers to our first camp, which we found deserted; the men who had occupied it being in two long trains of cars. We got on with them, and waited indefinitely to take aboard officers' horses, and quartermaster's stores, etc., a roasting sun beating upon us, cheerful, yet longing for the cooling breeze from the east, which refreshes us every time the cars move. We start along a few miles farther, thinking that we are finally off, when, behold! we come to the Twenty-seventh, waiting for us in the forest. We thought our train was full, as great pains had been taken to pack us close together; but we were astonished by the brigadier in charge of the Twenty-seventh telling us to move forward so as to make room for his men. As our boys complied slowly, he told them quietly, that his regiment had got to come on, and the quicker we moved, the less time we should have to wait. It was surprising to see how soon the matter was arranged, and we were speeding at a high rate on our way to Newbern. It was quite an exciting ride. The road was not in the best of order, and the train swayed heavily from side to side. We were stowed so closely, that nothing was visible to us except the locomotive and the men. It did not require a very violent exercise of the imagination to suppose ourselves to be a gigantic serpent, spitting fire and smoke, intent upon an assault on Newbern.

At Newbern there was another tedious delay, as all but our own regiment left the cars here. When this was accomplished, we went through one of the principal streets of the town, and over the railroad-bridge, across the Trent, stopping at the nearest point to our own camp, where we left the cars, and reached Camp Rogers about four o'clock P.M., having been gone nearly five days.

The birds whispered to me very early on this march, that there was a good deal of buncombe to it. Many of the men thought our hundred rounds meant an advance on Kinston, and plenty of fighting. I did not think any such thing. The repair of the road was a mere sham, only sufficient to give the impression, at a distance, that we were in earnest; and other things, such as running the trains up and down, blowing whistles, setting fire to forests, moving troops, etc., were all on a scale to alarm the enemy, and quite give them to understand that we did really intend to move on Kinston. Our ammunition was an awful load in such warm weather, weighing nearly ten pounds. This department is

notorious for loading men in this way, in consequence, it is said, of some of the principal regiments at the battle of Newbern being reduced to one or two rounds, having gone in with only forty, and nearly losing the fight by it.

This was our last marching experience in North Carolina. On the 23d of May the regiment was under orders again, but was not sent out. The occasion was as follows. Five regiments were out on the railroad on a similar errand to the one we had recently been. They had obtained very marked advantages in breaking up a picket-post. Stung by repeated assaults of this sort, the rebels rallied in large numbers from Kinston, and followed the column, on its return, up to the Newbern forts; our force being considerably demoralized, its commander, the brave Col. Jones of the Fifty-eighth Pennsylvania Infantry, being killed.

CHAPTER X.

NEWBERN.

THE following extracts from letters written during May and June outline the experiences of the company and regiment during that time : —

CAMP ROGERS, May 9, 1863.

If the Forty-third were all Catholics, I should say that this was carnival week; for, with the exception of guard-duty and dress-parade, we have had nothing to do (but fatigue-work) since we arrived in camp a week ago yesterday, making it more than a month since we had any drilling. We had two days of intensely hot weather the first of the week; but the rest of the time has been quite comfortable.

Lieut. Bradbury has been busy erecting shelters on each guard-beat; and during the heat of the day we loop up the bottom of our tent, and lay back.

One feature of our experience is not so agreeable. The flies are as numerous and annoying as we have them in August. In the course of the forenoons, the different forts, apparently commencing over across the Neuse, and coming to those nearest to us, begin practice in firing. This is facilitated by the fact that the fields are not occupied by infantry.

BRIGADE HEADQUARTERS, NEWBERN,
May 19, 1863.

Sabbath before last, in company with three comrades, I walked about four miles, to the battlefield of Newbern. When we reached the place, we followed the earthworks down to the fort on the bank of the Neuse. It was an exceedingly interesting trip to me. I was able to understand all the prominent features of the engagement, even to ascertaining, within a few feet, of where Adjutant Stearns of the Twenty-first fell. The field is covered now with the decaying remains of equipments which the rebels abandoned, so sudden was their flight.

BRIGADE HEADQUARTERS, NEWBERN,
May 23, 1863.

Matters seem to be working very favorably in the formation of the colored brigade. It was only on Monday that the officers, under Col. Wild, reached here; and they have one regiment already. There seems to be a rush on the part of the blacks to join. I have no doubt of their ability to make at least fair soldiers, and, in many cases, after drill and experience, superior ones. We are not without mean, and, I may almost say, half-witted efforts to defeat this noble movement. But they will prove abortive, for the exigencies of our position, by an irresistible logic, are working out the kind designs of Providence: in fact, opposition is being silenced.

CAMP ROGERS, May 30, 1863.

The fields about us, so sterile last November, are yielding blackberries in profusion. Great quantities are picked by the men. The latest excitement in camp is the recruiting and obtaining commissions in the new heavy artillery regiment (Second), which it is proposed to raise out of the nine-months men here, to garrison forts in North Carolina. Gen. Foster has been round to each regiment, offering a hundred and fifty dollars bounty, thirty days furlough, and three months in camp in Massachusetts. They are making a fair start in our camp, though most of the activity is in getting commissions. Many of the men who have a fair disposition to re-enlist prefer to make up their minds in Massachusetts.

CAMP ROGERS, June 14, 1863.

I am seated outside of my tent, under a canopy of leaves, which, although somewhat dry, still answer their intended purpose of excluding the sun while they admit the air. The day is cloudy, though still hot. We feel the mitigation of the temperature very sensibly, as until yesterday, which was rainy, there has been no intermission, for long weeks, of clear skies and burning suns. We have been, however, favored with light breezes, which have set up the valley of the Neuse with sufficient force to afford partial relief.

The dates of two of the preceding letters indicate a detail which came to me for a ten-days' course of guard-duty at Gen. Amory's house in Newbern, thus bringing me slightly in contact with the corporate life of the place; for more than

this could not be said of a town deserted by its inhabitants, and under such strict military control, that a pass must be shown to sentries at every corner.

I noted in this connection, however, the remarkable incongruity of the transfer, by immigration, to North Carolina, of the hardy mountaineers of Switzerland. Holland itself would hardly appear to be in greater danger of submergence than a large part of eastern North Carolina is; yet to these swampy precincts came the men and women who were born and reared under the awful shadow of Mont Blanc. The universal local spelling of the name of the town is New Berne. They must have had vigorous health and stout hearts to resist the combined forces of malaria and homesickness.

The moral character of the influences to which they and their descendants were subjected were even more strangely unfortunate than the material; for, if my memory does not much deceive me, they were Huguenot refugees, the last persons in the world who would have looked forward with approval to the complicity of their descendants with slavery.

I had always understood that the relation between master and slave was much ameliorated in North Carolina by the fact that the manufacture of the various descriptions of naval stores, tar, pitch, etc., was carried on by small employers, many of whom labored with their slaves on terms of greater intimacy than prevailed in the cotton States. It is quite likely that this was to some extent the case; but, if it was, then I say that I do not wonder that the divine patience with the South was exhausted, and that he launched the fearful retribution of war against the oppressors of his children; for even in North Carolina the public conscience had become imbruted. There was a revolting deliberateness of wickedness in which the colored people were universally alluded to. When we asked any of the whites about the wealth of the owner of a plantation, the answer generally came, "He had so many head of *black cattle* before the war!" I make the following extract from one of my letters, in order that those who come after us will have a directly realizing sense, as

they read this account, of the fearful curse which brought us from our homes into scenes of violence and bloodshed.

"As I was strolling around yesterday (in my second visit to Newbern). I found a colored man, a little rising fifty years of age, engaged upon a wharf in siding an oak-knee. I entered into conversation with him, and found that he had been a slave until the battle of Newbern. (He was nearly white.) He was doing his work excellently; and in a quiet and prepossessing manner, in answer to a question of mine, said that he was thoroughly acquainted with his trade, and had worked at it all his days in Newbern, Beaufort, and other North-Carolina ports, paying his owner about three hundred dollars a year, retaining only enough for the bare necessaries of life for himself and family. I asked about his children, to which he replied, that, when the secesh went off, they took three of them away. It was quite an experience to me to see a man evidently as intelligent, respectable, and skilled as any of our Northern mechanics, handling the familiar tools of my own calling, and yet so recently delivered from so abject a condition. I felt more than ever, that, if the South rules, it will ruin."

Whenever I was in Newbern, I found myself drawn irresistibly to the contemplation of one of the most interesting natural objects upon which my eyes ever rested. This was the palm-tree, growing in the open air, on the southerly border street of the town, near the point of the peninsula. It was in the front-yard of a fair-sized, two-story house, with which it compared well in height; so that it must, I judge, have been as tall, at least, as thirty feet. Its exquisite symmetry formed its chief attraction to the outward sense. There were no angles about it, as in ordinary trees. I have no doubt but that an expert in the use of compasses in the delineation of curves could construct a palm, on paper, which should very nearly approximate the living tree. The manner in which the trunk passes by imperceptible gradations into the branches, and from them into the leaves, is wonderful. The trunk is massive at the base, giving the impression of the solidity of the oak in its hold upon the earth; but, as the eye followed the lines of the tree upward, its perception insensibly alters, as it finds itself viewing curves as delicate and graceful as those of the weeping-willow.

But my chief pleasure in looking at it came from a higher source. In my youth I had made a visit to the remote group, called the Magdalen Islands, lying in the central portion of the Bay of St. Lawrence. While there, I was told that nothing but potatoes would grow, so bleak were the climatic exposures of the sea-girt isles. The location was about seven hundred miles north of Boston, and, when I stood before the palm in Newbern, I was nearly the same distance south of my home. I was impressed, as I gazed upon the tree, with the thought that the narrow belt of fourteen hundred miles, as it sweeps around the globe in the northern hemisphere, includes the homes of nearly all the people who have as yet risen out of barbarism. The potato and the palm are in some sense the sentinels of civilization. As I recalled my youthful visit northward, my mind was repelled by recollections of the chilly atmosphere of the arctic region; and the equally depressing warmth of the tropics was brought sensibly before me by the association of the palm with the intense heat which forced itself upon us in the early spring months of North Carolina.

The visit to the battlefield of Newbern quickened a latent faculty of the existence of which I had hitherto had no realizing sense. I refer to the power to enter appreciatively into those military combinations which lie mostly outside of tactics, which are understood to be confined to the actual movements upon the field of battle, without any reference to the theories upon which a general of an army decides upon the plan of a campaign.

In entering North Carolina through the Sound and Slocum's Creek, instead of the harbor of Beaufort, or by the Neuse, Burnside really got into the house through the unguarded back door, which was comparatively open, instead of the front one, which, in either case, was strongly fortified by Fort Macon at Beaufort, and the obstacles of various kinds which were placed in the river to hinder a direct attack on Newbern by the way of the Neuse.

The astonishment and alarm of the Confederates must have been as great as that of the French at the Nile when Nelson

sailed around their fleet, which lay at anchor, and engaged them on the side of the ships toward the shore: most of their guns had been removed from this side to an island in their front. The surrender of the whole coast-line of North Carolina was a matter almost of necessity the moment that Newbern was captured, and it did, in fact, follow with but little bloodshed in a few weeks. The victory at Roanoke Island uncovered Norfolk, and compelled its evacuation.

I had a very peculiar experience in another respect, as I strolled over the battlefield, with every sense open to the heroic and elevated impressions which naturally affect all thoughful visitors to such scenes, and above all those who have themselves experienced the strong emotions which swell the breast where every thing is hazarded against a chance shot or shell.

Our dead were buried together upon the field of action, a graveyard being improvised; but most of them had not been permitted to remain. Lying as they did in immediate proximity to water transportation to the North, the affection of friends overcame all obstacles in the way of their removal. The locality was unfrequented, and there was therefore no occasion to incur extra expense or labor in refilling the graves. The effect, as matters were at my visit, must have been rather sensational to all believers in the literal resurrection of the body; for it looked very much as though Gabriel had made a beginning of his work in a manner very encouraging to their phase of faith. I was not open to that class of influences; but I rather revolted, in spite of myself, at a certain air of ghastliness which so many yawning graves presented.

A retrospective view of the history of the regiment calls for a notice of the universal exposure of soldiers to the accidental discharges of fire-arms. Immediately after our arrival at Newbern, the casualty on board of "The Merrimac," by which we were deprived for a time of the services of our quartermaster, was duplicated by a similar one to private John W. Fracker, who had the misfortune to mutilate his hand by the accidental discharge of his piece while engaged

in foraging a few miles from camp. He was sent to the hospital at Newbern, and on his recovery accepted a permanent detail; so that we saw but little of him afterwards.

On the morning of the 1st of February, as I came off duty as guard, about sunrise, I sat down on a pile of wood between two of the guard-tents. I had been there about fifteen minutes, when I was startled by the report of a musket and the whiz of a ball, from some quarter close by me, though I could not for the moment tell where. For an instant or two I was petrified with astonishment. As soon as I could collect my faculties, I was drawn by a deep groan of distress into the middle tent, the entrance to which was but a few feet from me, and there lay one of the guards, private Calvin Williamson of Company F, with a ball through his foot, the sole of his boot being blown apart, and the flesh and bones protruding. He was rheumatic, and in the effort to recap his gun while lying upon his back, through some stiffness of the joints, or sudden twinge of pain, he managed to discharge his piece in this disastrous manner. The day before, I had sat on the wood, when I came off duty, twice, in a spot that would have brought me directly in range, but was led this morning, by inward experiences which afterwards recurred at once to me, to a place which just cleared me from the range of the shot, which could be traced quite directly by the hole it made in the tent, and other tests; as follows, the bullet passed over the camp, so close to the heads of the men who were flocking to the sink as to cause them to dodge, and struck in the Trent. It brought a large part of the regiment out to the parade-ground, and I received many congratulations on my narrow escape. Certainly it was so; for one step only was needed to place me just where I should have been hit in the body.

On Tuesday, March 31, as we were going on dress-parade, we noticed our chaplain hurrying out of camp with a musket in his hand. This was an unusual proceeding on his part; but it did not excite special remark, until, as we stood in line, as motionless as so many statues, we were startled by the report of a gun, and the passage, over the heads of the

right-flank companies of the regiment, of a ball: it was sufficiently close to the men to cause an involuntary shrinking. The colonel immediately detailed a corporal and two men, who proceded to arrest the chaplain. He was brought into camp, and conducted up the street of Company H, just as we "broke ranks;" the members of the adjacent companies crowding in upon us to witness the novel sight of a staff-officer under arrest. There was much suppressed mirthfulness, sympathetic and respectful, however, in its character. The profound regret of the chaplain was very significantly shown in his concealment of his face by drawing his visor down. He was conducted to the colonel's tent, reprimanded, and dismissed. He had a very narrow escape from the sad reminiscences which would have harassed him in case of injury to any one of us. He was supposed to have fired into the water, from which the ball glanced in a manner which he did not anticipate.

As we are about taking our leave of North Carolina, I will here insert some climatic and personal exposures, beginning with a tropical storm.

Some time in the early spring, a large body of conscripts passed by our camp, and took the road to Trenton, presumably on a march of the same character as our own in the preceding January. They had been gone a day or two, when, just at nightfall, we were visited with one of the most imposing thunder-storms of this locality. The coast of North Carolina thrusts itself abruptly into the ocean, and seems to be the focus of atmospheric disturbance. A sailor's ditty to this effect has become almost a proverb:—

> "If the Bermudas let you pass,
> You must beware of Hatteras."

On this occasion, darkness came on prematurely, the clouds hung so low and so heavy. The forests across the plantation cast the blackest of shadows; and although we were for the moment free from wind or rain, yet it was evident that the elemental war was being waged with fearful fury a few miles inland. The peals of thunder were so frequent and so well

defined, that, in spite of our better judgment, we could hardly help believing that a deadly action was going on at no great distance from us. We knew better; yet really our sympathies, for a time, were excited in behalf of our friends who were "out."

I was on guard that night, and, as the hours moved on, I noted the passage of the storm-cloud northward, along the inner coast-line, until it appeared to have reached Plymouth or Suffolk. There it lingered for a while, the sound being deadened by distance. Then it began a retrograde course southward, following the Sounds and the Hatteras banks. Somewhere in the small hours of the night it was upon us, at Newbern, in all its fury; and we walked our stations, with our guns under our coat-capes and blankets, enveloped alternately in the blazing light of noonday, and at the next instant in pitchy darkness, in drenching torrents also of rain, and thunder so loud and so incessant as to mock the heaviest artillery.

It was a night long to be remembered by those who were exposed to its violence. When at Hill's Point, in April, we had another of these characteristic storms. The flashes of lightning were so brilliant, it seemed as though we were wrapped in flames. Men who would have resented the slightest charge of cowardice were appalled at the awful display of Almighty Power which we witnessed on these occasions.

We had a brigade picket-post across the Trent, on a road running through a thick forest. I had a personal fight with an army of mosquitoes here one night, just before we left for home. Their size and ferocity was something fearful. They attacked in massed columns, with an energy that was surprising. While off duty, I wrapped my head and face in my coat-cape, and lay down, thinking that I had got the better of them, surely; but, to my horror I found, after it was too late, that they had bored through the knees of my stout army pants, and had drank their fill of blood, to my intense discomfort. I was driven to desperation by them, and was obliged to walk back and forth on a sultry night, swinging

my arms in the vain endeavor to avoid their thrusts. Singular as it may seem, we were not annoyed by them in our tents on the open plain, on the other side of the Trent.

Another pest of our army-life may as well be brought to the front now as at any other time. We had a common Sibley tent for the reserve-post at this same picket-station. It was as dirty and neglected as was usual in such cases. One day, while I was on duty at the nearest post, I noticed that the members of the guard who happened to be occupying the tent, all at once, and without any apparent provocation, sprung out of it with a haste which could not have been excelled if a live shell had dropped in their midst. They then straightway proceeded to level it to the ground, working with a zeal that showed that they were in earnest. After I came in, I tried, in an indirect way, to ascertain what the matter was; but *nobody knew*. For this reason, I fear that I shall be obliged to leave the reader to evolve the cause out of his or her inner consciousness.

There may have been a few who escaped this fearful nuisance, one of the greatest humiliations of our soldier-life: if there were any such, they were fortunate indeed. Come they would, in spite of the utmost care of our persons. With the indifferent and thoughtless, they stopped. By perpetual vigilance, those who were energetic in their personal habits of cleanliness managed to resist, with more or less of success, this Egyptian plague.

CHAPTER XI.

THE RETURN HOME.

THE ensuing letters detail the order of events by which the regiment found itself transferred to Virginia, and made, to some extent, a participant in the interest attaching to the occurrences which culminated at Gettysburg.

CAMP ROGERS, June 21, 1863.

Yesterday was nine months since our company took the oath for that length of time, and, by a coincidence somewhat singular, we marched to the barracks of Company H, Seventeenth Regiment, and stacked our arms, while they served us the same way. They have got our splendid arms, in the most perfect order; and we take such a set of Brummagems as you never put eyes on, mostly Belgian smooth-bores. We are glad for their sakes, however.

We have received to-day New-York newspapers to the 17th inst., in which the North seems to be in full blast for another scare; and items from Boston look as though the Forty-fourth would be off again (back to the scene of war). We look upon it as somewhat exaggerated, though it may be, that, in sheer desperation, the rebel forces are moving north *en masse*. It is thought possible that it may effect us, even to the extent of going home by way of Virginia or Pennsylvania; though of this we know nothing, and there are various theories as to our possible movements. All drill is stopped on account of heavy picket and fatigue duties (in building forts) and the heat.

MONDAY, A.M., 22d.

So far as we can ascertain, the Fifth and Forty-fifth leave between now and Wednesday, and are ordered to report at Fortress Monroe. We suppose they may be kept there, or sent up to Washington or Philadelphia, or, quite as likely, sent home (which last proved true). If we are needed, we may follow in their tracks.

ON BOARD TRANSPORT STEAMER "VIDETTE,"
YORK RIVER, VA., June 28, 1863.

If you received the letter mailed on the 22d, I presume your minds are somewhat prepared for this. On Wednesday morning, the 24th inst., the Forty-third, and all the other nine-months regiments remaining in Newbern, received notice to be ready to go on board of transports, in heavy marching order, at four hours' notice. And at noon we had orders to fall in at half-past four P.M., when we took our final leave, with three rousing cheers, of Camp Rogers. Our friends of the Seventeenth Regiment swarmed out of their barracks as we passed them to bid us a hearty good-by. After the usual delays incidental to such movements, four companies, including our own, got on board of this steamer; the rest of the regiment finding accommodation on the steamer "Emilie" and the schooner "Skirmisher." We drew the most water, and, in coming out of Hatteras Inlet, we grounded, and remained for six hours, until noon of Friday, the 26th; our consorts having passed out the same morning. We were directed to report at Fortress Monroe for orders. We reached that place about three o'clock on Saturday P.M., and, after waiting about three hours, had orders, with the rest of our regiment, to come up this river, as we understand it, to White-House Landing, where a force, under Gen. Dix, is menacing Richmond, in order to relieve the pressure upon Pennsylvania. Ostensibly we are going to Richmond. But I have got to be too old a soldier to believe all that I hear. Our colonel is reported, on good authority, to have stated to the officials at the fortress, that we were provided with but forty rounds of ammunition, and he was told that we should not need twenty; so it would appear that the movement is only a feint. We were ordered to leave our sick, and our heavy baggage, at Newbern, to be sent direct to Boston. Malarial sickness is fast increasing in the regiment, and there are some with us who ought to have gone directly home.

ON BOARD STEAMER "VIDETTE,"
IN CHESAPEAKE BAY, June 30, 1863.

I am on my return with my regiment, to Fortress Monroe, from White-House Landing, on the Pamunkey River. We have been ordered back on account of our complete destitution of every thing except the personal outfit of the men (our quartermaster and all heavy material having been left behind at Newbern), and also for the reason that our time is too near out for an advance;

in addition to which, the fact that we have condemned arms and a large sick-list has also been taken into account. It is understood that we are to report at the fortress for such transportation to the North as can be furnished; we don't know when, what, or where.

Gen. Dix had reported the same muskets unfit for use a year previously, while the Seventeenth were at Baltimore. They had been two years in service, and their numbers were less than ours by several hundred men. This gave them an opportunity to lay aside the poorest of the muskets as fast as they became injured. But, when we took them, the old condemned traps came out of the quartermaster's dust-holes, and were placed in our hands. I have reason to speak very definitely of one of them, which failed regularly three times out of five in attempts to snap a cap; and the general appearance of the piece was in harmony with its conduct. This transaction, I am assured, would not have taken place, if the remotest idea had existed that the regiment would go to the front in Virginia and Maryland.

The letters above quoted have taken me a little in advance of my narrative. When we reached Hatteras Inlet, we found Gen. Foster there in his despatch-boat, to see us off, and we took our last look of him, until years afterward, when he came to Boston. We had the vexation to see " The Emilie " go through the inlet with the schooner in tow; while we had a reminder, as we lay aground, of the annoyances and dangers which came near rendering Burnside's expedition abortive. We managed, however, to press through on the flood-tide, and followed our companions.

Two sea-going steamers of the largest size were lying outside of the inlet. They were understood to have been sent South with orders to bring up troops. They were not at anchor, but lay listlessly in the long ocean-swells; their heads pointing all round the compass, with motions as graceful, as they rose and fell, as if engaged in waltzing, — an illusion which was all the more suggestive from the glassy smoothness of the water, which answered well in its flowing undulations to the polished spring floors upon which gay

assemblies of pleasure-seekers pass the flying hours. I heard no music, unless the measured pulsations of the surf as it broke upon the beach might be supposed to supply the place of a band. I apprehend that my sense of hearing was too dull to catch the sound of the subtle harmonies which are said to pervade nature.

We found that "The Vidette" was a slow coach. At intervals of just twenty minutes, all the way up to Fortress Monroe, she blew off steam. When the boys growled at the delay, word came up from the engine-room that we had better hush up, and consider ourselves fortunate that we were in careful hands, as the boat was needing repairs, and would not bear a full head of steam.

We passed Hatteras Light at a distance of a few miles: it compares well in its elevation to Bunker-Hill Monument. The low coast-line and the extremely stormy seas of the winter in this locality, make its height a necessity.

We were very much crowded; but our quarters were above the water-line, and well ventilated, so that there was no actual suffering. We were obliged to sleep on the deck, in two rows, on each side of the boat She was not wide enough for us to occupy twelve feet; so that we lay with legs interlocked, something like clothes-pins when shut into each other. This was all very well as long as we lay still; but irregular efforts to change our positions snarled our legs as badly as if our heads had been full of "tangle-foot" whiskey. We found ourselves obliged to systematize matters. When a number of us had lain so long on one side that we wanted to change over, some one would stand up, count off a "platoon," and announce it in regular military style: he would then give the order "About-face!" whereupon we would all "flop" at once, with precision and ease, avoiding the unpleasant predicament of confounding a comrade's leg with our own. Of course, we were all "sober;" that is, nobody laughed, or made any effort to extract any fun out of our surroundings.

One experience, however, happened to us, which was any thing but laughable: in fact, it came near costing some of us

our lives. The boat, in all probability, had not had so many men on board before, since she bore Burnside's heroes to the scene of their exploits, more than a year previous. Her cooking apparatus was drawn upon to its full capacity: in doing this, a large copper-bottomed boiler was used without due regard to its condition. The consequence was, that twenty or thirty of us were attacked with severe pain and vomiting, with indications of poison. I was one of *les miserables*. We all recovered; but the effects in my own case were permanent, so far, at least, as to unfit me for duty, and, in connection with the malarious influences with which my system was already charged, I was finally prostrated.

We entered Hampton Roads during Saturday afternoon. A small fleet of merchant-vessels lay at anchor, and we could see "The Minnesota" at the mouth of the James River, opposite Newport News. At the moment of our arrival, a bank of thunder-clouds was in the western horizon, obscuring in partial darkness the tall masts and heavy spars of the great ship. Their gloom was enhanced by the smoke and noise of her guns; for she was engaged at the moment in firing a funeral salute to the honored memory of Commodore Foote, the gallant man who won the first naval victories of the West.

The scenery, and the associations of the vicinity of the fortress, are of the most interesting character. The land is so low, that it makes little or no claim upon the attention. The ocean asserts its supremacy by the absence of islands or peninsulas. The swell broke angrily on Willoughby Spit, outside of the anchorage, revealing the terror of the waves when lashed by storms; but in all other respects the bay and the outlying sea with which it mingled were quiet, presenting no impressive indication of power to the senses, except their magnitude: this, however, was impressive in the extreme. The broad expanse of water stretching magnificently seaward from the majestic fortress as far as the eye can reach, toward Capes Henry and Charles, seemed a fitting arena or foreground for the naval conflict in which, a year before, "The Cumberland" and "Congress" had been sunk under

circumstances of imperishable honor, and where "The Monitor" appeared unexpectedly upon the scene, and vanquished her huge antagonist, "The Merrimac." The hull of the frigate "Brandywine," in use as a storeship, was a conspicuous object in the roads. She was associated in my mind with the visit of Lafayette to America, having been placed at his disposal when he returned home. By a very grateful and tender reminiscence I thought, at that moment of terror and gloom in our national affairs, of the bright aspirations of the young republic, and felt in my heart that it could not be that our sun was to set in irrevocable disaster.

We received orders on arrival, as previously stated, to proceed at once up York River, and report to Gen. Dix at White-House Landing on the Pamunkey. We arrived there early the next day, remaining over night, without leaving our vessel, and started on Monday, on our return to the fortress.

During the twenty-four hours of our visit to White-House Landing we had very interesting calls from prominent friends and acquaintances in our Chelsea company, G, of the Fortieth Regiment. "The Vidette" lay close to the shore, the banks of which were near enough and high enough to permit our main boom to be swung over our quarter, so as to furnish a bridge upon which we could pass and repass. Our friends were strongly impressed with the idea that it was possible for the column (supposed to be about eighteen thousand men which had been gathered there) to make a sudden dash upon Richmond while Lee was in Maryland, and capture the place. We smiled at their ardor; but we said nothing calculated to chill it. During the next year their magnificent record had extended from Upper Maryland to Olustee in Florida, including the siege of Charleston. I presume that when, a year afterward, they came back to White-House Landing, they were not so eager to rush upon the impregnable fortifications of the rebel capital.

This column, or a part of it, did actually advance ten miles toward Richmond a day or two after we left them, but were repulsed. Col. Porter states, that "it may be truly said, that to the Fortieth it was due that lasting disgrace was not inflicted upon the entire corps."

The scene upon the York and Pamunkey Rivers was a very animated one. It was well calculated to deceive distant or superficial observers, and for the moment I was a little puzzled myself; the item that confused me the most being the fact that a large locomotive went up the river on a schooner's deck, and was in process of transfer to the York-river Railroad while we were there. Large numbers of steamers, some of them of great size, were passing up and down the river. They were often visible across the beautiful meadows for miles before we met them; and, when we came opposite to each other, a large amount of cheering was indulged in. I recollect that one boat had quite a number of rebel prisoners on her forward-deck, — sour-looking fellows, most of them, in butternut clothes. On the upper-deck of this boat, in front of the wheel-house, was a smart-appearing Union soldier, a sergeant. He leaned over toward us, and pointed with great earnestness and much gesticulation to the after-part of the boat. We could see that he had some piece of information that he was longing to impart; but, on account of the noise, he was obliged to confine himself to pantomime. We learned, when we reached the landing, that, if he could have said in ordinary language all he wanted to, his talk would have been about as follows : —

"We've got one of the biggest toads in the rebel puddle aft there in the cabin;" the fact being, that Gen. Fitzhugh Lee, an officer of cavalry, a brother of Robert E., had just been captured, and was on board.

On the passage up the river I noticed the ruins of a large ship upon the stocks. Her frame had been completed when the hand of the industrious artificers had been stayed, no doubt, rudely. Nearly a third of the timbers, including the whole bow, had fallen over bodily to the ground, presenting a sad emblem of the distress which the great State of Virginia had brought upon itself.

On our return to Fortress Monroe we landed, and went into camp at Hampton, remaining a day or two. On the afternoon of July 2 the whole regiment went on board of the steam transport "Kennebec," and landed at Baltimore,

near Fort McHenry, early in the afternoon of the 3d, at the precise moment of the final desperate and disastrous charge of the rebels at Gettysburg.

We marched a short distance to the barracks, which were provided for us in a large unfurnished upper-room of a substantial building which had been used as a tobacco-warehouse. One of the most unpleasant incidents of our whole term of service happened during the ensuing night. It was impossible to prevent the men who wanted liquor from obtaining it. They had been so long without stimulants, that it seemed to fly into their heads at once, and with fearful power. They were not ugly nor malicious; but it made them delirious with excitement. There were no accommodations for commissioned officers in the building, and none of them were present; so that the roughs had everything their own way as long as the "hoorosh" lasted. It was confined to a hundred, more or less, of the illiterates of the regiment (not one of them belonged to our company); and the way that they raced around the great room was a caution to windmills. All that the rest of us could do was to pick up our equipments, and pack ourselves as closely as we could against the walls, holding our traps in our hands. This wild scene lasted for several hours, until nature was exhausted, and the foolish fellows, one by one, dropped off to sleep.

My vitality was failing me very fast at the time, from causes already stated. Being too weak to stand, I made a rush alone for the centre of the room, which was comparatively secure, but not altogether so. As the drunken crowd swept close by me, I attracted the attention of one of their number, who sympathetically inquired the reason for my conduct. He was an entire stranger personally to me, and I was the same to him; but he kept his eye upon me, and acted in the most friendly manner whenever I was in danger, actually saving me from being trampled under foot.

The next morning was the Fourth. The victory at Gettysburg was known in Baltimore. There was a certain air of exhilaration manifested in the business portion of the city, occupied mostly by Northerners, but, with that exception,

no exultation was visible. Early in the forenoon the regiment started through the city to its northern suburb, locating at Camp Bradford.

We marched for miles, through streets occupied by costly hammered granite buildings, without seeing an open window, a waving handkerchief, or hearing a single cheer.

Our camp was on a steep hillside, in beautiful private grounds understood to belong to a party compromised with the Rebellion. We were placed under strict orders not to injure or mar the property in any respect: a heavy rain which came on in the night obliged us to disregard this order. The soil was so hard, that we might as well have been on the roof of a building, as all the water that fell above us ran down the surface of the hill, and drove us at midnight out of the fly-tents which were given us, with bayonet and dipper to trench ourselves.

Fifty miles away from us, at Gettysburg, the same rain was falling upon the bodies of poor wounded men, unsheltered and uncared for, so great was the number to be attended to. We remained in this camp three days, nothing of interest occurring, except the arrival, at a depot in the vicinity, of large numbers of prisoners from the battlefield.

Those of us who returned home saw another depot, just as we left the city, occupied by five hundred wounded officers of our own army: their injuries were in the upper part of the body, and all of them could walk. They had been furloughed home until recovery. Their spirits were buoyant and impressible to the last degree. The thunder of the great fight was still ringing in their ears. As I mingled with them, I saw another illustration, just as I had done when I passed into the ranks of the Twenty-third at Kinston, of the influence of deep feeling in giving eloquent impressiveness to commonplace utterances. My last letter home was written from here.

BALTIMORE, July 4, 1863.

I am sitting on my blankets, in a beautiful grove, among elegant residences in the northern suburbs of this city. We reached Baltimore from Fortress Monroe yesterday noon, went into

the barracks of the Union Relief Association, and this morning marched out here, ostensibly to remain until the first part of next week, and then start for home. I do not dare to fully believe this, as we get quite direct intimations that Gen. Schenck, who is in command here, will wait to see the result of the battles to the west of us before he relinquishes his hold upon the four regiments of nine-months men in this vicinity, as, if they prove to be disastrous, Baltimore will be in imminent hazard. We found it difficult to get out of the place this morning, as all the streets are barricaded on account of their dread of a cavalry attack. The accounts for a few days have come in so favorably, that public confidence seems to be restored, and most of our men think we shall be at home next week. As I have said before, you must try and restrain your feelings so as not to be disappointed, as, in these times, nothing is certain until it comes to pass.

The next event that happened was as follows: —

"On the 7th the regiment received orders to report to Gen. Naglee, who, understanding there was some dissatisfaction in the regiment, on account of the expiration of its term of service, issued an order leaving it optional with the men to go to the front, or return home. [Eight hundred men were sixteen days over time.] Under this order 203 officers and men voted to go to the front." — REPORT OF ADJUTANT-GENERAL, 1863.

During the latter part of the afternoon of the 8th, the returning members of the regiment retraced their steps through the city, and took the cars for Philadelphia, riding all night. I was with this portion of my comrades. We were under the command of Lieut. Lysander Poole of Company G. Our orderly was with us, but too sick to fill his place, which was occupied by comrade George W. Geary, who was unanimously chosen to take command of the company, in the absence of the officers. We received very thankfully the hospitalities of the Cooper's shop restaurant; and, after a short march through the city, we crossed the Delaware, and took the cars for Perth Amboy. Early in the afternoon we reached this place, and went on board of a steamer for New York. A very pleasant passage through the narrow channels

lying west of Staten Island brought us to Castle Garden late in the afternoon, from which place we passed to the Battery, just adjoining. We lay upon the grass here for several hours, taking much needed rest, as we had slept none on the preceding night. After sunset, we formed line, and marched up Broadway a short distance, turning to the right, and going on board the steamboat "Elm City," for New Haven. This latter place was reached at daylight on the morning of the 10th, and the cars were taken for Boston, by the way of Springfield, where we arrived in due time. After reaching Boston, we were marched to the armory of the Boston Light Infantry, in Boylston Hall, and furloughed.

My health and vigor had given out entirely. On the passage home I became rapidly worse, but managed to keep with my comrades until we reached the armory, when I sank exhausted on the floor. I was assisted by friends to a horse-car, and came to my home in Chelsea to go upon a sick-bed, and remained there for weeks, hovering between life and death; my whole system thoroughly pervaded with malaria; my body corpse-like, so that the impression of the fingers in the flesh would remain for a considerable time; digestion absolutely suspended, the most tempting food being placed before me without the slightest effect upon the appetite; the brain itself, sunk in lethargy, or in feeble, delirious wanderings, taking no intelligent note of my surroundings. Most of the time I was with the comrades at the front. I finally recovered, being indebted, under Providence, to the skill of Dr. Wheeler, aided by the most assiduous domestic care.

The experience of the comrades who passed up into Maryland is pleasantly described by Corporal C. M. Coburn, now of Titusville, Penn., — the present commander of Post 50, G. A. R. Department, Pennsylvania, — in a recent letter composed from a diary.

BALTIMORE, July 8, 1863.

According to orders issued to the regiment last evening, we were to move forward this forenoon toward the front. The fact that our time of service had more than expired, many of our comrades having made their business arrangements to return home,

caused Col. Whiton, in making an address to the regiment, to give the opportunity (under orders from superior officers) to those who could not stay longer to go to Boston. The result was, that some went home. The balance of the regiment took up line of march *en route* for Harper's Ferry, leaving Baltimore about nine A.M., July 9. on platform-cars, passing the historical places of Relay House, Ellicott's Mills, Frederick Junction, Point of Rocks, etc., and arrived, without special incident, at Sandy Hook, opposite Harper's Ferry, after dark; the last few miles having been run rather cautiously, fearing trouble from rebel guerillas, our locomotive being an iron-clad one, running in rear of the train.

It was said that several of the train-hands had been shot, picked off by rebel sharpshooters, within the past few days.

Upon reaching Sandy Hook, we camped upon the hillside, tired and dirty. On the next morning I started off early to look around. I found we were at the base of the famous Maryland Heights, commanding the surrounding country. The fortifications at the summit were in a sad state, having been left in a demoralized condition since the unfortunate Col. Miles's surrender. A large hundred-pound Parrott gun, which must have taken great labor and expense to put into position, was pitched over into a deep chasm hundreds of feet below.

The view from this elevation is magnificent; the lovely Loudon valley extending for miles to the south-west. Returning to camp, I found that the Thirty-fourth and Thirty-ninth Massachusetts Regiments were in our vicinity, together with the Thirtieth and Thirty-second New-York Batteries and the Eighth New-York Heavy Artillery.

About noon, our regiment was called upon to do provost-duty, and Major Lane was made provost-marshal; Gen. Naglee being in command.

On the 14th we assisted in the laying of a pontoon across to Harper's Ferry; and the rebel pickets were driven out of the place by our batteries, who opened fire, at a preconcerted signal, about nine A.M. We watched the effect of the artillery-fire from the heights with considerable interest, and noted the telling accuracy of some of the shot.

The mounted rebel pickets were not slow in getting back into the country, to the south of Harper's Ferry. One party started out in a buggy, and, when out on the road a short distance from

town, he made a good mark for our artillerists. Several shells were sent whizzing after him, and one burst near enough to overturn buggy, horse, and rider, down an embankment, where they lay, very much demoralized. We saw no signs of life for a few moments; but presently a man was seen legging it to the best of his ability, leaving the horse and vehicle to take care of themselves.

Upon the completion of the pontoon-bridge, many of our boys went over, and visited the ruins of the government arsenal.

Gen. Gregg's cavalry came in sight soon after the bridge was completed, and crossed over. They had left the main body after the battle at Gettysburg, and were swinging around to intercept and capture what prisoners they could from Lee's retreating army.

From late this afternoon, all through the night, groups of prisoners were coming in under guard: they were put on trains, and sent to Baltimore.

On the 16th our army began to arrive, and we were glad to find old friends in the Second, Third, and Twelfth Army Corps, as they passed over the bridge to-day. Among the different regiments we saw the First, Second, Fifteenth, Nineteenth, Twentieth, and Twenty-eighth Massachusetts Regiments. Company H of the First Massachusetts was heartily welcomed by our boys, and the air rung with cheer upon cheer as the old veterans of so many hard fights marched by. We also got the news to-day of the surrender, to our forces, of Fort Hudson, and we really began to think that the war was about over.

On the 18th we were relieved by the Nineteenth Maryland Regiment, and orders given to start for Boston. Before leaving, Gen. Naglee made a neat speech, and issued a complimentary order, which was read on dress-parade this evening. He also directed us to wear the corps-badge of the first brigade, second division, Sixth Army Corps. We left by rail this afternoon, and arrived in Baltimore at midnight.

On the 19th, Sunday, we were well fed by the parties in charge of the relief rooms, and left at six P.M. for Philadelphia, continuing to New York, where we arrived at five P.M. on the 20th, and immediately went on board the Sound steamer, "Plymouth Rock."

We arrived in Boston on the 21st, and were received at the depot by the Boston Light Infantry Association, who escorted us up State Street to Boylston Hall, where a bountiful collation was served to us.

We were also welcomed at the depot by the Boston Light Dragoons and the Chelsea Rifle Corps: the latter being our own special escort. After our banquet, the Rifle Corps escorted us to Chelsea, where we were dismissed, and granted a furlough until the 30th, when we were mustered out at Readville.

The "Boston Journal" (of the 21st) and "The Chelsea Pioneer" reported these receptions as follows: —

RETURN OF THE FORTY-THIRD REGIMENT.

The detachment of the Forty-third Massachusetts Regiment which volunteered to go to the front, and remain until the rebels were driven out of Maryland, arrived in this city this morning, about eight o'clock, by the Stonington route, and met with a most cordial reception by their friends. They arrived some two hours earlier than they were expected, and were marched to the Boylston-street Mall on the Common, where their muskets were stacked, and, under their captains, they proceeded to obtain breakfast at the nearest convenient place. Many of their friends met them on the Common.

The following is the complimentary order issued by Gen. Naglee, at the time of their return home from Maryland: —

HEADQUARTERS, HARPER'S FERRY,
July 17, 1863.

SPECIAL ORDERS, No. 14.

I. The term of service of the Forty-third Regiment Massachusetts nine-months men, under Lieut.-Col. John C. Whiton, being about to end, they will leave for Baltimore at noon to-morrow, and Col. Whiton will report for further orders to Major-Gen. Schenck. The quartermaster will furnish the necessary transportation.

II. The general commanding is happy to acknowledge the generous offer of the regiment to remain in service as long as the late emergency should exist, and thanks them for the services rendered as fully as though they had been called to the field.

He would further acknowledge with satisfaction the excellent conduct of the regiment while attached to the department of North Carolina, under Major-Gen. Foster.

By command of
BRIG.-GEN. NAGLEE.

GEORGE H. JOHNSTON, *Capt. and A. A. G.*

The battalion of Dragoons, Major Wilder, who had volunteered to do escort-duty, arrived, and formed on Boylston Street about eleven o'clock; and the Boston Light Infantry Association, under whose auspices the reception was given, soon appeared, headed by Gilmore's Band, and under command of its president, Major C. O. Rogers, as chief marshal.

The Dragoons, who were accompanied by the Chelsea Brass Band, mounted, took the head of the procession, and were followed by the Chelsea Rifle Corps, Lieut. Blake. Next came the Infantry Association, and then the guests of the day, — the Forty-third Regiment, under Col. Holbrook. Their war-worn uniforms attracted much attention; and their soldierly bearing and prompt movements won them much commendation, and loud and repeated cheers from the crowd who lined all the streets.

The route of the procession was through Tremont, Winter, Summer, Arch, Franklin, Devonshire, Milk, India, State, and Washington Streets, to Boylston Hall. Large numbers of people were assembled along the route; and the greeting of the regiment was most enthusiastic.

At Boylston Hall a collation had been prepared by the city authorities for the regiment, and, after their arrival, they were drawn up in line around the hall.

His Honor the mayor then came forward, and was introduced by Major Rogers as follows: —

Mr. Mayor, after an absence of over nine months in the field, the Forty-third (Tiger) Regiment has returned to you and to the city of Boston, which has nurtured and cared for them, and remembered them, through the whole time that they have been gone. I have the pleasure of presenting to you Col. Holbrook, and of saying to him, that whatever words can be uttered for the gratification of the regiment will now be uttered by you.

[Mayor's address not reported.]

[Pioneer, July 25, 1863.]

MILITARY AND CIVIC RECEPTION.

That portion of the Forty-third Massachusetts Regiment which volunteered, at the expiration of their nine-months enlistment, to march under Gen. Naglee to the front, and were attached to the Sixth Army Corps, forming a part of the Army of the Potomac, arrived in Boston on Tuesday, where they met with au enthusi-

astic reception. Capt. Hanover's command, Company H of Chelsea, was subsequently received by members of our city government and a large concourse of citizens at the Ferry, where they arrived under escort of the Chelsea Rifle Corps. They thence proceeded, amid the enthusiasm of the people, expressed in repeated cheers, to Winnisimmet Square, where they halted for a few moments, were grasped by ready hands in fits of Northern shakes, and soon after entered the armory. Here they were received by the Rifle Corps, who presented arms, and, through Lieut. Blake, greeted their return with a few brief and fitting expressions of welcome. Capt. Hanover replied.

E. C. Fitz, Esq., president of the Common Council, welcomed the returned soldiers in behalf of the city. He said, that in the absence of the mayor, and in consequence of the diffidence(!) of the chairman of the Board of Aldermen (Churchill), it devolved upon him to give to the returned soldiers a few honest words of welcome. The incidents of the day brought to his mind a reminiscence of 1862, when Chelsea was called upon to supply a quota of troops which seemed to her disproportionately large. I remember when you, Mr. Commander, unfurled your banner in yonder Square, and called upon the citizens of Chelsea to enroll their names in the defence of their country. How they responded, let the muster-roll make answer. Never will the people of Chelsea forget the sensation of pride which animated their souls, when, after days of anxiety inseparable from such a demand upon their hearts and homes, we received the gratifying announcement that Chelsea's quota was full. Nobly have you done your duty. The battlefields and swamps of North Carolina testify to your faithfulness. Permit me to allude to an act of heroism on your part that should not be overlooked. When absolved from further duty by the limitation of your enlistment, and while your hearts were yearning for and anticipating a speedy return home, in this moment of expectancy your country claimed an extra service at your hands. You felt that that claim was paramount. You obeyed the call, were ready for the sacrifice; you went again to the front, nobly determining to do your duty. [Enthusiastic cheers.] No words can adequately express the gratitude that lies deep in our hearts. I congratulate you on your safe return to your homes. As you lay aside the soldier's garb, and resume the costume and occupations of peaceful life, in your own hearts you will find a

gratifying approval of your course. We rejoice that Chelsea's escutcheon remains untarnished. May that kind Providence which has led you through the dangers of the conflict ever smile upon you and your command! [Cheers.]

Capt. Hanover replied, that his heart was so full he could not express himself. He thanked them for their kind reception. A thousand thoughts had possession of him; but he could give expression to but one, — that Company H had ever been ready to do their duty. [Cheers.] In the hour of trial no man quailed, no man proved craven. God in his providence had brought them back in safety. They felt deeply thankful. The joy at their return was reciprocal: they had had hand-shaking to the aching of their bones. [A laugh.]

William G. Clark, Esq., proposed three cheers of welcome on behalf of the citizens. Given with a tiger.

Sergeant Perry of Company H here stepped out from the ranks, and said, " I propose three cheers for our good, kind-hearted captain." They were given by the men, with " one more."

Thus ended the reception. The weather was rainy and unpleasant, which abridged much of the out-door arrangements of the committee.

It may be worthy of note that the returning twenty-seven bore on their caps the distinctive mark of the Sixth Army Corps, — the cross. They have a right to be a little proud of belonging to the Army of the Potomac.

[All the nine-months men on the quota of Chelsea were afterwards welcomed home at the City Hall.]

Some information upon which I had depended in reference to the movements of a large detail of invalids from Newbern to Boston by sea, at the time of our departure from North

Carolina, has failed me at the last moment. They were in charge of Lieut. Turner and Assistant Surgeon Henry O. Marcy. There were probably twelve or fifteen, at least, of our own company among them. They reached Chelsea a day or two before any of the rest of us, after a pleasant passage, unmarked by any incident, except that their vessel, "The Consort," grounded in a fog on the beach at Scituate, at which place they landed.

I desire to say, in conclusion, that a very unreasonable prejudice rested upon the nine-months men from the outset, in respect to the matter of bounties. With regard to the large sums of money which we are credited with receiving, I respectfully ask to have the facts reviewed in the light of figures. My "bill," if I had been called upon to present one, would have been as follows: —

CHELSEA, Aug. 31, 1863.

The State and National Governments to ...., DR.
For one year's services, at a low average of the earnings of his calling at the time ($3 per day) $750 00

CR.

By Cash, and other items received: —
Local Bounty $200 00
State Aid, eleven months, at $4 . . . . 44 00
Monthly wages, eleven months, at $13 . . . 143 00
Rations, per week, $4 . . . . . . 192 00
Clothing 40 00
───────
619 00

Balance due to me $131 00

My earnings for several years after my return were from eight hundred and fifty to nine hundred dollars. Board for a married couple at the time was from eleven to twelve dollars per week. The fact was, that every soldier with a family to support needed, under the inflated prices of the war, every cent that was available, and even then he would fall several hundred dollars short of the ordinary income of the average citizen. Among the social fallacies which the war exposed, none were more conspicuous than this; namely, that multitudes of respectable and presumably well-meaning people

thought it not wrong to force large numbers of their fellow-citizens into the army without equitable reward. Many men who would have filled the State with their clamor, if they had been drafted into the jury-box for a few weeks, at any less price than three dollars a day, were unwilling that the families of soldiers should have more than that sum for a week.

Some who read this will be surprised to learn that Adjutant-Gen. Schouler states, in his "Massachusetts in the Civil War," that the average amount of bounty paid the seventeen thousand nine-months men was a fraction over *one hundred dollars a man*. These bounties were in great part re-imbursed to the local governments from the State treasury, to the total amount of $2,300,921.

It is but fair, in this connection, for me to recall the fact already noted, that all the Chelsea members of our company — which was a very large majority of our whole number — were brought into town from Readville, just before we left the State, and dismissed in the Square, upon our own recognizance, to report at the same place the next day; and we did it. Before the war closed, recruits were not, as a rule, trusted out of sight after they got their bounty. I can myself certify to the fact that prudent citizens avoided bodies of newly enlisted men as they passed through our cities under the care of officers who marched by their sides with their revolvers in their hands. The reason was obvious: pistol-balls are no respecters of persons; and a citizen was quite as likely to be hit as a bolting recruit.

The change for the worse in the public mind, as the war progressed, will be evident on comparing the following flier, bearing date July 30, 1864, with the one dated August, 1862, already quoted in my opening statements.

WAR MEETING No. 3,

TO FINISH UP THE WORK,

WILL BE HELD IN THE CITY HALL,

On Saturday Evening, July 30 ['64],

AT 8 O'CLOCK.

$2,500 yet to be raised. One grand, united effort will do it.

There are 1,800 legal voters in this city who have not yet contributed.

Come in, ENROLLED MEN, pay $10 each, and make up this balance.

Subscribers to the recruiting-fund are requested to pay in the amount of their subscriptions at this meeting.

STAND BY THE FLAG!

Another flier, dated a month later, calls upon all citizens to contribute five dollars each. A noticeable feature of both of the circulars of 1864 is the fact that no appeal is made to volunteer. It is money that is wanted at these last gatherings; whereas at the former ones it was men.

In these remarks I do not mean to discredit the whole-souled patriotism of many who enlisted during the last year of the war, and took the bounties then offered, which in some cases amounted to nine hundred dollars. My opinion is, that every man who did his duty to the best of his ability earned every cent he received. It was unfortunate that the last war-meetings took such a mercenary aspect. The tongue

should not have been divorced from the sword: the stirring appeals to the patriotic sense of the community ought to have been continued to the end. They were not inconsistent with impending drafts or with large bounties. All these elements were necessary, and should have been blended together.

I have now reached the end of my history. Before closing, it is due to the memory of the Chelsea Rifle Corps, out of which our company originated, to acknowledge our indebtedness to them in more ways than can be recounted here. I have the impression that we went to Readville with a larger number of experts in company movements than any other organization outside of Boston in the regiment. We were followed by them to the scene of war with sympathetic courtesies, showing that we were not forgotten, and cordially welcomed home.

Our acknowledgments are also due to the ancient and honorable military organization known originally as the Boston Light Infantry, later as the Second Battalion. Certain elevated associations connected with their origin during the last century; their motto, " Death, or an honorable life ; " their emblem, a couchant "tiger," closely connected with the characteristic savage pronunciation of the word with which we sometimes made the jungles of North Carolina ring, — were always present in some inspiring form suggestive of patriotic obligation.

To the officers of the Second Battalion we were largely indebted for instruction in regimental organization and drill. Nearly all of them were men of high character. We had, as has been intimated, the good fortune to be on the most acceptable terms with our company officers of every grade. So far as the field and staff were concerned, it is deserved praise to say of all of them. that their bearing toward the men of the regiment was fully consistent with their position, and yet equally kind and considerate with the officers of our company toward us of the ranks. They were of such habitual self-command, that my feelings were not for an instant ruffled by any harshness of manner, or hasty language, from either of them during the whole term of service.

I cannot close without saying a word in the spirit of charity toward the South. Their whole course, at the time of the war, seemed to me to be one of pure diabolism; but my opinion in the course of the years that have since elapsed has been modified.

The South can only be judged properly by those who are, to some extent at least, diligent and candid students of the social question.

The triumph of the Republican party in the election of 1860 demonstrated the determination of the North to restrict slavery to the States where it already existed. The South believed that their prosperity depended upon its extension. A series of influences extending over more than two centuries, going back, in fact, to the first cargo of slaves which entered the James River, and connecting themselves inextricably with race-antipathies, and with the excessively onerous conditions under which labor must be performed in the South, had led them to believe that slavery was essential to social order. Under these circumstances they resisted, with the whole organized power of their communities, in every possible way, the imposition of a policy upon them from without, which they honestly, and I must almost admit religiously, believed to be fatal to them. Their position, in short, was very similar to what ours would be if the great mass of the working people of the North should attempt the abolition, by the ballot, of our present industrial system, and should succeed in the effort, in spite of the wishes, and against the votes, of the cultivated classes of society, united in one compact body in resistance.

In seceding, the South set itself not only against the North, but really against Christendom. We were absolutely forced to fight; but advancing knowledge now compels the admission, that the situation of the South was essentially different from that of the rest of the civilized peoples of the world. The abolition of chattelship has passed the social question one stage further along, leaving it still an open one, but so comprehensive in its aspects as to relieve it from sectional and race antagonisms. The lower classes of the whites of

the South are but a shade less ignorant and degraded than the colored people. In their regeneration this fact must be recognized, and the measures taken should be of such a character as to admit of application throughout the national domain, wherever ignorance and poverty are cursing the people.

We are struggling against disastrous odds in our present reliance upon legislation to bring peace throughout our borders. The final solution of the social problem lies in the direction of practical religion rather than politics. Chattelship went into a bloody grave, because the issue was too momentous and intricate to be controlled or adjusted by the civil power. The Church will finally, and as I truly believe at no distant day, find the real grandeur of its mission in merging law and love together in institutes which shall combine the principles of the Decalogue with the utterances of the Sermon on the Mount. The vast energies that found expression in the Christian and Sanitary Commissions will yet be permanently devoted to the redemption of man from the material and moral evils which still fester in human society. Herbert Spencer, in his "Data of Ethics," joins the forces of natural to those of revealed religion in expressing "the humble hope and faith, that some reasoned form of the ethics of the New Testament may yet become the life-core of society."

Something more than a year and a half after we returned, the citizens of Chelsea thronged our City Hall, and offered a joyous oblation of praise to Almighty God for the restoration of peace. I have forgotten nearly all of the speakers, and most of what was said; but a leaflet of songs and hymns which was distributed at the meeting is still at hand to quicken my memory, and to revive some of the most grateful and profound emotions which I ever experienced.

A stalwart colored man was present, one of the preachers of Newbern, named George A. Rue. He sang with stentorian voice, and with a pathos which commanded all hearts, the verses of the grand oratorio of "Egypt," which follow: —

SOUND THE LOUD TIMBREL.

Shout the glad tidings, exultingly sing,
Jerusalem triumphs, Messiah is king!

CHORUS.

Sound the loud timbrel o'er Egypt's dark sea!
Jehovah has triumphed: his people are free.

Sing, for the pride of the tyrant is broken —
His chariots, his horsemen, all splendid and brave!
CHORUS.

How vain was their boasting! the Lord hath but spoken,
And chariots and horsemen are sunk in the wave.
CHORUS.

Praise to the Conqueror! praise to the Lord!
His word was our arrow, his breath was our sword!
CHORUS.

Who shall return to tell Egypt the story
Of those she sent forth in the hour of her pride?
CHORUS.

For the Lord hath looked out from his pillar of glory,
And all her brave thousands are dashed in the tide.
CHORUS.

Te Deum Laudamus.

APPENDIX A.

HISTORICAL PORTION OF THE ADDRESS OF HON. R. C. WINTHROP ON THE PRESENTATION OF THE COLORS OF THE FORTY-THIRD.

COL. CHARLES L. HOLBROOK, — You have been honored with the command of a regiment which has been enlisted under the auspices of the old Boston Light Infantry, and which has recognized its filial relations to that corps by calling itself "The Tiger Regiment." The officers and members of the Boston Light Infantry, past and present, and of the Second Battalion, of which it has recently formed a part, have accordingly desired to manifest their regard for your command by some substantial and visible token, which may accompany you on your tour of patriotic service, and which may serve to remind you that there are those at home who will watch your movements with an eager interest and a jealous pride, and whose hearts will be with you in every hour of prosperous or adverse fortune which awaits you, — whether of endurance or of struggle, of tribulation or of triumph.

Sir, I need hardly recall in this presence the history of that old corps, whose familiar designation you have adopted, and whose character may seem in some sort committed to your keeping. You yourself, certainly, — who have risen to the successive command of a regiment in peace, and now of a regiment in war, after so long and honorable a service in its ranks, — must know its history by heart. You have not forgotten how it sprung into existence just four and sixty years ago, in that memorable year 1798, when our infant republic was menaced, and more than menaced, by the madness of revolutionary France, and when it seemed as if that gallant and generous nation which had done so much to aid us in establishing our independence, and whose arms had so

recently been united with our own in the crowning and consummate glory of Yorktown, were about to be made the instrument of a despotic directory in subjecting our youthful energies to a cruel and perhaps fatal test. Our own John Adams — John *Yankee* he was sometimes called — was then seated in the executive chair; and the august and venerated Washington, having finished a career of military and civil service which has no parallel in the annals of mankind, had nobly consented to waive all considerations of previous rank, or present dignity and ease, and to assume the subordinate position of lieutenant-general of the provisional armies of the United States. The pulse of patriotism, at that hour as at this, beat high throughout the land, and every bosom was animated with the same desire to do something for the defence of the country, which is burning at this moment in every heart around me It was then, that, the young men of Boston having united in one of those patriotic addresses which were among the peculiar features of the period, a reply was received from the President, containing those memorable words, "To arms, to arms, my young friends!"

To that appeal, which was publicly read at Faneuil Hall by the first elected commissioned officer of the corps, Ensign Francis J. Oliver, the establishment of the Boston Light Infantry was the immediate practical response.

You have not forgotten, sir, the solemn agreement which was forthwith adopted among the fundamental articles of its constitution, — "that every man should pledge himself to support at all hazards his country, and the government which protects him, and that, unless commanded, he will never quit his standard till forced from it by an honorable death," — a pledge which was afterwards inscribed upon that standard itself in the simpler and more compact phraseology of "Death, or an honorable life."

Sir, as I have looked many a time and oft on that old motto emblazoned on the colors or accoutrements of our corps in those piping times of peace when I had the honor of being one of its officers, I have thought to myself that the sentiment was perhaps rather superfluously stern and solemn; and that so little probability was there that it would ever again become applicable to any circumstances which could arise in our free and happy land, that it might better be changed for something less heroic and defiant. But I rejoice this day that it never was changed. I rejoice that no

false confidence of our own, and no flippant ridicule of others, ever induced us to obliterate that time-honored legend from our banner or from our breasts. The day and the hour have at length arrived when we comprehend and appreciate its full significance,—"Death, or an honorable life." You can go forth to the field of duty under no more appropriate or impressive motto, endeared to you, as it will be, by so many memories of the past, and breathing, as it does, the precise spirit which should animate the present. Adopted with a view to sustain the civil authority of John Adams and the military lead of George Washington, it will ever be associated with their noble names and glorious examples, and cannot fail to inspire you with something of that devoted constancy and courage in the defence of our Union, which they so signally displayed in establishing it.

It was in the spirit of this pledge and this motto, that our old corps, at their dinner at Concert Hall, after their first public parade, on the 18th of October, 1798, gave utterance to their earliest recorded toast: "The United States of America: as they have drawn the sword of justice with reason, may they never sheathe it with disgrace!" O sir, if, at that festal board at which our honored first commander, Daniel Sargent, presided, and around which were gathered more than one of those who bore the names and the blood of the patriot-mechanic, Paul Revere, and the patriot-statesman, James Otis, and the patriot-martyr, Joseph Warren,—for each one of these illustrious men had a son, or a nephew, or a near relative, on our original roll,—if, in the midst of that festal scene, a vision of this day and this hour could have been unrolled before the eyes of those ardent and patriotic volunteers of '98, with what mingled grief and pride, with what contending emotions of agony and exultation, would they not have contemplated it!—grief and agony, that the grand triumphal arch of Constitutional Union, which it had cost so much toil and treasure and precious blood to construct and cement, was so soon to be assailed, and threatened with overthrow, by an unnatural and an unholy rebellion,—pride and exultation, that, when that dark day should arrive, the noble battalions of patriotic young men should be heard responding, as they had responded to another President's appeal, "To arms, to arms!" and should be seen mustering, and marching forth to the defence of the country and the support of the government, under the influence of their example, and under the very motto of their banner.

In view of such a scene as this, destined in the decrees of a mysterious Providence to occur while at least one survivor of their patriotic band is still living to witness it, — in view of such a scene as this, could it then have been unfolded to their aching sight, with what renewed fervor, with what redoubled emphasis, with what reiterated cheers, would they have responded to that first toast, and that original pledge, "Death, or an honorable life!" "The United States of America: they have drawn the sword of justice with reason: may they never sheathe it with disgrace!"

I think it requires no stretch of imagination to conceive, that, if the founders of our corps had been initiated into the mysteries of a certain unearthly sound which has almost become an *institution* with their successors, there would have been added to those cheers more than one tiger-growl.

Nor, Mr. Commander, will this name of Tiger, which you have adopted from the more recent history of our corps as the distinctive designation of your regiment, be without its own peculiar significance, now that your martial exercises are to be transferred from the parade-ground to the battlefield. There are those around me who remember how often, in years long past, we have recalled at our anniversary festivals those familiar lines of the immortal dramatist: —

> "In peace there's nothing so becomes a man
> As modest stillness and humility;
> But, when the blast of war blows in our ears,
> Then imitate the action of the *tiger*."

Little did we dream in those hours of recreation, that we should ever have occasion to apply those lines to any exigency more serious than the skirmish or sham-fight of a militia muster. But we find them rising to our lips this day in all the solemn earnestness and stern severity in which they were first put by the great poet into the mouth of the monarch-hero of Agincourt. We feel that they are the very words for the hour, embodying the exact idea of that quick, sharp, strenuous, and overwhelming onset, which alone, so far as human eyes can reach, and human instruments are concerned, — would to Heaven we could see any other way! — which alone can bring this deplorable and dreadful war to an early and successful conclusion.

APPENDIX B.

ROSTER OF THE COMPANIES COMPOSING THE FORTY-THIRD REGIMENT, M.V.M.

[Lieuts. FLETCHER of Company K, and SCHOULER of Company D, joined the expedition to Charleston, S.C.]

COMPANY A — AT LARGE.

Henry J. Hallgreen, Captain.
George Chadbourne, First Lieut.
Lucius A. Wheelock, Second Lieut.
James A. Blanchard, " "
Thomas R. Appleton, First Serg.
A. S. Farquharson, Sergeant.
Charles I. Crabe, "
Robert B. Palfrey, "
J. Horace Kent, "
Horace D. Mack, Corporal.
E. F. Simmons, "
Frederic D. Flagg, "
Charles M. Cook, "
Edwin T. Nash, "
S. H. Burroughs, "
Charles A. Rice, "
John R. Cozzens, "
James E. Gilman, "
Frank E. Atkinson, Musician.
George H. Pierce, "
Hiram F. Hilton, Wagoner.

PRIVATES.

Allen, John.
Allen, John, 2d.
Allen, Patrick.
Burgess, Robert.
Brennan, Dennis F.
Balch, George E.
Bacon, Frederic P.
Billings, J. Quincy.
Bly, Charles F.
Bailey, Martin, jun.
Burke, Joseph J.
Beckler, Frank M.
Brown, James.
Bartlett, John.
Brooks, Richard.
Callahan, Dennis J.
Chisholm, Alexander W.
Coe, James A.
Considine, Michael.
Carpenter, James R.
Crabe, William S.
Conlan, Bernard.
Coles, Jacob.
Caloney, James.
Dunn, John W.
Dilloway, William H.
Dennison, Albert E.
Dodsworth, George.
Davis, William.

200   HISTORY OF THE FORTY-THIRD REGIMENT, M.V.M.

COMPANY A — Concluded.

Foley, John W.
Finn, Thomas F.
Field, Frederic A.
Flaherty, Patrick.
Feeley, James.
Grace, Thomas.
Grace, Joseph.
Gowell, Sylvester C.
Grady, Albert.
Hall, Thomas H.
Hobson, Robert.
Howard, Nichols.
Hutchinson, Thomas.
Harlow, James.
Harwood, Otis F.
Henderson, Thomas.
Johnson, James.
Johnson, George T.
Kingston, George.
Kelling, Charles.
Kimball, Frank.
Kenney, James L.
Keller, James E.
Lenhurst, John.
Leroy, James.
Mullin, Patrick.
Morris, John.
McLaughlin, Thomas J.
McDevitt, Hugh.
Mooney, Michael J.
Mellen, Henry.
McAuliffe, John.

Murphy, William.
Nason, William J.
Nugent, John.
O'Conner, James A.
Oremay, Francis.
Pendergast, William.
Petterson, John.
Rice, Jerome F.
Rider, William H. H.
Roberts, Watkins W.
Russell, William.
Robinson, James.
Reed, Rudolph.
Riley, John.
Shanahan, Michael.
Sprague, William W.
Smythe, Wayland R.
Smith, John W.
Sabin, Ralph J.
Shaw, George.
Sullivan, David.
Tiusnni, James.
Trafton, Charles A.
Vial, Samuel H.
Walsh, John E.
Welsh, James.
Wylie, Charles.
Wilson, Henry.
Wilson, George.
Wilson, William.
Wiley, Emery.
Young, George A.

COMPANY B — AT LARGE.

Edward G. Quincy, Captain.
William Jordan, First Lieut.
John C. Sanborn, Second Lieut.
James M. Dunn, First Sergeant.
Robert E. O'Brien, Sergeant.
Philip Dolan,   "
Edward H. Mellus,   "
Rufus M. Easton,   "
John Q. Bicknell, Corporal.

Charles W. Bean, Corporal.
George Goodale,   "
Charles Arnold,   "
Thomas Stoddard,   "
J. Henry Fearing,   "
Luther W. Bixby,   "
Pierce J. Babbington, Musician.
Edward D. Barton,   "

COMPANY B — Continued.

PRIVATES.
Abbot, Hiram E.
Boodnee, John.
Bicknell, Ansel F.
Burns, Henry.
Bacon, C. H.
Baker, John.
Carmichael, John R.
Clark, Horace.
Christian, Henry.
Cummings, Robert M.
Campbell, James.
Corkery, Patrick.
Crane, Silas D.
Clark, Jonathan R.
Conway, Patrick.
Conroy, John.
Casey, James.
Carle, John.
Carson, James.
Casey, Michael.
Denton, William B.
Dow, James H.
Dennison, Jerry.
Dailey, Michael F.
Davis, John.
Durgin, Daniel.
Doyle, James.
Davy, John.
Dow, Daniel.
Fisher, Edward A.
Foley, Cornelius.
Foley, Patrick.
Fontaine, S.
Friery, Richard.
Fay, John.
Green, Patrick.
Gavin, John.
Higgins, Andrew.
Hill, William G.
Hayden, Hosea B.
Henius, Max.
Hollis, Lemuel.
Hollis, Albert O.

Hennesey, Edward.
Hanley, John M.
Homey, Thomas.
Howe, George A.
Hennison, William.
Johnson, William.
Jackson, William.
Kearns, John.
Leonard, Charles B.
Leyden, Daniel.
Lawrence, George.
Mower, William W.
Mower, George A.
Marks, M.
Murphy, John.
Morgan, Cornelius.
Maher, William.
Masters, Edward.
Milan, John.
Newton, Antipus, jun.
Norton, Shubael M.
O'Brien, Cornelius.
Oakley, George.
Ogden, John.
Pool, John F.
Peacock, Lewis.
Palmer, George W.
Rowe, William H.
Roe, Patrick M.
Rowley, Thomas.
Ricker, Alpheus.
Reed, George.
Snow, Jacob C.
Sylvester, Gideon Y.
Schenkle, Antoine.
Sprague, George H.
Smith, James.
Somers, Henry G.
Sullivan, D. J.
Sayers, William.
Tangney, Daniel.
Taylor, William H.
Troupe, George H.
Troupe, Charles A. S.

COMPANY B — Concluded.

Thorp, William R.
Turner, John.
Williams, Morrill.
Wild, John F.
Wallace, Cranmore.
Wallace, Frank.

Winslow, Henry.
Woodman, Edward.
Walker, Samuel.
Wilson, John M.
Wilson, James.

COMPANY C — AT LARGE.

William B. Fowle, jun., Captain.
Augustine Sanderson, First Lieut.
John F. Thayer, Second Lieut.
William F. Rayne, First Sergeant.
Joseph E. Fiske, "
Lucius A. Wheelock, "
James McCallum, Sergeant.
George O. Sanderson, "
Obed M. Fish, "
Joseph H. Dewing, "
Charles Everbeck, Corporal.
William S. Friend, "
Charles H. Kelly, "
John E. McGlinn, "
Edward F. Littlefield, "
John Peck, "
George W. A. Langley, "
John Curran, "
Eugene A. Holton, Musician.
Robert M. McCloud, "

PRIVATES.

Ambrose, Robert.
Acton, John T.
Baker, Theodore L.
Boynton, Richard F.
Belcher, Charles H.
Bell, Solomon L.
Bullard, William P.
Bryant, Snow.
Bent, Thomas D.
Cameron, John.
Cooper, Hugh.
Clough, Leonard N.
Copeland, James.

Carven, Patrick H.
Donhiser, John.
Davis, Charles M.
DuBois, Lewis.
Donavan, Michael.
Eccles, George.
Flock, Charles.
Ford, John B.
Frye, Samuel G.
Flagg, George W.
Fessenden, Albert.
Fitzgerald, Andrew M.
Guyot, Joseph.
Grady, Edward F.
Gormley, William.
Gilbert, Clinton.
Gove, William B.
Gassett, Oscar.
Gardner, Henry J.
Grous, Daniel.
Hardy, William H.
Hunting, Emery F.
Howland, Allen.
Hawes, Solomon L.
Hussey, Charles H.
Johnson, George W.
Knapp, Cyrus W.
Kuhlig, Julius.
Kinsler, Charles C.
Keating, William J.
Knight, Henry D.
Kingsbury, William H.
Levy, Morris.
Lewis, George.
Murphy, James J.

APPENDIX B.

COMPANY C — *Concluded.*

McFay, John.
Maguire, Hugh.
Morris, Charles C.
Marshall, John P.
McLane, William H.
Morgan, Walter J.
McCann, Jeremiah G.
Newman, Frederick.
Nolan, Andrew.
O'Connell, Timothy.
Oakes, Joseph.
Phillips, George H.
Penniman, Isaac H.
Pratt, Francis L.
Russell, William L.
Robinson, Edmund B.
Ropes, Charles A.
Short, Thomas.
Soule, Marcellus.

Sherman, John S.
Severance, Charles R.
Simmons, John S.
Seagrave, Gilbert H.
Staniford, John W.
Seeley, Christopher.
Tuttle, Abram D.
Tucker, Henry S.
Taylor, James H.
Towers, William F.
Ward, Joseph T.
Weeks, Charles H.
Wisner, George P.
Whitney, William H.
Wilder, George S.
White, John.
West, William A.
White, Henry B.
Zittle, Koncart.

COMPANY D — DEDHAM.

Thomas G. Whytal, Captain.
Edward A. Sumner, First Lieut.
James Schouler, Second Lieut.
Cornelius A. Taft, First Sergeant.
John E. Webster, Sergeant.
Alvin Fuller, "
Joseph H. Lathrop, "
Francis W. Haynes, "
Charles B. Fessenden, "
Elbridge P. Boyden, Corporal.
William Chickering, "
John McDonald, "
Emelius A. Everett, "
G. Phineas Guild, "
Isaac A. Cox, "
Samuel D. Cobb, "
Charles D. Marcy, "
Melvin A. Galucia, Musician
Frank D. Hayward, "

PRIVATES.

Alexander, William H.
Babbitt, Willard.

Babbitt, Samuel M.
Barrett, William F.
Baker, Addison G.
Baker, Charles A.
Broad, Nathaniel W.
Ball, James E.
Carroll, William F.
Carter, Frank.
Clifton, John D.
Collins, James.
Cox, Patrick.
Cox, Samuel H.
Coy, Albert M.
Cheney, Rufus F.
Clements, William H.
Eagan, Patrick.
Edmands, George W. S.
Ellis, Lewis.
Fairbanks, Albert F.
Fairbanks, Benjamin A.
Fairbanks, James G.
Fisher, Edwin E.
Gay, William H.

204 HISTORY OF THE FORTY-THIRD REGIMENT, M.V.M.

COMPANY D — Concluded.

Guild, Clarence M.
Guild, Joseph.
Guild, Charles J.
Guild, Edward W.
Golden, Michael.
Guy, Henry M.
Hann, Jno. A.
Houghton, Joseph.
Hathaway, R. Ellis.
Howard, Martin.
Hooker, George E.
Hooker, James B.
Hartshorn, Charles E.
Hawkins, James J.
Ide, Francis P.
Johnson, Willard L.
Kieman, John.
Lincoln, Herbert R.
McGlone, Patrick.
Marsh, William.
Morse, A. Mason.
Morse, Charles H.
Morse, Josiah E.
Morse, Sanford O.
Meagher, Patrick.
Nichols, John H.
Perkins, Charles M.
Pond, Charles E.
Pratt, Edwin.

Rhoades, George A.
Rhoades, George L.
Richardson, James H.
Richards, Bennett O.
Randall, William H.
Shapleigh, James F.
Shapleigh, Alfred M.
Shapleigh, Nathan E.
Sheridan, William N.
Smith, George N.
Stone, George M.
Soule, Francis E.
Shackley, Charles H.
Shaw, Henry A.
Talbot, Nathaniel H.
Tibbetts, Joseph N.
Tibbetts, William R.
Tucker, James.
Tracy, Andrew.
Towle, Horace E.
Temporly, Thomas.
Urry, James.
Webb, Albert G.
Weeks, Henry.
Woolley, Edwin A.
Wood, James M.
Woods, John S.
Wight, John K.
Woolley, Frederick J.

COMPANY E — ORLEANS.

Henry Doane, Captain.
Joseph W. Paine, First Lieut.
George H. Nickerson, "
Charles M. Upham, Second Lieut.
Irving Emerson, First Sergeant.
John W. Atwood, Sergeant.
Joshua S. Sparrow, "
Henry A. Whittemore, "
William H. Harley, "
George H. Collins, Corporal.
Charles G. Rodman, "
James B. Cook, "

John A. Gross, Corporal.
Charles E. Atwood, "
Luther Crowell, "
Alonzo N. Bearse, "
Morton Fuller, "
Joseph L. Kenrick, Musician.
Samuel Levi, "

PRIVATES.

Bassett, William H. H.
Baker, Winslow.
Brown, Charles.

APPENDIX B. 205

COMPANY E — Concluded.

Brown, Francis.
Crowell, John W.
Cook, David.
Connelly, John.
Casey, John M.
Cahoon, Thomas Y.
Cahoon, Benjamin S.
Chase, John S.
Crabbe, Joseph.
Clark, David P.
Connell, James G.
Drown, Alvin L.
Dow, John N.
Dill, Albert F.
Donovan, Patrick.
Doyle, Lawrence.
Eldredge, George.
Eldredge, Ephraim.
Emery, Cyrus.
Ellis, Alvarado C.
Ebrenstan, Max.
Freeman, Charles S.
Freeman, Gideon H.
Finn, John W.
Freeman, Jonathan S.
Grozier, John P.
Higgins, Thomas R.
Higginns, Sparrow S.
Horton, John M.
Hayden, Caleb.
Harding, David.
Hammond, Franklin D.
Hamilton, James S.
Hamilton, Josiah J.
Hamilton, James T.
Hopkins, Daniel P.
Hopkins, William M.
Higgins, Elisha A.
Howes, Samuel H.
Illingsworth, Henry.

Johnson, Charles.
Kenrick, Benjamin C.
Kelley, George F.
Keeler, Owen.
Lee, James W.
Lyman, Storrs L.
Lewis, Horatio F.
Lockwood, George.
Mayo, Andrew S.
McVea, David M.
Paine, Henry R.
Paine, Amasa E.
Parker, Thomas H. R.
Powers, John.
Ray, John G.
Rogers, Joshua N.
Rogers, Benjamin.
Rogers, Francis B.
Robbins, Samuel.
Rich, Jeremiah H.
Rogers, Ensign.
Smith, Daniel P.
Snow, Samuel.
Snow, Isaiah.
Schilling, William.
Sullivan, William.
Small, Joshua.
Smith, Simeon L.
Snow, Freeman.
Silver, Nathan B.
Smith, Isaac Y.
Taylor, George A.
Townsend, James A.
Tripp, Francis M.
Tripp, Edwin.
Verge, Thomas K.
Wilson, Charles.
Young, Henry, 2d.
Young, William H.

COMPANY F — AT LARGE.

Charles W. Soule, Captain.
Henry S. Bates, First Lieut.
Nathan S. Oakman, Second Lieut.
Samuel J. Simmons, First Sergeant.
William E. Thompson, Sergeant.
Dexter Grose, "
Peleg S. Sherman, "
Edwin Curtis, "
Peleg F. Clapp, Color-Bearer.
Charles W. Sparrell, Corporal.
Thomas B. Whiting, "
Edward H. Davis, "
Benjamin Brown, jun., "
Henry T. Jenkins, "
Eleas A. Pratt, "
John E. O. Prouty, "
Joseph W. Morris, "
Jotham W. Bailey, "
Samuel Chamberlain, Musician.
George H. Stevens, "
Thomas Alden, Wagoner.

PRIVATES.

Alden, James, jun.
Beal, Walter M.
Bailey, Charles W.
Baker, James E.
Bates, George S.
Bouve, William J.
Brown, Henry L.
Brown, Charles E.
Curtis, George W.
Curtis, George M.
Curtis, Joseph H.
Church, William, jun.
Carver, Israel H.
Cudworth, Elijah F.
Clapp, Henry O.
Damon, Israel D.
Damon, Alfred C.
Damon, Virgil.
Doherty, John.
Ewell, Daniel E.
Ford, Thomas P.
Falvey, Edward A.
Grose, Henry A.
Grose, Charles.
Gardner, Stephen N.
Hobart, Alonzo C.
Hatch, Edward.
Hatch, Charles R.
Hatch, Samuel F.
Hatch, Calvin O.
Hatch, John F.
Hatch, George A.
Holmes, Samuel.
Hooper, Charles A.
Hyland, Thomas W.
Harrington, Lorenzo D.
Hewett, Asa W.
Keene, John A.
Lawrence, Thomas R.
Lewis, John W.
Little, William B.
Litchfield, Francis M.
Litchfield, Milton G.
Litchfield, Otis.
Litchfield, Liba W.
Litchfield, Warren, jun.
Mann, Howard F.
Mann, Albert G.
Mann, Charles D.
Merritt, William O., jun.
Osborn, George T.
Peterson, Phineas P.
Pool, Benjamin B.
Pratt, Bryant C.
Perry, George W.
Porter, William S.
Raymond, Thomas A.
Randall, Josiah.
Spencer, John H.
Simmons, Jonathan J.
Sherman, Warren H.
Sherman, Joseph.
Studley, Alfred H.
Southard, Francis E.
Sylvester, Gideon Y.

COMPANY F — Concluded.

Thomas, Lucius.
Thayer, Lucius.
Tyler, Franklin.
Turner, John II.
Turner, Henry A.
Tolman, George S.
Thomas, Josiah.
Vinal, George O.
Vinal, Seth H.

Vinal, Amos.
Vining, William H.
Williamson, Peter.
Williamson, William.
Williamson, Andrew J.
Woodward, George W.
Williamson, Calvin, jun.
Wright, James A.

COMPANY G — ABINGTON.

Everett Lane, Captain.
Josiah Soule, jun. "
Lysander Poole, First Lieut.
Joseph B. Warne, Second Lieut.
Brainard Cushing, First Sergeant.
Joseph B. Merritt, Sergeant.
Ansel B. Randall, "
Anson V. Whiting, "
Alexander Blaisdell, "
John Burrell, 2d, Corporal.
E. Walter Burbank, "
Shepard F. Eaton, "
Joshua S. Grey, "
James B. Studley, "
Daniel G. Wheeler, "
William M. Walker, "
Edward G. Hunt, "
Frank Granville, Musician.
Gustavus E. Lane, "

PRIVATES.

Arnold, William D.
Burrell, James H.
Burrell, Benjamin A.
Burrell, Charles M.
Briggs, Nathaniel B.
Briggs, Joseph W.
Beal, David.
Beal, Nathan A.
Beal, Franklin.
Bates, Edwin, jun.
Baldwin, Elza.
Bisbee, Zenas M.

Cushing, Urban W.
Curtis, George E.
Curtis, Warren C.
Curtis, Samuel G.
Curtis, Edmund B.
Chubbuck, Charles H.
Caplice, Maurice.
Carney, Richard.
Crook, Patrick.
Conlan, Edward.
Church, Robert.
Connell, Cornelius.
Crowell, Joel.
Connell, James O.
Chubbuck, Hosea.
Damon, Washington.
Damond, Piam.
Donovan, Daniel O.
Doane, Simeon K.
Davis, Joseph W.
Elmes, William.
Fenno, James A.
Fuller, Henry E.
Foster, Lorenzo D.
Gammon, Horatio H.
Green, Patrick.
Groce, William R.
Gurney, James S.
Hook, Charles O.
Hughes, Robert J.
Harwell, Elisha.
Hurley, Patrick.
Hunt, Joseph W.

COMPANY G — *Concluded.*

Hallet, Charles G.
Hobert, John T.
Joyce, Leander R.
Kennedy, Hugh.
Kenney, Elijah F.
Lane, Josiah W.
Lane, Charles H.
Lewis, George H.
Lowell, Henry H.
Loud, Samuel M.
Mitchell, Robert.
Mansur, Andrew J.
Mullaly, James.
McMorrow, John.
McMorrow, Michael.
Phillips, Gideon B.
Poole, William W.
Payne, Elbridge.
Rush, John.

Rogers, Andrew.
Studley, Andrew H.
Studley, George S.
Sullivan, Daniel F.
Shaw, Micah R.
Shaw, Otis R.
Smith, Zenas.
Stoddard, George W.
Stoddard, David.
Shurtleff, Solomon H.
Sullivan, Eugene.
Tower, James A.
Taugney, James.
Turner, Luther.
Warner, Henry.
Wetherbee, Joseph M.
Wheeler, Elijah H.
Young, Edwin R.

COMPANY H — CHELSEA. See p. 19.

COMPANY I — CAMBRIDGE.

George O. Tyler, Captain.
Robert Torrey, jun., First Lieut.
Oliver H. Webber, Second Lieut.
Gustavus A. Smart, First Sergeant.
Leonard Arkerson, jun., Sergeant.
Daniel A. Buckley, "
William J. Dowd, "
Leonard B. Wilder, "
William H. Arkerson, Corporal.
Charles A. Patch, "
John J. Dowd, "
James K. Odell, "
Martin J. Keating, "
Charles E. Herbert, "
Ruel W. Hanscom, "
Thomas Lackey, "
William F. Sparrow, "
Benjamin Calley, Musician.
Alexander H. Clapp, "
Mark J. Fulsom, Wagoner.

PRIVATES.
Adams, Charles A.
Ashworth, Charles.
Boyle, Henry F.
Bagley, John.
Brooks, Sager.
Burke, James.
Clapp, Edward J.
Casey, James.
Clark, Thomas.
Cummings, Patrick R.
Cronin, Daniel.
Campbell, Edward F. A.
Cane, Lewis.
Currier, George W.
Collins, John J.
Casey, Michael.
Christie, Addison G.
Colzi, Pietro.
Doherty, Michael.

APPENDIX B.

COMPANY I — *Concluded.*

Daley, Michael J.
Davis, Daniel.
Dolan, Matthias J.
Dolan, William.
Dowd, Christopher.
Dallenger, Samuel W.
Doherty, Robert.
Fallen, Daniel.
Frizell, Joseph P.
Ford, George R.
Fellows, DeWitt C.
Fisher, Edward P.
Ford, Howard J.
Gallagher, Owen.
Gallagher, Patrick.
Grammo, John.
Grammo, Francis.
Geier, John.
Green, William.
Glenn, Michael.
Hawkes, John.
Hewins, John A.
Hardman, James J.
Hamilton, John.
Jackson, David A.
Klidelin, George.
Kane, Michael.
Laha, John.
Lakin, James T.
Lynch, Thomas.
Linney, John.
Leary, Michael.
Laredo, Luigi.

McDonough, Joseph R.
McNally, Frank.
Moesehlin, John F.
Murray, Timothy.
Mahoney, Jeremiah J.
McIntire, John B.
Norris, William H.
O'Neil, Thomas.
O'Toy, Hugh.
Prescott, Charles E.
Paradi, Charles.
Park, Charles T.
Quirk, James W.
Quinn, Michael.
Quinn, Maurice.
Redfern, John H.
Ryan, John A.
Rollins, Albert W.
Rollins, Francis E.
Rorke, Joseph H.
Rhuling, E. Frederick.
Storer, William.
Stone, William A.
Sarsfield, Patrick.
Snow, Russell L.
Smith, John N.
Strickland, John.
Turner, Jonathan G.
Warren, Edward E.
Williams, Edward.
Williams, George S.
Wilson, William F.
Young, Stephen.

COMPANY K — AT LARGE.

J. Emery Round, Captain.
Lucius P. Kimpton, First Lieut.
John W. Fletcher, Second Lieut.
Albert A. Day, First Sergeant.
James Emerson, Sergeant.
Edward O. Fisher, "
George W. Nichols, "
James A. Coles, "
Daniel B. Lovell, Corporal.

Martin V. B. Dunham, Corporal.
John N. Collier, "
Benjamin F. Stone, "
Joseph C. Marshall, "
Warren T. Heillman, "
Alfred A. Presbrey, "
George W. Fearing, "
Caleb F. Bates, Musician.
Minot S. Crane, "

COMPANY K — Concluded.

George E. Frederick, Wagoner.

PRIVATES.

Beekman, Cyrus A.
Bliss, Warrence.
Brown, Joseph.
Bryant, James A.
Boswell, Joseph P.
Birch, Joseph.
Campbell, Thomas M.
Cammitt, Warren.
Christian, James.
Chubbuck, Henry H.
Cole, Ebenezer.
Collins, John.
Cooke, Orin C.
Copeland, Cyrus F.
Cotton, Frederick W.
Coiteux, Joseph.
Crane, Samuel S.
Cushing, Henry F.
Cushing, Loring H.
Cully, Eli.
Durant, Charles H.
Durr, Thomas E.
Dunham, Sheperd.
Dalton, John.
Evans, Isaac S.
Farnum, Samuel M.
Ferris, Job T.
Fiske, Noble.
Fitz, Edward S.
Fullerton, George H.
Goodwin, Isaac F.
Gurley, Jacob B.
Hadley, Albert F.
Hawes, John A.
Hayward, Henry J.
Henderson, William.
Harlow, Aaron S.
Hersey, Hollis.
Hillman, Beriah T.
Hough, George H. S.
Hunt, Ira J.

Hurst, William.
Hyde, William H.
Hutchins, Cornelius W.
Johnson, James P.
Johnson, James.
Jones, Harvey.
Keough, Henry J.
Koff, Frederick.
Livingston, William A.
Loring, Peter.
Lunt, George W.
Mayhew, John W.
McKenna, Daniel.
McCullough, James.
Meara, Sherman T.
Morgan, Roscoe G.
Miller, Jacob.
Mason, Thomas.
Moore, Fitz H.
Oakes, George H.
Oliver, Henry A.
Perry, John S.
Pratt, Thomas W.
Puffer, Jonathan.
Rawlings, James D.
Remick, Augustus.
Remick, Henry A.
Robinson, Charles S.
Rogers, John R.
Souther, Thomas.
Souther, Samuel C.
Spear, John B.
Sumner, Louis N.
Smith, Joseph.
Taft, Andrew.
Tidd, Joseph S.
Tilton, Charles W.
Tower, Charles.
Thayer, Otis E.
Tilley, James B.
Wilson, Eliphalet H. S.
Walker, Albert.
Weeden, Warren D.
Watson, James.

www.ingramcontent.com/pod-product-compliance
Lightning Source LLC
Chambersburg PA
CBHW032142010526
44111CB00035B/860